Essential Sociology

Jay Mullin, Ph.D.

Professor of Social Sciences (Sociology)
Queensborough Community College, City University of New York

PEARSON
Custom
Publishing

Cover Art: *Subterranean 02*, by Michael Lary.

Printed in the United States of America

10 9 8 7 6 5 4 3 2 1

ISBN 0-536-39771-6

2007540064

CS

Please visit our web site at *www.pearsoncustom.com*

PEARSON CUSTOM PUBLISHING
501 Boylston Street, Suite 900, Boston, MA 02116
A Pearson Education Company

To Roseanne

1 Thess. 4:13 ". . . That you may not grieve as others do who have no hope."

I would like to thank Delia Uherec, my editor at Pearson Custom Publishing, for her help and encouragement, both on this book and its companion volume, *Beyond Gender Prejudice*.

CONTENTS

PREFACE

Why does an introductory sociology textbook have to read as though it were written by a committee? Why does an introductory sociology textbook have to include the *same* chapters, in the *same* order, as all other ones? The answer to both questions is the same: it doesn't.

The aim of this book, expressed positively, is to give students the conceptual tools they need to analyze the world (including themselves) sociologically.

Readers will notice that there is no chapter on gender in this book. This fact does not reflect the author's belief that gender equality has been achieved and that we therefore live in a gender-blind society. Far from it. What it does reflect are two things: (1) gender inequality, and so gender-relevance, is taken to be so pervasive that a single chapter on it would be like a woman's page in a bygone newspaper; instead, the topic of gender inequality is weaved throughout the book, and (2) a separate book on gender equality exists by the author, namely *Beyond Gender Prejudice: Toward a Sociology of Male Domination*.

1

WHAT IS SOCIOLOGY?

Sociology is the study of society. Why is the study of society important? Because we are members of society; we are formed by our membership in society; and so, to study society is to study ourselves. Sociology is important, therefore, to the extent that self-understanding is important. We cannot "prove" that such an undertaking is important. Obviously sociologists think it is. But one can live an entire lifetime, and even achieve "success," "happiness," and so on, without ever seeking to understand the life one has led. Insofar as sociology has to do with self-understanding, disciplines such as philosophy and psychology (because they are about selves, persons, "rational beings") are closely related to it, while disciplines such as biology and physics (because they are about organisms, matter, etc.) are not. The latter sciences, though useful and even indispensable in their place, may even interfere with human self-understanding, since they inadvertently encourage people to understand themselves as though they were essentially organisms or collections of matter.

Sociology, then, is one of the social sciences. In Europe, the social sciences are sometimes called the "human sciences," and in German the word is *Geisteswissenschaften*—sciences of the spirit. Those terms seem to express the essence of the matter better than "social sciences": after all, we are talking about human beings and human behavior, and not all entities that are social are human. Not only does sociology address human beings and human behavior, it addresses these things *as human beings behaving* in a particular way (i.e., as sociologists). We cannot escape the fact that we are enclosed within our own humanness; there is no trans-human standpoint we can adopt from which to survey human beings and human behavior. In this respect sociology and the other social sciences differ from the natural or physical sciences, whose object is external to the investigator. Is this feature of the social sciences a *limitation* (since we are trapped within our own humanness and so cannot view our object "objectively") or an *advantage* (since our similarity to what we are studying means we may become intimately familiar with it)?

Then, of course, there arises the question: how can *any* subject-matter be addressed unless the one who addresses it stands *in some sense* outside it? So it is not sufficient to say that the natural sciences stand outside, the social sciences inside: to be more precise, we must say that—paradoxical as it may sound—social scientists, while not sacrificing their humanity (and in that sense staying "inside") can and must detach themselves from their subject-matter, i.e., they must make phenomena objects of study. The social scientist, then, is both a member and an observer of societal membership.

To sum up: the social scientist differs from the natural scientist by being both the same as yet not the same as her/his object of study. (The reason why this is paradoxical may not be evident yet; we will explore this theme further in Chapter III.) But whether they are able to leave the human realm or not, sociologists are committed not to; a chief implication of this commitment is the sociological principle that human behavior can only be understood in human terms. A second principle is that anything human beings do can (eventually if not immediately) be understood by other humans. (This is known as Max Weber's principle of *verstehen*, or "sympathetic understanding.") Now understanding and agreeing are two different things; anyone who, because they equate the two, wishes not to understand is cautioned not to read further in this or any other sociology book—or any book written from the standpoint of *any* of the social sciences, for the *sole* purpose of such books is to help us understand.

SOCIOLOGY AND SOCIAL ORDER

Sociology treats human behavior as a product of the society in which it occurs. According to sociology, human behavior is in every case a reflection of society; thus in studying individuals sociologically we learn about the society in which they live, and vice versa.

Consider the following mundane example:

Students enter a classroom for the first class meeting of the semester; they take their seats and wait for the professor to enter the room. While they freely choose which seats to take, their choices nevertheless follow a pattern: they all choose seats other than the one reserved for the professor. This behavior pattern is visible; but following it means making use of something that is invisible—namely, the students' knowledge of how they are supposed to choose seats. The students' knowledge of how they are supposed to behave is **shared**; and their behavior can be seen as **an expression of** their shared knowledge. It is as if they entered the classroom with a shared image of what it is supposed to look like with regard to seating arrangements and then proceeded to align their behavior with this shared image. The shared image, then, served as a guideline for behavior; it provided the students with shared **rules** for behavior. But while the rules for behavior exist in the students' minds, the fact that they are shared indicates that they did not originate in individual minds but are the product of **society**. These socially produced rules or guidelines for behavior are called **norms**. Insofar as behavior tends to be a patterned reflection of the norms of society, we can say that social order is a basic characteristic of society.

We can depict various aspects of the social order of the classroom. After all, students not only follow seating rules but a variety of other rules as well. For instance, the professor says she welcomes student participation—but the norms tell us what counts as "normal" class participation. Students know that behaving "normally" means asking questions and offering comments that bear some relation to the topic at hand; not intentionally interrupting the professor in order to speak; knowing more or less when one has talked long enough and should yield the floor; responding to questions the teacher may ask in response to one's own comments, and so on. And then there are other rules: face the front of the room rather than the sides or back; appear attentive or even interested in the lecture as long as the possibility of eye contact with the professor exists; remain seated for the whole period unless it becomes necessary to leave the room, etc. The list could go on. The point is that by behaving normally in the classroom—that is, by behaving thoroughly unremarkably—we show that we are not merely individuals but members of society, following societal rules that we have at some point learned. Ordinarily we do not have to be told what to do; the invisible social order exists within us, so to speak, and our visible behavior—the fact that we go through our daily routines without hesitating or doubting—proves it.

Of course, in listing all these classroom rules we do not mean to suggest that they can't be broken; but even breaking a rule only makes sense and can only be understood with reference to the rule being broken. Behavior looks rude only with reference to norms of politeness.

Norms may vary according to the social position, or **status**, you occupy. The professor, for example, has somewhat more freedom of action than the students—she can stand or sit, lecture or initiate discussion as she chooses—but she too has rules to follow, even if they are different from the students'. She must sit in the professor's chair if she sits, just as the students must not. She is expected to be the first speaker and the last speaker; she should not allow silences to last for more than a "normal" interval; she should make at least some eye contact with the class during each period; when she does so, it should be more or less random (she shouldn't look at the same student for an entire period), and so on.

And then there are rules which apply to student and teacher alike: stick to topics related to the subject of the course; appear attentive while someone else is speaking, etc. But even those rules that apply only to the teacher are **known** as such by the students, so that the students can recognize "normal teacher behavior" when they see it—and vice versa.

Norms, in short, guide our expectations of our own and others' behavior, and these expectations serve to enforce normal behavior. People who don't behave normally—who violate our societally produced expectations—are subject to varying degrees of ridicule, hostility, and other forms of ill treatment. (We know we are dealing with a norm when a violation provokes a reaction.) This informal policing tends to keep us all in line.

Through knowledge of and adherence to norms, we participate in a shared universe of mutual expectations, or what sociologists call "common culture."

Of course in everyday life we do not usually take note of the structured or patterned aspects of behavior. To perceive patterns—and so the influence of society—where normally we would tend to see behavior in terms of individual choice (or see it as sheer randomness) is to exercise what C. Wright Mills called the "sociological imagination" (Mills, 1959). It is something to which the sociologist is by definition committed.

If this is the sociological view of human behavior, is there any place in it for individual uniqueness? Is normal behavior as drably uniform as our description so far might suggest?

Obviously there are individual differences in normal behavior; the question is what difference these differences make. The students in our example **choose**, as individuals, where to sit—that is, where to sit **among the students' chairs**. That is, they make choices **within a range of normal choices that they don't choose**. Similarly, you choose what to wear to class—from within the range of "normal classroom attire" choices, a list whose items you didn't choose. There are a lot of choices on the list (beach wear, formal wear, cross-sex dressing) that you will not make.

Furthermore, within the normal limits you are not only **allowed** to exercise free choice, you are **obliged** to. It would violate the norms to wear an evening gown to class; but it would also violate the norms to ask your classmates to tell you what to wear. Not only must you choose **within the range**; within the range you **must** choose. In other words, "individual uniqueness" **is itself a rule or norm**. Thus, to be a unique individual is to be a typical (normal) member of society; individualism, that is, is not a product of the individual but of society. Otherwise it couldn't be found in some societies but not others. But it is: modern Western societies in general, and American society in particular, place great emphasis on the importance of people acting as individuals.

SOCIOLOGY, SOCIAL SCIENCE, COMMON SENSE

Sociology is only one of a number of disciplines that study human behavior. The other social sciences include psychology, anthropology, economics, and political science.

Psychology can be defined as the study of individual mental and emotional states and their effects on human behavior. Sociology has assimilated many of the basic insights of psychology—including some main ideas of Freud, Piaget, and Skinner. Still, there are fundamental differences between the sociological and psychological approaches to behavior. Psychology tends to locate the cause of behavior in the individual—as when, for example, suicide is explained as the result of an individual emotional disturbance. When it does look beyond the individual, psychology for the most part limits itself to examining the influence of small, intimate groups—as when, for example, suicide is seen as the result of disturbed communication patterns within the family. But ultimately this kind of explanation too comes down to the individual: the family may have caused the child to be disturbed, but in any case suicide is to be **understood as an expression of that disturbance**. Suicide, in other words, "tells us" about particular emotional disturbances. The difference between sociology and psychology is not that sociology is interested in the group rather than the individual—sociology too wants to understand why individuals commit suicide—but that it locates the source of individual behavior in society. So, for example, teenage suicide could be explained in terms of intensified pressures to excel academically in an increasingly competitive society. And in our classroom behavior example we attempted to explain individual behavior-where students choose to sit, what they wear, how they participate in class discussions, etc.—in terms of the influence of societal norms. Now one could object that such an explanation only works for behaviors that are **typical** of a whole class of students rather than ones that are unique to individual members—that is, group behavior rather than individual behavior. But from the sociological point of view virtually all behavior is group behavior, no matter how individual it may look. As we said, your individual choice in dress is really a choice-within-the-normal-range—"normal" being defined for you by your society. Thus the question "Why is he or she dressed that way?", posed by a sociologist, means: what does this choice of dress tell us about the society we live in? What do we learn about our society from the fact that, for some people, it is **normal** to spend hundreds of dollars on sneakers? What societally approved values were projected by the "Preppie" look? And repudiated by the "Goth" look? While such questions bring out the fact that different groups in our society behave differently, the task of the sociologist in every case is to explain the particular behavior in terms of the structure and values of American society as a whole.

Finally, since for sociology the meaning of "normal" is given by society, it follows that sociology views normality as **subject to change**. Psychology, on the other hand, tends to regard the meaning of normal as fixed and objective—the way medical doctors regard the meaning of "healthy."

Another social science with which sociology can be compared is **economics**—the study of the production, distribution, and consumption of goods and services. Economics is relevant to sociology because economic developments give rise to particular types of social relations and institutions. For example, the modern "nuclear family" (now in eclipse) composed of a breadwinner-husband, homemaker-wife, and children, emerged as a result of the rise of an industrial manufacturing economy in the West. And particular social classes are clearly products and expressions of particular economic structures. Only in historically specific economic contexts, in other words, do we find a peasantry, a working class, a class of professional managers, an urban underclass, Yuppies, and so on. But the relevance of economics to sociology is limited by two factors. First, while a variety of social phenomena can be traced to economic factors, **these factors themselves require explanation**; and most sociologists believe they are rooted in non-economic factors. For example, according to Max Weber's theory, the rise of modern industrial capitalism was in large part the result of certain developments in Western religion—namely, the rise of ascetic Protestantism. Why people want to be "successful" rather than simply survive; how they define success or being "comfortable"—these attitudes, which sociologists believe are socially produced, motivate particular kinds of economic behavior. The **motives** behind economic behavior—the **need and desire** for success or survival—and so economic behavior itself, differ from one society and historical period to another. Thus economic behavior is not an expression of "natural" acquisitiveness rationally applied (what economists call "rational self-interest"), for the degree and kind of acquisitiveness and rationality is determined by a variety of social forces. The norms of society can restrain or release human greed, encourage or discourage altruistic behavior. Insofar, then, as economics treats self-interest as a natural rather than a social fact, this constitues a second factor limiting its relevance to sociology.

Political science is the study of the structure and process of government, and the distribution and administration of power in society. It touches on questions relevant to sociology when it analyzes political behavior (e.g., voting) and the motives underlying it. From the sociological point of view political science can seem at times to overstate the importance of formal, official seats of power. Who really wields power in our society? What institutions exert the greatest influence over people? Which of them most accurately reflect and most effectively promote societal norms and values? These questions need to be raised especially in an era of wide-spread political indifference such as our own. Some analysts believe that the **mass media** wield more influence today than any other institution (Kellner, 1989). It could be said that television plays a greater role than political institutions in shaping and transmitting societal values; politicians, after all, have to learn to play by its rules in order to win the public's approval. (The overwhelming influence of the media in shaping our perceptions of reality—an influence that is both symptom and cause of our increased estrangement from the "real world," in the sense that we tend increasingly to respond to images of reality rather than reality itself—is a major theme of post-modernist thought. It seems fair to say, then, that the continued relevance of political science to sociology will depend on its ability to focus on the radically altered nature of power and influence in contemporary society.

Finally, we turn to **anthropology**. Anthropology is so closely allied to sociology that at many colleges the sociology and anthropology departments are combined. Anthropology is ordinarily defined as the study of societies of the past or pre-industrial societies of the present. The field is subdivided into **physical anthropology**, which studies the physical evolution of the human race and the influence of the physical environment on human anatomy; and **cultural anthropology**, which analyzes socially structured ways of living in their geographical and historical contexts. Anthropology as the study of pre-industrial society is thus ordinarily contrasted with sociology as the study of modern industrial society. But the difference is deeper than that. While anthropological studies have provided enormous amounts of data for sociology—since much can be learned about modern society by comparing it with pre-modern society—anthropology is so concerned with making societal beliefs and practices intelligible as responses to environmental challeges and as expressions of universal human needs that the **substance** of the difference between one society and another tends to be overlooked.

Certainly geographical and other external factors do make certain societal responses understandable. For example, it has been observed that the harsh climate and widespread poverty of the Indian subcontinent helps explain the development there of two religions—Hinduism and Buddhism—both of which teach that life consists of suffering and that salvation consists in achieving a meditative transcendence of the earthly, bodily state. But does that mean that ultimately the only differences between one religion and another are the physical environments they originated in? If different religions express different basic beliefs about the meaning of life, aren't these differences worth taking seriously in themselves? The sociological study of the influence of society seems more attuned to the differences between norms in one time and place and another. And norms—which include normal religious beliefs and practices—establish differences between one society and another; they do not, like physical environmental factors, explain them away.

SOCIOLOGY AND COMMON SENSE

There is one more "perspective" we should compare with sociology: common sense. After all, the average person is as likely to have opinions on many of the subjects discussed in this book as practitioners of the various social sciences are. Poverty, crime, the changing role of women, race relations, the changing definition of "family," bureaucracy—all these topics studied by sociologists are topics for common sense too.

The usual distinction made between sociology and common sense—at least by sociologists—is that common-sense views are held regardless of whether thay have been **tested** and found to be valid. Thus, they may be held not because they are true but because they are pleasing. For example, there is no evidence that deliberate efforts by employers to recruit minorities—so-called "Affirmative Action" programs—have led to the routine hiring of unqualified people at the expense of qualified people. But many people want to believe this, so it has become common sense to view Affirmative Action that way. And as a result the beneficiaries of Affirmative Action have to be constantly prepared to defend themselves against a baseless charge.

In this example common sense not only does not test, it **resists** testing its views. How many opponents of Affirmative Action would accept evidence that Affirmative Action does not empower the underqualified? Popularity and truth are obviously different qualities.

On the other hand, common-sense views naturally provide sociology with many of its **topics**. Affirmative Action is interesting not only because it has contributed to the growth of a black middle-class but because so many people are so vigorously opposed to it. Thus the common-sense view, however distorted, is itself "news." There is much we can learn from the persistence of the anti-Affirmative Action view: about the level of economic anxiety in society (people wouldn't be upset, after all, if there were enough good jobs to go around); about the apparently widespread belief that the employment opportunity system normally works strictly according to merit (until Affirmative Action came along to mess things up); and, perhaps, about current methods for expressing impolite sentiments, e.g., racial prejudices, politely ("I'm not aginst black advancement, I'm against favoritism for blacks").

But the main problem with common sense—that it does not examine its own views—would remain a problem even in cases where the views in question were true. Common sense is inadequate not because it is incorrect but because it is unreflective. Sociology is sometimes ridiculed for telling us "what everyone knows"; but the fact is, we need to be made aware of what we know.

"Common sense" also refers, not to the **opinions** of the majority, but to the taken-for-granted understandings of everyday, routine matters that all members of society share—the kinds of understandings displayed in the classroom example, about where to sit, when to ask a question, and so on. In this sense common sense provides a rich source of data—about apparently trivial things.

ORIGINS OF SOCIOLOGY

Sociology originated in Western Europe in the 19th century as an attempt to understand the nature of life in **modern industrial society**.

The three most important of the early sociologists—thinkers whose work exerts a decisive influence on the field to this day—were Emile Durkheim, Karl Marx, and Max Weber. (Comte and Spencer were significant forerunners; see Box I.) These three thinkers all agreed that thought and behavior patterns in modern society were historically unique, although each perceived the nature of this uniqueness differently. We will now briefly describe the principal themes of their work.

Emile Durkheim (1858–1917). Durkheim is generally regarded as the actual founder of sociology; it was he above all who achieved recognition for it as a legitimate, specialized field of academic study.

According to Durkheim, the principal challenge facing any society is how to promote and maintain **solidarity** among its members. The very existence of society, after all, depends on the extent to which individuals are able and willing to co-operate with each other. In traditional societies this task is not especially difficult, since members of such societies tend to be united by the deep, in-destructible bonds of ethnicity and religion—and, consequently, of shared values.

In such a society, there is little or no **tension** between the standpoint of the individual and the standpoint of the group. Each individual is more or less a replica or microcosm of the whole. Durkheim uses the term **mechanical solidarity** to describe this kind of unity based on common beliefs and lifestyles, and on indifference to individual differences.

And what about modern industrial societies? The most salient characteristic of such societies, according to Durkheim, is the **diversity** of their populations. Yet in one respect, at least, this diversity is actually itself the source of solidarity. As Durkheim points out, the modern **division of labor**, in which more and more individuals, as society advances technically, are engaged in occupations that differ more and more from those of their neighbors, makes individuals more **dependent** on each other than at any previous time in history. Society more than ever begins to resemble an **organism** in which each specialized part functions to ensure the survival of other parts and the system as a whole. Think of how a strike in one industry can paralyze an entire society. Or ask yourself how many people we depend on every day in order to perform our roles as teacher or student. We don't build or repair the roads that get us to school. We don't arrange for the transporting of food and drink to the school cafeteria (let alone produce the food in the first place). Obviously many more examples could easily be given. Durkheim uses the term **organic solidarity** to describe this kind of unity based on the modern individual's acute lack of self-sufficiency and the interdependence of social roles.

In one sense this modern form of solidarity is deeper than the traditional one, for our **daily physical survival** now depends more than ever on the labor of others. But in another sense it is shallower since it is based only on mutual need rather than shared sentiment. After all, the division of labor is only one type of division in modern society; and the other types—ethnic, racial, religious, linguistic—often give rise to conflict rather than co-operation. And occupational diversity diminishes the sense in which people feel they have something in common with their neighbors. For these reasons solidarity in modern societies tends to be fragile. Often it exists alongside ominously high levels of indifference and even hostility between groups and a growing sense of isolation and alienation from society on the part of many individuals. In such a situation societal and psychic breakdowns are ever-present possibilities. (Durkheim's classic study of suicide shows just how serious the consequences of modern disorientation can be.)

Yet despite all this society under modern conditions has remained relatively orderly. The vast majority of the people obey the vast majority of the rules the vast majority of the time. Even in today's notorious big cities, where violence is rampant and where "nothing works," people wait patiently on lines, stop at red lights even when no one is looking, and in general participate in a great number of socially prescribed routines of varying degrees of significance every day. Many of the early sociologists, but especially Durkheim, believed that society's capacity to reproduce order had been drastically weakened by modern conditions; they studied social order because they were anxious about its future. A more recent trend among sociologists is to be **awestruck** at society's apparent capacity to achieve order under any circumstances. (This attitude is characteristic of phenomenological sociology.)

Karl Marx (1818–1883). Marx was as much an economist as he was a sociologist, but his contributions to these two fields cannot be separated from each other, for his economic analyses are informed by the conviction that societal norms and values—and so individual thought and behavior—are in fact shaped by economic forces.

For Marx the definitive characteristic of modern society is its **capitalist** economy. Capitalism is an economic system in which private individuals compete against each other in pursuit of capital—that is, a form of wealth that exists not for the sake of immediate use but in order to **produce** things of immediate use (and more wealth). In industrial society the most significant example of capital is the factory. To own a factory is to own the chief source of wealth in such a society; it is to own what Marx calls the "means of production." Now to maximize their wealth, it is important to the owners of the means of production—the "capitalist class"—to minimize costs, including, of course, the cost of labor. According to Marx, by the very logic of capital accumulation, workers tend to be exploited by those for whom they work. For what is the **source** of profit? Marx asks. It is the **work** done by the worker. The worker produces a pair of shoes; the owner sells the shoes on the open market; the price the shoes command, minus production costs, is the owner's profit—what Marx calls "surplus value." While the worker literally produces surplus value by producing the shoes, the owner is under no obligation to share the profits with the worker. But more than that: the less the owner pays the worker, the greater the owner's profit. Thus there is an **inherent conflict** between owner and worker in a capitalist system. In the short run, observed Marx, the workers are necessarily the losers in this conflict. As long as employers are under no obligation to pay decent wages, and as long as workers can be easily replaced—two conditions that existed in Marx's lifetime—workers have no choice but to accept low wages and submit to harsh discipline, or starve. In the long run, however, workers will win by uniting to overthrow the capitalist system. But that's another story. Here we are interested only in Marx's analysis of the dynamics of modern society, i.e., of capitalism.

The deprivation experienced by workers according to Marx is not only economic. Indeed, industrial workers under capitalism are completely dehumanized—that is, deprived of their humanity. Not simply the monetary value of their work but **their work itself** is taken from them. Unlike the traditional craftsperson, factory workers don't own what they make; and, typically, what any one individual worker makes is merely an infinitesimal part of the finished product. Instead of their work being a manifestation of their freedom and creativity, it is the sign and seal of their exploitation. It is what should be most their own yet under capitalism is least their own. The entire work process is set in motion, organized, and directed by the capitalist, who at the end of the process appropriates the product. This self-estrangement Marx calls **alienation**. Human beings under capitalism find their own lives—even their own selves—foreign to them, for it is their minds and their bodies that become no longer theirs as they exhaust themselves in alienated labor.

Just as workers suffer in more than an economic sense, capitalists reap rewards other than purely economic ones. The economically dominant elements of the population shape their society's norms and values, which then come to permeate the society's basic institutions—politics, religion, the law (and very importantly today, the mass media). According to Marx, the role of these institutions is to **reflect the interests of the capitalist class**, making it harder for exploited workers to recognize their oppression, let alone fight it. Workers who are permanently laid off as owners seek higher profits through automation are driven to steal out of desperation; but the law recognizes only the thief, not the owner who made him into one, as guilty. The endless tedium and meaningless of his job leads a worker to suffer a breakdown; but psychiatry recognizes only the worker, not the system that routinely consigns people to meaningless work, as sick. Another worker flees the cruel reality of working life through drinking; but the TV movie on the subject focuses only on the disease of "alcoholism" rather than the disease of alienated labor.

Max Weber (1864–1920). Weber coined the term "rationalization" to describe how modern societies differ from pre-modern ones. Rationalization refers to **the process by which ideals of efficiency and calculability have come to determine the way work and other activities are conducted in society.** It is a process which is at work everywhere in modern life, but can be seen most clearly in the way large-scale businesses, and similar enterprises such as government agencies, operate. The best way to understand rationalization is to contrast it with the **traditional** methods it has replaced. What were some typical features of traditional business activity before the trend towards rationalization set in? For one thing, **personal considerations** permeated every aspect of the typical enterprise. Hiring decisions were made on a personal basis, and bonds of mutual loyalty characterized relations within the firm as well as those between the firm and its clientele. Secondly, the process by which business was conducted was not methodically planned and executed but followed a more **spontaneous, informal, "rule of thumb"** type of pattern. Think of the difference between a traditional "organization" such as an open-air market and a modern supermarket. The teenager that the fruit vendor has hired to assist him may be a family member or a friend of one; supermarket personnel are in most cases complete strangers to top management, and have been hired only after submitting a written application. Insofar as job security exists for the supermarket employee, it comes as the result of management's continued need, rationally assessed, for the employee's services, as well as continued satisfaction with the employee's performance, re-inforced perhaps by formal protection against arbitrary dismissal provided by a labor union contract; "job security" for the vendor's helper exists to the extent that the personal relationship between the two parties remains intact. And the contrast in the relationship between organization and customer are even sharper. Even in cases where the customer is not a friend or acquaintance of the vendor, the typical transaction includes a fair amount of casual conversation, as well as some bargaining over prices; in a typical supermarket visit, few if any words are exchanged between customer and employee, and the customer pays prices that have been pre-determined, i.e., there is no bargaining allowed.

There is nothing wrong with this arrangement as long as we define "going to the supermarket," "working in a supermarket," and "managing a supermarket" not as occasions for human beings to converse with their fellow humans but simply as practical tasks to be accomplished as efficiently as possible. Here buying and selling is rationalized in the sense that personal sentiment is removed from the process and **technical** considerations of how to get the job done—from the point of view of the customer as well as the store—become the only relevant ones. We **may** think of a "good" supermarket as one in which the personnel are "friendly" (i.e., not rude or otherwise "unpleasant"). But if the "friendly" supermarket is at the same time one where items are hard to find, and the check-out lines move too slowly, we are easily persuaded that it is not so good after all. In other words, the primary criterion for evaluating the supermarket is efficiency, not friendliness.

And of course management sees things the same way. How can we "move" the most "product" in the shortest amount of time? How can we get the most out of each employee? These questions of efficiency lead to an emphasis on planning, calculating, evaluating, assessing, reviewing—in other words, efforts to bring as much of the operation as possible under **rational control**. This, to Weber, is the essence of the modern. The problem is that the fully rationalized world, in which no time is "wasted" on superfluous interaction and in which the unanticipated never happens, is, just as capitalism is for Marx, a dehumanized environment.

As human beings become increasingly oriented towards efficiency rather than humanness, the modern rationalized world becomes bland and colorless. And the social landscape becomes increasingly standardized: supermarkets and other chains operate on the same principles, sell the same products, and train their staffs to say "Have a Nice Day" in the same pleasant, robotic way.

Weber's analysis of modernity is quite intricate and complex—for example, in its emphasis on the ambiguous legacy of modernization. The same forces that have led to unprecedented dehumanization have, simultaneously, brought about significant improvements in the quality of life. Our impersonal, efficiency-oriented world is, for that very reason, one which is well-stocked in consumer goods of all kinds; modern dehumanized lives are made more comfortable than people in previous centuries could ever have imagined. More significantly, the same world that Weber decried for its impersonality is one which, because of its impersonality, has achieved unparalleled levels of **fairness**, **equality**, **and impartiality** in social relationships. To an employer you may just be a payroll number; but that means that, in principle at least, you will be treated the same as your fellow employees, who are also mere numbers. The rise of impersonality implies the decline of bias. In a rationalized world, ability begins to count—for the first time in history—more than personal connections (but, of course, only those abilities which suit the needs of a rationalized world). For Weber the rationalization process reaches its pinnacle with the rise of modern **bureaucracy**. The analysis of bureaucracy as the epitome of rationalized action—in all its ambiguity—is one of Weber's main contributions to sociology.

THE MODERN AND THE POST-MODERN

Throughout the first century of its history sociology has continuously analyzed the dynamics of modern society by examining the transition from traditional to modern life in the Western world and through cross-cultural comparisons between the West and other regions of the globe. Sociologists continue to build on the work of the originators, often in creative and surprising ways; we will discuss these contributions in detail throughout the following pages. But our task is complicated by the fact that the modern age, according to many observers, is coming to an end and that society is now entering a "post-modern" phase. What does this mean?

"Post-modern" is not easy to define. Over the past few years, the term has been used by a variety of authors in a variety of ways, creating a rather confusing situation in a number of disciplines including sociology. But this confusion should not be regarded as scandalous—nor should it come as a surprise. It would be far more surprising and scandalous, in fact, if there were no confusion at all over the meaning of the term. "Post-modern," after all, refers to the **end of modernity**. But how can we precisely define the essence of the modern? And who can say precisely in what sense the modern period is coming to an "end"—especially since all of us, no matter how smart we are, are living in the midst of this process of transition, a process which is apparently unfinished and which has already included incredible and unforeseen changes of various kinds—everything from global political upheavals to transformations in the sphere of intimacy. No one can predict where these developments will lead, or what further ones lie in store. Generally speaking, it seems easier to identify those aspects of modern life that are fast disappearing than to pinpoint what will take their place. In other words, it is easier to define post-modernity by what it is not than by what it is.

So we will begin trying to define post-modernity by considering further the meaning of modernity. While acknowledgement of, and interest in, the emergence of post-modernity is more common among philosophers and literary theorists than sociologists, formulating the meaning of the end of modernity, and hence the meaning of modernity, is a chief concern of these theorists, and for this reason the understanding of modernity worked out by classical sociological theory (as represented by Durkheim, Marx, and Weber) is a major resource for post-modernists regardless of their field. Practitioners of the post-modern, as we shall see, incorporate an essentially sociological perspective into their disciplines.

Post-modernists tend to identify modernity with the belief that **rationality, as defined by modern Western science,** is the key that not only unlocks all truth, but, in so doing, leads to steady and limitless improvements in the human condition. The modern age, then, is characterized by a strong belief in **progress**. The modern age is the age in which **humanity's self-confidence reaches its historical peak**—so that part of what "the emergence of the post-modern" means is that we are past this peak in confidence. Certainly our world today is one in which faith in progress through technology is being treated with growing skepticism. Yet it is difficult to exaggerate the **faith in science** that characterized especially the second half of the 19th century. Indeed only in the 20th century did people begin to suspect that faith in science is just that—namely, faith, and often blind faith. The disastrous effects of scientific technology in the 20th century (nuclear armaments, environmental devastation) provoked this skepticism—a skepticism that may be regarded as one of the principal symptoms of the end of modernity.

Of course it is easy to understand why such faith in science existed—and why even today most people do not want to abandon scientific knowledge but only the attitude of un-questioning faith in its benefits.

Where did belief in the value of science come from in the first place? There is general agreement that it stems from the Enlightenment, an 18th century French philosophical movement that in many ways epitomized the spirit of the modern age. The Enlightenment identified human dignity with the capacity for **reason**. The philosophers of Enlightenment believed that humanity is destined for greatness but that we do not realize our potential because we allow ourselves to be governed by alien forces—such as religious superstitions—rather than **governing ourselves** by the light of reason. To become truly free we must learn to pursue knowledge and truth even if that means questioning hallowed assumptions or criticizing traditional authority. To gain knowledge and truth we must make active use of the power of reason. But reason that is in the service of human freedom and dignity can only be **scientific** reason. Theologians in the service of the Christian church also use reason, but their use of reason is circumscribed by religious dogmas of various kinds. Science, on the other hand, reasons without making any prior assumptions. Its goal is not to defend a particular view of nature but simply to understand nature. The more we understand nature—as the scientific method of observation and experiment rather than religious faith illuminates it—the more we will be able to **control** nature for the sake of human well-being.

This Enlightenment faith in human emancipation through scientific reason led to extraordinary developments in science and technology over the past 200 years. Few of us would be willing to give up what the modern age has given us, whether this be polio vaccines or indoor plumbing, automobiles or heart surgery. It is modern science that produced the modern printing methods that make it possible for you to read this discussion of what's wrong with modern science. A wholesale rejection of modernity would therefore be hypocritical. More importantly, the Enlightenment, by emphasizing the **universality** of human reason (and therefore of human freedom and dignity in principle), also lies behind the rise of modern democratic political systems; of belief in racial and sexual equality; of attempts to establish civil and human rights for all; of systems of universal public education, and many other important advances.

Yet this same Enlightenment faith has led to other, darker developments. The term "post-modern" tries to address this ambiguity; it tries to capture the sense that the Enlightenment faith is no longer convincing even though no one is quite sure what to replace it with. At the very least, then, the term "post-modern" points to the fact that for many people naive trust in the wonders of scientific rationality is no longer an option. How can we believe that technical development equals progress now that we aware of its catastrophic effect on the environment? How can we believe that hatred and evil are expressions of "primitive" urges that can be overcome by reason (i.e., education) when the experience of the 20th century proves that being highly educated and "advanced" may simply mean being capable of committing murder on a grander scale (the Nazis in the Holocaust, and the Americans—many say—in Vietnam).

Most analysts of the post-modern agree that all the talk about the post-modern at least signifies a crisis of sorts—not only a loss of confidence in scientific progress, but, perhaps as a consequence, a general sense in society of a loss of intellectual and moral clarity. For the public at large, and not merely intellectuals, questions without answers abound. Our world seems to oppress us with a sense of the complexity and many-sidedness of every issue. Is abortion good or evil? It's more complicated than that. "Pro-choice" doesn't mean "pro-abortion." Under what circumstances should abortion be permitted? Should parental notification be required of teenagers desiring abortions? And do you mean parental notification or parental consent? The list of questions goes on and on. It seems that the more we know the more difficult the questions become. You're pro-choice but you don't believe the government should be required to finance abortions. That seems a clear enough moral position. But doesn't such a policy in effect discriminate against poor women? Why should the affluent have easier access to abortion than the poor? Where is the morality in that? Again: you are pro-choice but feel teenagers should have to inform their parents first. But, at the same time, you are aware of the fact that parents are not always as wise and understanding and loving as they tend to be depicted as being on TV. What an odd situation: we **know too much** to be able to answer questions! And even if we do manage to arrive at an answer that satisfies us, there is no guarantee that others, who have had to go through this same agonizing process, will reach conclusions similar to our own. Thus the modern explosion of knowledge, coupled with the modern emphasis on individual freedom leads, again, to ambiguous results. In place of an ethic we can all subscribe to as rational modern citizens, we see the erosion of societal consensus on questions of morality (as indicated by controversies over pornography, "family values," and a host of other issues, not only abortion).

Yet a positive meaning can be seen even in this. Negatively, "post-modern" signifies division and disunity—within individuals as well as between them. But the positive side of this chaos is an unprecedented increase in the number of **different voices** that are beginning to be heard—in the abortion example, we might think of the voices of poor women and abused children. To take another example: Demands are being made that world history no longer be taught as if it were the history of Europe; that this new global history tell us about the struggles and achievements of ordinary working people, women and men, rather than focusing exclusively on the momentous actions of kings and generals; that psychologists no longer describe the process of human psychic development in terms of the psyches and experiences of males (and for that matter male heterosexuals); and so on.

This growing pluralism could be regarded as either a threat or an opportunity: a threat to existing unity or an opportunity to build a more inclusive unity than has so far existed. But even where it is welcomed this post-modern pluralism raises questions that are not easy to answer: Is feminism a form of "male-bashing" or an attempt to build a society that values the experiences and abilities of women as well as men? Is Affirmative Action for minorities "reverse discrimination" or an attempt to build an opportunity system in which built-in advantages for whites cannot be taken for granted? Does the relative decline in the social power of the Christian churches signify a collapse of values or the dawning recognition that no religious institution has a monopoly on correct moral teaching or the correct way to worship God?

Different people will answer these questions differently, and for many people the answer will be yes and no. In short, the post-modern period is characterized by a widespread ambivalence concerning some of the basic questions confronting society. To avoid facing the complexity of the issues involved, many people take refuge in extreme, either-or type views (abortion is murder; feminists are witches, etc.), thus contributing to a growing polarization of public opinion. But the complexity will not go away. Does criticism of the "Eurocentric" approach to history mean that there can no longer be such a thing as History—that is, a story with a unified theme (e.g., the evolution of human freedom)—but only histories of various regions and cultures, each with its own "moral" or none at all? And how would the replacement of History with histories affect our sense of sharing a common culture despite our differences? Is society unavoidably on the brink of fragmentation—and if so, is that necessarily bad?

The principal early sociologists, as we have seen, shared a fundamental interest in the phenomenon of modernity. Their work remains relevant not only for the obvious reason that any analysis of the post-modern requires an understanding of the modern but because their work in particular draws our attention to certain aspects of modern society that make the crisis of modernity understandable. When we examine the classical sociological analyses of modern society, in fact, we can begin to see how modernity itself points beyond itself towards post-modernity (and thus, at the same time, we can appreciate how these analyses anticipated some of the basic insights found in contemporary works on post-modernity). For example:

- Durkheim's analysis of modernity in terms of the growing complexity of the division of labor helps us understand post-modern fragmentation as a symptom of a crisis in modernity that is at the same time a logical consequence of modernity.
- Marx's analysis of capitalism's need to continually generate profits by expanding markets for its goods helps us understand why society encourages a consumerist ethic in which images generated by advertising and purveyed by the mass media become more influential than reality: a major symptom of post-modernity, according to post-modern theorists, that is at the same time a logical consequence of modernity. (The role of the "culture industry" in reducing artistic products to the level of mere consumer goods which distract us from reality, is a basic theme of the Frankfurt School of Marxists. Adorno, 1975.)
- Weber's analysis of modernity as rationalization, in which the discussion of efficient means drowns out all debate on the worthiness of the aim, helps us recognize an enormity such as the Holocaust, not as an inexplicable eruption of barbarity in the midst of modern civilization, but as an expression of modern civilization itself (i.e., as a grotesque exercise in "rational planning" or "social engineering" (Bauman, 1991). Thus post-modern **skepticism**

with regard to the high ideals and grand designs of politicians and other would-be saviors becomes understandable.

SOCIOLOGY AND SCIENCE

If the work of Durkheim, Marx, and Weber are examples of sociology, and sociology is a science, the reader may be inclined to ask: in what sense are their analyses scientific? Or, more generally, the question is: in what sense is sociology a science? There is no single answer to this question to which all sociologists today would agree, not because sociologists don't believe that sociology is a science but because they disagree on the **meaning of science** as it pertains to sociology.

Many sociologists, for example, would claim that sociology (and social science as a whole) is (or should be) scientific but **not in the same way** that the natural or physical sciences, such as biology or chemistry, are. And this is true, according to this view, because the subject-matter of the social sciences—human beings—endows these disciplines with a different **aim** than the "hard" sciences: the aim of the social sciences is to **make sense** of social reality, to help us **understand** our behavior rather than to establish causal relationships or formulate law-like truths about the way the human animal operates. Such truths—like physical laws—may command our assent but they do not help us understand ourselves; they are not, as Weber says, "subjectively meaningful." Think of the difference between a causal explanation of depression in terms of the neutralizing effects of certain enzymes on the body's neurotransmitters, on the one hand, and an analysis of the circumstances under which depression can be seen as a reasonable or understandable response (which doesn't mean harmless or healthy) on the other. Now if we were to ask **why** a decreased concentration of serotonin causes depression, the only answer is: because it does. But if we were to ask why, say, failing to get a particular job one had applied for caused depression, the answer would be more elaborate: as sociologists we would describe the importance of material success in American society, its consequent relation to "ego" needs, etc. In other words, in the second case we make depression meaningful.

But isn't meaningfulness something we expect and require of explanations of human behavior? Sociology, in this view, is concerned with the **reasons** for our behavior rather than the **causes** of our behavior.

More traditional sociologists would argue that this way of defining the discipline undermines sociology's claim to being a science. How do we know that what is "meaningful" is also **true?** How can sociology not strive to discover general laws and yet still be a science? And why does the search for meaningfulness have to preclude the search for such laws?

And, while chemical theories of depression might be sociologically insignificant, that doesn't mean that formulating general laws of behavior from a sociological standpoint is necessarily a waste of time. For example, what if, instead of a correlation between depression and serotonin, we discovered one between depression and social class? The first type of sociologist would say: fine, but what is interesting still is not the law but the **reasons** why it holds (i.e., the reasons it **makes sense** that the poor are depressed).

But all parties would agree that, even if it is not like the hard sciences, sociology is scientific at least in the sense that it attempts to **derive its insights from an examination of data generated by research**.

This formulation too leads to a number of questions. Are a sociologist's conclusions drawn from the data by some sort of logical necessity? Or do conclusions represent merely a "reasonable interpretation" of the evidence? But then how do we determine whether an interpretation is "reasonable" or not? More fundamentally we could ask: Isn't the data itself discovered through a process—called "research"—which itself involves an element of selectivity, that is, of interpretation? After all, the things sociologists "observe"—capitalism, bureaucracy, modernization, racism, sexism, homophobia—are only noticeable if our **way of looking at reality** is open to them. But then how do we distinguish between this inevitable "selectivity" and outright bias? Most sociologists today agree that interpretation is a basic element in the research process (although there is disagreement, for example, over the question whether interpretation influences the entire research process or just the selection of a research topic).

In other words, while sociology involves continuous contact with and reference to the actual social world we live in, most sociologists acknowledge that this "contact" is mediated by a **perspective**—a set of basic assumptions that gives meaning to the otherwise incoherent facts of social life. There are four main perspectives in modern sociology, to be described in the next section. Now the word "theory" can and will be used interchangeably with "perspective" but the reader should keep in mind that this word carries certain connotations drawn from its use in the natural sciences. These connotations include the idea that to be valid theories must yield "objective" findings that are subject to "proof"; that they must have the capacity to predict future events; and that their findings must be reproducible (meaning that any researcher, regardless of his or her perspective, should be able to conduct the same research study and arrive at the same results). But are these criteria appropriate for evaluating theories in the social sciences? To answer "yes" is, in effect, to claim that sociology ought to be a hard science because to not be one is to be unscientific, period. As we suggested, many sociologists do hold this view, but many others do not.

2

THE PERSPECTIVES

We have described the sociological perspective, distinguishing it from the perspectives of the other social sciences as well as from common sense. As we have noted, there are a variety of perspectives within sociology itself. In this section we discuss the four major sociological perspectives: functionalism, conflict theory, symbolic interactionism, and phenomenology. There are areas of overlap among these perspectives as well as major points of divergence. No matter how wide the differences among them, however, all of these perspectives reflect a distinctly **sociological** to reality. Thus an examination of them will enable us not only to appreciate the variety of possible viewpoints that sociology can encompass but, by recognizing what these viewpoints have in common, we will be able to gain a sharper, more concrete sense of what distinguishes sociology from other disciplines.

We should already be prepared to discover that these perspectives all share the basic view that human behavior is a patterned reflection of societal norms. Differences arise over such questions as: where do the norms originate? what is their purpose? under what circumstances and by what processes do they change? etc.

FUNCTIONALISM

From the time—roughly 100 years ago—that Durkheim formulated its basic principles until the social upheavals of the 1960s prompted its decline, the functionalist perspective dominated sociology, especially in the U.S. Today, while it is still influential, it no longer occupies the commanding position in the field that it once did.

The basic idea of functionalism is that societies tend to be organized in such a way as to ensure equilibrium or stabilty. Why? Because society is like an organism: its basic aim is to preserve itself, and the primary purpose of its various parts is to contribute to the preservation of the whole. To understand any one social institution means to understand its role in maintaining the whole system. Also, as in the case of organisms, if one part of the system breaks down, so that its particular function is not being fulfilled, other parts of the system will be thrown off balance.

The functionalist question, then, is: How do the particular parts of society contribute to the maintenance of society as a whole? As an example let us ask: what is the function of the school system, as a part of society, in making society as a whole work?

We can identify a number of such functions. First, schools provide individuals with the training they need for employment. This includes not only the technical skills provided by the higher education system that are directly applicable to the job market but also the basic literacy and numeracy skills that are taught from pre-school on. While all this is obvious, the point is that this is a function the schools perform **for society:** our society needs a skilled work force—now more than ever. And so it is no accident that now more than ever society is encouraging (and the government is helping) students from all backgrounds to go to college. Thousands of college-bound students who, if they were 18 years old 40 years ago, would have gone straight from high school (if they went to high school at all) to working in a factory, are in college today because increasingly the skills Americans must have in order for America to be a major economic power are "high tech" skills that only the colleges transmit. Our manufacturing sector has been in sharp decline for decades. Thus, for sheerly practical reasons educational opportunities have expanded.

But while opportunities have expanded because such an expansion is functional, they remain limited for the same reasons. In other words, a second function of the schools is to produce individuals who not only are trained but **credentialed.** The schools perform a **processing** or **sorting** function for society; that is why we are not only taught but tested throughout our school careers. Graduates possess not only knowledge but records, and this too is vital to society. An employer needs to know whether to interview you for the position of sitting behind a particular desk or the position of cleaning the floor after the person behind the desk has left for the day. If society did not have this need, all the testing and evaluating that goes on in schools—a time-consuming headache for teachers and a source of intense anxiety for students—would be pointless. (And worse than pointless, for without tests there would be more time for teachers to teach, and the freedom from anxiety could make it easier for students to learn.)

The individual produced by the school system is not only trained and credentialed but **socialized:** this is a third function of education in society. Especially in the early grades it is apparent that part of the schools' job is to transmit social skills; and as more and more couples (particularly among professionals) are deciding to have only one child, this responsibility, which is in a sense shared with the family, is increasingly left to the schools. In day care many children learn for the first time how to interact with other chlidren, including how to resolve conflicts, how to share the limelight that in the one-child household is exclusively theirs, and so on. Perhaps the most important social skill the schools transmit is the ability to **accept the process of being evaluated**—to adjust to getting a "C" when your neighbor has gotten an "A." Inequality of grades prepares students for the inequality of income, power, and prestige that awaits them in the "real world"—something the all-supportive, non-evaluating environment of the family often does not. But the schools not only provide practice in inequality; they prepare us to regard future inequality as **justified** by encouraging us to understand it as a further instance of the rational evaluation process we were first exposed to in school. We accept that our social status, high or low, has been "earned" the way our grades were.

Finally, no matter how inadequately schools may educate and socialize children, they at least keep them off the streets. Sociologists refer to this as the **social control** function of education. Public education means free baby sitting if nothing else—but this is essential in a society with an increasing number of single-parent families, as well as dual-parent households in which both parents work. But while the social control function is important, it is not the purpose for which schools are built (playpens or prisons would be just as appropriate in that case); although the fact that schools do perform this function is nevertheless one reason why we want there to be a school sysytem. The difference between the "training" and "social control" functions, then, is not that one is important and one is not but that one is **recognized** and the other is ordinarily not—or, in the standard sociological terminology coined by Robert Merton (N), one is "manifest" while the other is "latent." This is an important distinction for functionalism because it points to the fact that to understand the importance of a social institution we must look at the functions it actually performs and not merely at the ones people acknowledge.

Functionalism is often criticized for its overly **conservative** implications. By paying so much attention, for example, to the ways schools contribute to society, functionalism tends to overlook the **harmful** consequences schools may have. Functionalists respond by pointing out that they do look at the negative side—the harmful effects, or **dysfunctions**—as well as the positive side. A function of American industry is to provide jobs; a dysfunction is that it may pollute the environment. A function of the military is to defend the nation (and to provide jobs); a dysfunction is that it diverts resources from domestic needs. A function of religion is to generate group confidence and pride; a dysfunction is that it engenders intergroup hostility. Throughout this book, to be sure, we will see examples of the functionalist analysis of dysfunctional aspects of our major institutions—so much so that the reader may well wonder, in particular cases, whether an institution shouldn't be considered more dysfunctional than functional, and therefore in need of radical reform. **But functionalism never draws that conclusion.** This is where the problem lies—not in the fact that functionalism ignores dysfunctions (it doesn't) but that it seems to assume that the continued stable existence of an institution over the course of time is **proof of its being functional.** This equating of stability with health has been criticized by Conflict Theory, to which we now turn.

CONFLICT THEORY

The conflict perspective, which derives from the work of Marx, directly challenges functionalism by arguing that order and stability are not necessarily indicative of a well-run society. In fact, according to this approach, what appears to be order and stability is usually just a reflection of the fact that those in power have successfully silenced the opposition. Peace and quiet often occur at the expense of justice; sometimes people keep still because they are afraid to speak up—or, more likely (and perhaps worse), because they have been lulled into forgetting how miserable they are. To functionalism stability is a sign of societal health; to conflict theory it is a disguised form of disease. Furthermore, such artificial stability is not only unjust but inherently unstable: since it is built on suppression it is liable to give way to open conflict if and when those who are suppressed realize their situation and decide to do something about it.

But to understand conflict theory we must begin with its basic premise: every society consists of "haves" and "have-nots." Why is this so? Because every society consists of a number of different groups each struggling to acquire wealth and other, related social goods (political power, prestige, etc.). If social groups were driven by a spirit of communality rather than self-interest, or if there were more than enough of the goods to go around, then a perfectly just society would be possible. But as this is not the case, every actual society is characterized by structured inequality, in which some groups have been able to allocate to themselves a disproportionate amount of the society's resources. This inequality may be based on racial, ethnic, or religious differences, or on where people are placed in the economic production process, i.e., worker or owner. (This **class** difference is, as we saw, the one Marx focused on exclusively.)

We can get a clearer idea of conflict theory by comparing its approach to education with the functionalist analysis described above. The functionalist asks how any one part of society contributes to the well-being of the whole society; the conflict theorist asks how it contributes to the well-being of some groups in society at the expense of others. As for the schools, conflict theory would argue as follows: Our education system provides credentials for success (as functionalism also notes), **yet some groups have an unfair advantage in competing for these credentials.** For example:

- Children from affluent families are likely to receive better public education than poor children are. Public education is financed largely through local property taxes; and so neighborhoods with more expensive properties generate more tax revenue to contribute to local schools. Some people argue that money is of only secondary importance in determining the quality of schools; what really counts, they say, are the right attitudes and commitment. Education critic Jonathan Kozol offers two responses to this: (1) If in fact poorly funded schools did not tend to provide poorer quality education, why do we never hear of campaigns in affluent neighborhoods to reduce the level of funding for schools so that money could be spent more usefully? (2) Even if the argument were true, it overlooks the psychological impact dilapidated schools have on the students who are forced to attend them: teachers in poor districts told Kozol that their students felt "written off" by their society; one student told him that by sending students to such schools society "teach(es) you how much you are hated." (Kozol, 1992.)

- If the public education available to the affluent is still not good enough for them, they are free to purchase private education, which is likely to be better still. Until recently, this was an option exercised only by the upper classes; but now, with competition for good jobs increasing, many middle class parents too are investing in private education for their children. Political commitment to public education is likely to decline as fewer and fewer children from middle-class families use the public system. After all, according to conflict theory, the issues that tend to dominate public debate are those issues of most concern to more affluent members of society—if not the wealthy, then at least the middle class. (Presidential candidates, for example, spend a lot more time addressing the needs of these groups than of the poor.)

    (It is true that some parents who are not even middle class choose private education for their children, despite the often considerable financial sacrifice involved. One might conclude from this fact that affluence does not necessarily provide unfair educational advantages, since with the proper commitment even children of the non-affluent get to go to private school. But this doesn't erase the inequality, it merely shifts the basis of it. Instead of children of the affluent having an unfair advantage, children of "committed" parents have one. But why should a child's chances of having a quality education depend on the accident of who the child's parents are? Of course, if the public schools genuinely provided all children a high quality education, neither the wealth nor the commitment of parents would any longer be a major factor in determining the child's educational opportunity.)

- The quality of the credentials students acquire from the school system—and thus the kind of employment they will be eligible for—depends in part on the results of various standardized tests they take throughout their school careers. Whether you are considered "gifted"; whether you are placed in a college-preparatory "track" in high school; whether, consequently, you end up in college, and the kind of college you end up in—all these are influenced by standardized test scores. But, according to conflict theory, these tests are biased—against lower-income groups, minorities, and women.

- Finally, affluent students are taught a different set of "survival skills" than poorer students, according to conflict theory—to be precise, they are taught certain **attitudes that prepare them for the more desirable positions in society.** This transmitting of the right attitudes does not form a part of the official curriculum but of what sociologists call the "hidden curriculum." Upper middle class and upper class schools put a greater emphasis on independent work, initiative, creativity, and other traits that **characterize higher status professional jobs** than working-and lower class schools, which tend to focus on the importance of rule-following and obedience to authority—the kinds of traits that are important in working and lower class jobs. In this way the schools not only reflect but perpetuate economic inequality.

One clear advantage that conflict theory has over functionalism is that it is better equipped to understand social change. (This is why the influence of functionalism began to wane in the 1960s, a period of cataclysmic social change.) If society is based on inequality, an implicit state of conflict always already exists; thus when society breaks out into open conflict—as a result of which important social changes may occur—the conflict theorist is not caught off guard. And because functionalism assumes that stability indicates a well-functioning organism, it can never convincingly explain how change, when it does occur in a well-functioning system, may be **desirable,** let alone necessary. Instead, functionalists focus on the problems they feel social changes have caused—e.g., a higher divorce rate as a consequence of the women's movement. To a conflict theorist, however, while divorce in itself may be disruptive and painful, an increased divorce rate is nevertheless a sign of the increased freedom of women to leave husbands who, in previous eras, they would've had to stay with out of sheer economic necessity.

The real challenge for conflict theory is to explain, not why social change occurs, but why it occurs so infrequently. Why is a world that is seething with injustice so relatively peaceful? To answer this question Marx introduced two now-famous concepts: **ideology** and **false consciousness.** The basic idea behind these concepts is that the stability of an unjust system is ensured not so much by the use of force as by the use of propaganda. People are kept "in their place" because they are **led to believe in the legitimacy of the system. Ideology** means an organized set of ideas that serves to legitimate a social system; **false consciousness** means the acceptance of these ideas even though doing so betrays one's own class interests. An example of ideology would be the idea that American society is characterized by complete equality of opportunity, such that the achievement of wealth and success typically reflects talent, hard work, and other virtues (and perhaps a little luck); an example of false consciousness would be the acceptance of this ideology by poor people. For the poor to accept this ideology means that they must attribute their poverty to low intelligence or laziness or fate—which is just what those in power would like them to do—rather than to inadequate schools, discrimination, or any of the other factors which might inspire them to struggle to bring about a more just society. On the other hand, it is easy to see why the powerful would embrace such ideas—believing them, and getting others to do so, plays right into their hands, for it makes their own wealth and power appear to be merited. Thus, according to conflict theory, ideologies exist to serve the interests of those in power.

While conflict theory, by drawing our attention to the importance of power relations in society, seems more realistic than functionalism, its basic weakness is that it oversimplifies. If the powerful are governed by self-interest, how do we explain the existence of wealthy politicians committed to empowering the poor? (Some of the wealthiest members of Congress are among the most liberal.) Conversely, is support for the status quo among the non-affluent necessarily a sign of false consciousness? Could it be, instead, that the lives of ordinary people are not as miserable as conflict theorists suppose? Conflict theory distinguishes between the powerful and the powerless; but what if most of us are somewhere in between? And what if our reluctance to rebel shows, not that we are brainwashed, but that the present system represents more of a compromise among the interests of various groups than the domination by one group of all the others?

Despite such questions, the importance of conflict theory cannot be doubted. It urges us to analyze social arrangements by asking **who benefits** from them—a question that can yield both theoretical knowledge of how society works and the practical incentive to change it. If conflict theory describes the benefits and losses too simplistically—in assuming, for example, that only the powerful ever benefit from normal social arrangements—this should not deter us from facing the fact that society produces both winners and losers.

SYMBOLIC INTERACTIONISM

Despite their differences, the functionalist and conflict perspectives share this basic assumption: society is an external reality that influences our behavior (and the sociologist's task is to explain how individuals are shaped by this external reality). Symbolic interactionists, however, reject this basic view. Instead, they hold that there is no societal reality other than the one conceived by individuals in the course of their interactions with one another. Even the individual "self" is formed in the course of the interactional process and is inconceivable apart from it.

Symbolic interactionism is about **people**—ordinary people and the ordinary things they do. Instead of studying the classroom and its place in the larger social system, as both functionalists and conflict theorists do, it focuses on the individuals in the classroom and the way they interact with each other. How do teacher and student address one another? What kinds of cues does the teacher rely on to gauge whether the material is "going over"? How do teachers and students collaborate to get by embarrassing moments? What methods—gestures, tone of voice, and so on—does the teacher use to establish and sustain an appearance of authority? These kinds of questions aim at a close-up view of society; for this reason, interactionism (along with phenomenology) is sometimes referred to as **micro-sociology.** Functionalism and conflict theory, on the other hand, are **macro-sociological** approaches; they are interested in large-scale social institutions, forces, and trends.

The most important single premise of the symbolic interactionist approach is that human beings differ from the lower animals in that their world is a **meaningful** one to them. So, for example, we respond to an external stimulus according to the meaning it has for us. Our subjective experience of a thing—our point of view—determines our response to it; the thing in and of itself does not. A man wielding a baseball bat will evoke a different response from you depending on whether he is wearing a baseball uniform and standing at home plate in a ballpark or staring malevolently at you in a dark alley. The wooden stick in his hand may be the same in both cases; but its meaning is different. As George Herbert Mead, whose work laid the foundations of symbolic interactionism, expressed it, a wooden stick is a **thing,** while a baseball bat and a weapon are **objects.** Human beings respond not to things but to objects— i.e., things that have meaning. "Reality," then, is the product of the interaction between ourselves and the environment—an interaction in which we experience things and **invest them with meaning.** In this sense we **construct** the reality we live in; from the interactionist point of view, then, the human individual is much more of an **active agent** than functionalism or conflict theory allow.

A second basic point is that the meanings we give to things are **shared.** In fact, for the interactionist society **consists** of these shared meanings, such that membership in a particular society is defined by knowledge or ignorance of them. For example, in Great Britain an extended index and middle finger means what the extended middle finger means here; a typical member of either society is one who knows, and responds in terms of, the meaning the gesture bears in that society. In this example, a gesture of the fingers is used to convey a message—in other words, the gesture functions as a **symbol.** This leads us to a third basic point: the human world is a world of symbols. To know the meanings of things means to know how to interpret symbols correctly. That is because meaning is never communicated directly. Instead we are constantly **representing** what we mean. This is obvious in the case of gestures. A wink, a wave of the hand, applause—all these stand for, or point to, what we want to "say" by means of them. However, it is not only when we gesture but even when we speak that we communicate by referring, indicating, pointing, alluding. We rely on our conversation partners to understand what we are saying not in the sense of knowing the literal definitions of our words but in the sense of grasping the connotations the words carry. In other words, other people understand us not because they know the dictionary but because they are members of the same society as ourselves, and so are capable of correctly **interpreting** the meaning of our words (just as we interpret the meaning of gestures).

Take the everyday expression, "How are you?" As spoken by a classmate of yours as you pass each other in the hallway, it presents no problem; you immediately know what it means and, consequently, how to respond. But knowing what it means means knowing how to interpret it. For example, "How are you?" is **literally** a question but you know it isn't intended as one. Though it's difficult to say just what "How are you?" means, one thing it **doesn't** mean is "How are you?" Of course, if your doctor or your therapist asked you this question as you took a seat in the consulting room, you would respond differently; you would regard "How are you?" as a question, and a very serious one.

"How are you?" means what **we** (members of society) take it to mean; and its meaning for us as members of society will depend on the context in which it is used. All this should not be taken to imply that there is always only one correct way to interpret a symbol. Symbolic interactionism is interested in the variety of ways in which individuals make sense of their world, and how their particular interpretations of things then affect the behavior of others (who respond in terms of **their** interpretations, etc.). For example, if person A interprets a remark of person B's as an insult, A will respond accordingly; and this will in turn affect B's next response to A, and so on. In other words, we always act in accordance with our **definition of the situation.**

One of the refreshing aspects of symbolic interactionism is that it focuses on ordinary, everyday life—people and behaviors we can identify with. The major shortcoming of interactionism is not, as many macro-sociologists suppose, that it studies insignificant matters—unless you assume that the things most people spend most of their lives doing are insignificant. The real problem is that the emphasis on the interactional and interpretive process becomes monotonous after a while because the **process** is the same regardless of the setting in which it takes place. We can't compare the interactionist analysis of education with the functionalist and conflict analyses of education because there really is no such interactionist analysis. As we suggested, interactionism doesn't study the school system but the actions of the people in the school sysytem. Insofar as symbolic interactionism is committed to studying the process by which individuals interact with and make sense of their environment, the **particular** environment in which the process occurs is basically irrelevant. Whether the context is the school sysytem or the criminal justice system makes no difference, for institutions merely provide the backdrop, the occasion for the interactionist to examine the interpretive work being done by the people involved. (The same point can be made with regard to phenomenological sociology.)

There is one substantive area, however, to which symbolic interactionists—and phenomenologists—have made a significant contribution, and that is the study of **gender.** This makes sense inasmuch as gender is a feature of every interaction, every definition of the situation, and every act of self-definition. The meaningful world of social interaction is a thoroughly gendered world.

In addition, the interactionist emphasis on interpretive activity as the source of what we call social reality places it in a better position than the macro theories to take seriously the similar, though often more radical, claims of post-modernist thinkers. Indeed, a number of symbolic interactionists have recently turned their attention to the study of the post-modern world and have called upon sociologists to incorporate some of the basic insights of post-modernist thought in their work (Denzin, 1990).

PHENOMENOLOGY

We construct reality, according to symbolic interactionism, by giving meanings to things in collaboration with others, so that the things we perceive are experienced as objects. But **how** do we do this? After all, we only really perceive **things.** Our subjective experience of something as an object is constructed out of the data of perception but is not equivalent to that data. Phenomenological sociology seeks to get at the experience that is prior to, and which underlies, our everyday experience of objects.

Phenomenology originated as a philosophical movement; it was founded by the German philosopher Edmund Husserl (1859–1938). Alfred Schutz (1899–1959), the founder of phenomenological sociology and a German emigre to America, was a student of Husserl's. Technically, "phenomenon" means "appearance"; the task phenomenology set for itself was to describe, not what reality is, but what appears before the human consciousness as real. What appears before us may or may not be what is really real; but how can we ever know? We cannot; the human mind can examine and reflect upon its own contents, but it can never prove that these contents—namely, the sum total of what we perceive—corresponds to reality itself.

Now how did Schutz transform these highly abstract philosophical concerns into a social theory? Like the symbolic interactionists, he emphasizes the fact that human reality is a shared reality (the term he uses is "intersubjective"); the meanings we give to things must be more or less held in common for them to really seem meaningful. But he adds to this a further point which he considers equally important: the meaningfulness of the world we inhabit is not only shared under normal circumstances but **taken for granted.** Under normal circumstances, that is, we **suspend all doubts** as to the meaningfulness and reality of the world. We **could** doubt but we **don't.** Since we can never be certain whether what we take to be real is really real, it is a wonder that we don't ordinarily doubt. But under normal circumstances the fact remains— we are not philosophers. We are, instead, common sense members of society. The **attitude of common sense,** according to Schutz, is definitively characterized by the suspension of doubt about the meaningfulness and reality of the world.

While common sense is unphilosophical it is by no means empty-headed. If the common sense attitude is characterized by suspension of doubt, then, put positively, we can say that the common sense mind contains, so to speak, all the **undoubted assumptions** that continuously must operate in order to lend a sense of meaningfulness and reality to our experience, so that under normal circumstances we seem to have "no reason to doubt." These assumptions—the contents of the common sense view of the world—are not examined or even noticed by common sense because common sense is interested, not in **experiencing its assumptions about reality,** but in **experiencing reality.** If you experienced your assumptions about reality rather than the reality those assumptions make available to you, you could end up—like the philosopher—doubting whether reality was real, since you would then see it only appeared real due to the assumptions you were making. (Similarly, a prejudiced person wishes to criticize the alleged shortcomings of a particular group rather than examine the assumptions that were used in arriving at the criticism. Perhaps the assumptions are unfounded. Perhaps they are stereotypes that say more about this individual's need to be prejudiced than about the group in question.)

The contents of the common sense attitude are the object of phenomenological inquiry. They are normally taken for granted because for the world to seem meaningful and real we must continuously **employ** our common sense assumptions unhesitatingly rather than take them aside to examine. It is precisely the phenomenologist's task, however, to take our assumptions aside—to "bracket" them, as Schutz says. Like its philosophical counterpart, phenomenological sociology seeks to be a purely **descriptive** discipline—in this case, describing the common sense perception of the world. Schutz' work consists in large part of detailed descriptions of the various components of our "common stock of knowledge," i.e., our shared assumptions. For example, he describes how common sense assumes a **reciprocity of perspectives**—we assume, that is, that differences between people are due to differences in their location. Disagreement, confusion, and misunder-standing are neutralized in everyday life by attributing them to the fact that we are all "coming from" different "places." We pass over differences as ultimately non-existent because we assume that, if we were in the other person's position, we would adopt that person's perspective (and we can count on the other person to assume the same of us). So, for example, while there may be occasional tension and even conflict at work, it is minimized by the worker's and the employer's sense of each other's behavior as understandable given that it is the behavior of a worker or an employer. Through this assumption, then, we take for granted the rationality of the behaviors we encounter.

A second, related aspect of the common sense view of reality is the tendency to **typify.** The world that common sense experiences is a world populated by types rather than individuals. We continuously encounter typical situations, featuring typical people, calling for typical-behavior-under-the-circumstances. And this is true even when we are encountering a particular situation for the first time. (We know how to act as a customer and what to expect of salespersons even on our first visit to a particular store.) Life goes on with an appearance of normalcy to the extent that what we do and see conforms to **some** model, or typification, in our minds.

The common sense world as described by Schutz is, according to him, **the fundamental reality** for all of us, insofar as we are functioning members of society. Even philosophers, who are committed to raising fundamental questions about reality, rely on common sense assumptions in their pursuit of philosophy. In order to teach a philosophy course or write a philosophy book, I have to suspend all sorts of doubts about the rationality of the world and myself. I assume that the train will take me to work tomorrow just as it did today (barring a strike or a blizzard); I assume that my peers will either like or dislike my conference paper but will not declare it to be completely unintelligible to them; I assume that the activities called "teaching" and "writing" make sense, and that what I do in the classroom and in my study exemplify these activities. Of course this kind of list could go on indefinitely. The phenomenologist's point is that the common sense approach to the world actually underlies any additional attitudes we may come to adopt. Only on the basis of shared, taken-for-granted assumptions—and by constantly employing them—is it possible for us to engage in those activities which, like philosophy and sociology, supposedly transcend common sense.

The phenomenological sociology pioneered by Schutz remained marginal in the discipline until it was taken up and developed by Harold Garfinkel (1917–) beginning in the 1950s. While Garfinkel calls his approach **ethnomethodology,** his work is deeply indebted to Schutz, and he has acknowledged as much (Garfinkel, 1967). Some sociologists consider Garfinkel to be a symbolic interactionist—his work is often compared to that of the influential interactionist Erving Goffman, but Garfinkel rejects this interpretation. Actually the best way to understand ethnomethodology, we think, is to see it as having **combined** the principal insights of interactionism and phenomenology. From phenomenology Garfinkel takes the idea that the common sense attitude permeates human consciousness, and that under the influence of this attitude we habitually suspend all doubts as to the reality and meaningfulness of the world. The world, in the common sense view, is taken for granted; it appears as a matter of course, as **natural.** (Schutz often spoke of the common sense attitude as the "natural attitude.") Much like Schutz, Garfinkel sees the common sense attitude as consisting of an inexhaustible fund of "background assumptions" which members routinely employ in making sense of their world. Garfinkel emphasizes the fact that, regardless of the particular assumptions at work in particular circumstances, the common sense attitude is defined by the faith that **some** sense can be made of the situation at hand. The world may at times frustrate, anger, or disappoint us, but ordinarily we do not adopt an attitude of "One of us must be crazy" toward it. Like Schutz but perhaps even more emphatically, then, Garfinkel speaks of a fundamental sense of trust that the world makes sense as characteristic of the common sense attitude.

There is one basic difference between the two approaches, however. Schutz's emphasis on the taken-for-granted common sense assumptions that are accepted as part of membership in society implies a rather **passive** image of the individual—especially when we consider that the most basic of these assumptions is that fundamental questions about the meaningfulness and reality of the world we live in need never be raised. Here is where we see the interactionist side of Garfinkel's work. Symbolic interactionism, we saw, argues that people construct meaning in interaction with others. Garfinkel accepts this basic premise and seeks to **apply it to the background assumptions described by Schutz.** We do not simply accept the assumption that the world is sensible; we enact it. Just as, for Schutz, the common sense assumption that the world is sensible is operative in every interaction, for Garfinkel every interaction can be described as an interaction in which individuals are co-operatively **enacting the assumption** that the world is sensible, and in so doing make that assumption stick. The world appears real because in our actions we act as if it were real. Ethnomethodology, then, is the study of the methods members use to **accomplish the taken-for-grantedness** of everyday reality. Taken-for-grantedness is not something we merely believe in, it is something we "do."

Think of it this way. There is really nothing "natural" about the common sense attitude. After all, the idea that we can never know that what we experience is really real is not an idea only philosophers can have. The proof of this is that our common sense belief in reality is not based on evidence but merely on a **decision** not to doubt. Since in principle we **could** doubt, it is, to Garfinkel at least, amazing that we do not. Or more precisely: to Garfinkel the unquestionable reality of the world is an **achievement of ours that has to be continuously re-achieved.** We have to—and we do—**make happen** the everydayness of everyday life—the fact that it appears to make perfect sense and does not call for any "philosophical" doubt about itself. We achieve a world in which the sensibleness of philosophy is routinely called into question because it questions the sensibleness of the world.

Now the principal way we achieve our sensible world is through **common sense language use.** Through the way we use language, we make our world into a routine, sensible, reliable one. For example, Garfinkel notes that everyday language is permeated with "indexical expressions"—terms whose meaning is only implied or indicated by the terms themselves. In interaction we collectively make the connections between words and their meanings; the connection only exists to the extent that we posit a connection. If we fail to make the connection everyday life breaks down—which proves that its existence depended on our actions all along. To illustrate this Garfinkel has had his students do numerous "rule-violation experiments." The student is instructed to engage a friend in conversation and pretend not to understand the simple common sense expressions the friend utters. In the following example the student is a husband talking to his wife:

WIFE: All these old movies have the same kind of old iron bedstead in them.
HUSBAND: What do you mean? Do you mean all old movies, or some of them, or
           just the ones you have seen?
WIFE: What's the matter with you? You know what I mean.
HUSBAND: I wish you would be more specific.
WIFE: You know what I mean! Drop dead! (Garfinkel, 1967).

Now why did the wife take offense at the husband's questions? Obviously not because he doesn't understand her comment—since non-understanding **is not a possibility** in this context—but because he is refusing to. For "understanding" in this case doesn't mean seriously considering, to the limits of one's ability as a student of the history of cinema, the question of the validity of the wife's observation about set decorations, but simply **accepting her remark as unremarkable.** The husband's "mistake" was to act as though he were taking his wife's comment seriously—which had to be an act (i.e., a refusal to co-operate) because "everyone knows" that in this kind of situation we are not supposed to seriously examine each other's words but simply nod in assent to them. That the wife got angry shows that she had assumed she could **trust** her husband to **take for granted** the sensibleness (the unremarkableness) of her words. The ethnomethodological point is that **any** routine conversation could be disrupted by the simple maneuver of questioning the meaning of what is said; therefore the smooth flow of everyday interaction, and thus of everyday life, depends upon our **continuous willingness to actively co-operate with others** to achieve taken-for-grantedness.

Garfinkel's "experiments" show that sentences spoken in common sense discourse carry with them an implicit "You know what I mean." In the example cited, for instance, the wife uses the word "all" **not** to mean "all" but—well, you know what she meant. But the husband refused to acknowledge the implicit "You know what I mean" and proceeded to act as though "all" really meant "all"—which naturally led him to request further clarification.

Ethnomethodology has inspired an almost cult-like devotion among its followers (and an equally intense hostility among its detractors). Its emphasis on the **fragility** of everyday reality—on the merely agreed-upon and acted-out nature of social reality and, consequently, the omnipresent possibility of breakdown—can seem liberating (as well as relevant in the context of post-modern thought and the post-modern "condition"). The world no longer appears as an immovable object but as an illusion dependent on our constant certification of it as real. This insistence on the artificiality of reality is just what critics of ethnomethodology have against it. They attack it for ignoring the "centrality of power in social interaction" and other equally rock-solid facts of social life (Coser, 1975). Such criticisms, however, are beside the point; all they really show is that the critic has a different conception of what constitutes social reality than ethnomethodology does; they don't in any sense **refute** ethnomethodology's point of view but merely assert a different one. In general, phenomenology cannot be effectively criticized by simply saying it wastes time by studying common sense attitudes and behaviors and ignoring the larger aspects of reality, since phenomenology claims that ultimately there is no other reality than the common sense one.

This does not mean, however, that phenomenology is above criticism. Its principal weakness, we think, is that its emphasis on common sense undermines its own, quite non-commonsensical activity. If the non-reflective, unquestioning, natural attitude of common sense governs our lives as members of society, how does the blatantly **unnatural** attitude of the phenomenologist or the ethnomethodologist arise? Schutz and Garfinkel represent a commitment to **examining and reflecting rather than taking for granted** (although of course they have to do a lot of taking for granted just to get their work done, as we all do). But if they represent a non-common sense attitude—while obviously belonging to the common sense world as well—doesn't that mean that common sense is not **necessarily** unreflective? Doesn't it mean that being unreflective is a possibility but not a necessity for people in everyday life? But if so, then Schutz's and Garfinkel's description of everyday life is oversimplified and incomplete. It doesn't capture the fact that membership in society includes the possibility of being 'of' and yet not 'of' the everyday world one inhabits. For the sociological theorist fits that description. In short, the phenomenological and ethnomethodological descriptions of society fail to explain how the activities called "phenomenology" and "ethnomethodology" are possible.

We began this introductory chapter by raising the question whether and how sociology, a discipline originating in the modern world as an attempt to explain that world, is equipped to help us understand the post-modern era we are entering. Then we saw that, in formulating their differences from traditional macrosociology, the interactionist and phenomenological perspectives have developed notions which mirror some of the basic insights of post-modernist analysis (e.g., the emphasis on interpretation and reality-construction is mirrored in the post-modernist emphasis on plurality and ambiguity). And even the older perspectives in sociology paved the way for the post-modern consciousness by emphasizing the fact that norms and values are relative to specific cultures and epochs. Modern sociology has indeed alerted us to the fact that the norms and values we are liable to cherish as absolute are in fact merely the norms and values of modern, Western society—norms and values whose universal validity, therefore, cannot be assumed. Perhaps our conception of morality is just that—**our** conception, **our** preference, not necessarily better or worse than any other culture's (and certainly not to be forced upon others as though **we** knew what was good for them). This self-questioning attitude is as much a reflection of the modern sociological point of view as it is of the post-modernist one.

On the other hand, the older sociological perspectives —unlike interactionism and phenomenology—tend to be committed to a conventional methodology which makes it difficult for them to get at the more "subjective" or "experiential" aspects of life—aspects which are of central concern in a post-modern world in which the image of a unified, objective, shared social reality is no longer convincing.

And that of course is the test of the continuing significance of sociology: whether it can help us understand our experience as members of society today—including all the ambivalence, confusion, and skepticism, as well as the sense of new possibilities, of hope in the development of a truly inclusive society and of a sense of global responsibility, and so on. Whether we call this society "post-modern," and the thinkers and disciplines that help us understand it "post-modernist," is of secondary importance; if we insist on using these terms, it is merely to call attention to the fact that important changes are taking place here and now, at the close of the 20th century, that we must think about, and that it is wishful thinking—at best—to pretend otherwise.

With that in mind, we now turn to an in-depth analysis of a set of related themes: gender, sexuality, and family. There can be no doubt that **profound changes** are occurring in these areas, and that things are not as unambiguously clear here as they once were—things such as: what it is to be a 'real' man or woman; what a 'family' is; in what sexual morality consists. Are we experiencing in these areas today merely the **breakdown** of values—the end of modern family and sexuality, so to speak—or the emergence of a post-modern family and sexuality? And how do the sociological perspectives help us understand these changes?

In the following chapter, then, we take a second look at the main sociological theories, with the aim of doing something with them. We want to try to understand the changing world in which we live. This activity of seeking understanding we call **theorizing.**

The Frenchman Auguste Comte (1798–1857) coined the term "sociology," and argued for the importance of a scientific approach to the study of society, but his own approach was more philosophical than scientific. For example, he speculated that it is in the nature of all societies to pass through three evolutionary stages of development—the religious, the metaphysical, and the scientific. The Western societies of Comte's time had, according to his scheme, entered the scientific stage, and thus were on the brink of achieving full maturity. By contrast, non-Western, pre-scientific cultures were seen as, if not primitive, at least immature: they were either like children (the religious stage of civilization, where magical and superstitious thinking prevails) or adolescents (the metaphysical stage, where abstract speculation is regarded as the highest form of thought). Comte's main contribution, beyond inspiring people with the idea that society, and the forces operating on and within it, ought to be studied—for the sake of mastering them, just as nature and natural laws were being studied for the sake of the betterment of the human race—lay in his idea that the new science of society would have to focus on two fundamental aspects of social life: stability ("social statics") and change ("social dynamics"). How is social order produced and maintained? What provokes social change? These are the questions sociologists have contended with since the discipline's inception. But these, and similar questions, only began to be treated scientifically—in the sense in which the modern world understands that term—a generation after Comte's death, in the work of Emile Durkheim, who for that reason is generally considered the true founder of sociology.

Comte's style of thinking was characteristic of the times. Indeed, speculation about the nature and origin of society and social life was common in the 19th century—partly as a result of the thought-provoking transformations wrought by industrialization, the increased contact between Europe and the strikingly different civilizations of Asia and Africa, and the unprecedented advances made by the sciences, which convinced people that everything can, and therefore should, be understood, and understood comprehensively. Speculation in accordance with one or another evolutionary scheme was especially common; the impact of Darwin's theory outside biology as well as inside cannot be overstated. The Englishman Herbert Spencer (1820–1903), another early non-scientific sociologist, applied Darwin's concept of "survival of the fittest" to the difference between the rich and powerful, on the one hand, and the poor and powerless on the other. He believed that the process of "natural selection" could be seen in these different social outcomes, and therefore maintained that social reforms aimed at overcoming them were worse than useless: they were human intrusions in a natural process which, like other natural processes, would work out well if left undisturbed. Spencer can be viewed as a forerunner of Durkheim's (and of functionalist thinking in general) because of his belief that society should be seen and studied on the analogy of an organism—a system aiming at equilibrium, comprising various subsystems, all of which must function in interrelation for the entire system to survive.

3

SCIENCE AND RELIGION

Toward the end of the century before last, the German philosopher Friedrich Nietzsche wrote: "It is not the victory of science that distinguishes our nineteenth century, but the victory of scientific method over science." (Nietzsche, 1967). As the 21st century dawns, Western culture has begun to question its attitude of unqualified enthusiasm for the achievements of modern science—and, indeed, for the scientific mode of thinking itself. Philosophers and sociologists of various schools have begun to express ideas similar to Nietzsche's, although (usually) not in the spirit of utter disdain for modern science that characterizes his work.

But no matter what opinion one adopts on the question whether science has on the whole been a force for good or evil, there is no denying that that force has been significant. There can be no doubt, that is, that science is one of the constituent features of modernity. We have seen in the case of other basic ingredients of modernity—bureaucratic organization, the achievement ethic—that their legacy is mixed. We are going to assume that the same is true of modern science. We have all benefitted from the technological advances made possible by modern science. At the same time, we all face a similar risk of being victimized by them. Air travel and air pollution; nuclear medicine and nuclear fallout: these are all equally products of modern science. In short, we exist—and we write—in a post-modern situation, in which **the achievements of modern science appear irreducibly ambiguous.**

Before we evaluate modern science, however, we need to understand what, essentially, it is all about. While Nietzsche's statement may seem rather strange—we will come back to it later, when we are in a better position to evaluate it—its point of departure is a notion with which all scientists, including social scientists, would agree: a science is defined by its methods as well as its results. That is, the word "science" is ordinarily defined as a collection of systematic methods by which knowledge is attained, as well as the body of knowledge thus attained. **But if the application of scientific method leads to the acquisition of (scientific) knowledge, what led to the formulation of the method in the first place?** That is: scientific method produces scientific knowledge, but did scientific knowledge produce the scientific method? Obviously not, since the method had to first exist and be employed in order to yield scientific knowledge. This means that scientific method originated in a decision (or in an "insight" together with the decision to trust it) rather than in a (scientific) discovery.

Someone could say: perhaps the scientific method, while not a product of scientific knowledge, was a product of the insight that such a method would lead to the acquisition of scientific knowledge. In other words, the first scientists, while not possessing any scientific knowledge, nevertheless developed the scientific method because they anticipated that it would have certain results. They didn't have the results yet—but they didn't have nothing, either. They must have had an image of scientific knowledge—a blueprint of what the new method would produce. And of course that is the case whenever a new method is introduced: **one begins with a desired end,** and then a method which one believes will bring it about—and then, if all goes well, the desired end is realized. The carpenter doesn't begin with a table but with tools, materials, and, so to speak, an "imaginary" table—that is, a definite, if as yet unrealized, goal. While this might sound uncontroversial, the fact is that in the case of science (as opposed to carpentry), most people have a different idea: they seem to believe that the horizon of modern science, the field of objects it gazes on for potential study, is limitless. Yet science does observe limits—self-imposed ones. The limits of what science can research are set by **science's definition of its goal**—which is not simply "to inquire," but to inquire in such a way as to be in a **position to obtain scientific knowledge.** In the popular view—which scientists themselves have done little to discourage—the freedom of scientific inquiry is exaggerated, and its limits ignored. Science is seen as representing freedom from arbitrary constraints, especially religious and other ideological ones. Freed from the obligation to defend the religious belief, for example, that humans are made "in the image of God," science was able to discover that humans have ascended from apes, are perpetually under the sway of unconscious sexual and aggressive impulses, and so on. The contrast could not appear any sharper between traditional religious closed-mindedness and modern scientific openness. Indeed the belief that humans are made in the image of God led Western theologians to teach, as the Greek philosophers had before them, that the earth, as the home of God's loftiest creation, must be the center of the universe. The scientific discovery that the earth revolves around the sun rather than vice versa was rejected by religious authorities for centuries, just as Darwin's and Freud's discoveries would later be rejected.

Scientific inquiry is certainly free and open—but **within the domain of scientific inquiry, as defined by science.** (But then theology, too, is free and open within its domain. Christian theologians continue to analyze the meaning of the trinity, as Jewish thinkers continue to re-interpret the Torah. There is no more of a foreseeable end to discussions in theology than there is a foreseeable end to discoveries in science.) **Science does not allow itself to go where the scientific method cannot take it;** this humility is as essential to science as scientific pride in going wherever its method does take it. The "first scientists" referred to earlier are not hypothetical cave men but real historical figures who were quite clear about this. One of the most important of them was Francis Bacon, the 17th century British philosopher—important both in the sense that he fervently advocated the use of scientific method and was a pioneer in defining what that was. His advocacy was based on his conviction that such a development was necessary and desirable. Why? Because, he believed, what previously—from the time of the ancient Greeks down to his own day—had passed as science, and which was generally known as "natural philosophy," was fruitless. Like philosophy in general, Bacon argued, it was interesting but it didn't lead anywhere. Questions just led to—more questions. However, the proper goal of the study of nature, according to Bacon, should not be to appreciate it but to **control** it, for only this would be commensurate with human dignity. (Notice that the argument in favor of science is **based on a philosphical or religious** premise: **true humanity implies mastery of nature, since humanity is higher than nature**—i.e., made in the image of God.) For Bacon the only question is: Are we going to be continually subject to the whims of nature or are we going to exercise true dominion over it, by exercising that which lifts us above nature—our reason? Posed that way, of course, the question rather answers itself. From Bacon's time to the present, science has understood itself as methodical investigation of the universe whose ultimate goal is to increase humanity's power, our ability to control our destiny by controlling the environment in which we are placed. Indeed, all social science textbook definitions of the difference between humans and animals emphasize our ability to modify and control our environment (hence humans can live anywhere but animals only somewhere). All this means that modern science judges itself by its practical applicability. Science, therefore, is intimately linked to technology. Philosophy and religion meditate on the meaning of death; science prolongs life.

This simple difference has a lot of implications; one of them is that **the questions which science poses, since they are supposed to lead eventually to technological advances, have to be answerable.** Philosophical questions—such as, what is the meaning of life?—can be, and often are, given answers, but never in such a way that a particular answer can command the assent of other philosophers: a follower of Plato gives a different answer than a follower of Epicurus, and so on down through the centuries. **Science is committed to asking questions that have "correct" answers.** The prototype of such questions is "what causes x?" rather than (the philosophical question) "what is the meaning of x?" Thus the philospher asks, "What is human life such that there is pain in it?" while the scientist asks, "what is the cause of this pain?" Which means: what events were necessary and sufficient to produce this subsequent event? (Niebuhr, 1974). Thus, science is talking about **events in the world and their interrelations rather than about the nature of the world itself.** (This is true even when physicists speculate about the "origins of the universe": what they are doing is still to connect one set of events with a prior set of events.) For a question to be able to yield a correct answer—i.e., an indisputable one—it must not only be about the relations among things (as against the ultimate meaning of things); **it must be about things whose definition is also indisputable.** The question, what is the meaning of life?, yields innumerable answers because the thing it asks about—life—can be defined in many ways. So the things science asks about have to be things whose definition people can agree on; they will therefore tend to ne material rather than spiritual things—things we can observe as against things we merely conceive. Thus, medicine treats the body rather than the soul. If the body is an observable object, it should be able to be described the same way by different observers; what we think of it can be put aside while we describe what is there to be seen.

Now we begin to see what it means to say that science imposes limits on what it inquires into: Science asks **answerable questions,** which means questions about the **relations among observable, i.e. neutrally describable, things in the world.** Questions about meaning, value, reason, and so on are placed outside the boundaries of science. Only questions that can be expected to eventually yield undisputed answers are admissible.

In addition to this negative limitation—this exclusion from science of all unanswerable questions—science has developed a positive structure of norms by which scientific inquiry is supposed to be guided—an ideal culture of science, in other words. In an influential paper written in 1942, and in a number of subsequent writings, Robert Merton has described these norms as follows:

Universalism

This means that the validity of scientific research is to be determined independently of the identity of the researcher. The norm of universalism derives ultimately from the principle of observability. That scientific objects are observable means that the ability to describe them is a result of technical training rather than, say, some special moral sensitivity (as religious thinking, for example, could be said to require). Thus it is **open in principle to everyone** (though, of course, some may lack the technical aptitude).

Scientific universalism is not merely an ideal. During the Cold War, for example, while American and Soviet politicians did not do much talking with each other, American and Soviet mathematicians did, for math is a universal language in which political or national differences, even animosities, have no place. Math is math—there is no such thing as communist or capitalist math. Particularistic science is a perversion of science—as in the case of Nazi "biology," which sought to prove the superiority of the Aryan race, and which would not admit as evidence the findings of non-Nazi scientists. An example of science's commitment to universalism is the standard practice whereby a manuscript submitted to a scientific journal is evaluated without the reviewers knowing the identity of the author.

One question which has caused much soul-searching among artists and critics in this century especially—can good art be made by evil persons? (this comes up whenever a famous dead artist is found out to have concealed an ignoble past, such as the renowned conductor and Nazi supporter Herbert von Karajan)—answers itself in science: the answer is, of course. Doing science competently is a matter of expertise, not character.

Communalism

Science is a collective enterprise. Growth in scientific knowledge reflects the cumulative results of innumerable inquiries by innumerable inquirers. Even the work of scientific geniuses is inexplicable apart from the influence of the research of other scientists, and often even the geniuses make their famous discoveries in collaboration with others. More importantly, once a discovery has been made, it is not considered the private possession of the discoverer. Instead, it can be, and is supposed to be, tested, applied, expanded, and revised by others, and integrated into their own work, which is then taken up and re-formulated by others, and so on. This lack of privacy is captured in the practice of footnoting, where a present author shows her indebtedness to other scientists—to such an extent that her work can be seen as a collaboration, although not a literal one, between herself and previous researchers in her field. In this respect the culture of science is diametrically oppposed to that of art, where the image of the solitary genius is enshrined. While art works too cannot be understood apart from the influences exerted by previous artists—and the great artists are precisely the ones who accept these influences and try to build on them—it is the distinctiveness of each artist's voice, rather than the effect made by the sum total of works, that ultimately is supposed to stand out. The main point, again, is that the production of art is not normally a collective activity. Imagine trying to publish a novel that was actually a Hemingway novel to which you had added a new chapter; but that is basically how normal science works ("normal" as opposed to "revolutionary" science).

Art, unlike scientific knowledge, is the private property of the artist. That is because art supposedly expresses the unique viewpoint of an individual; it is not a description of observable reality but of the "inner reality" of imagination, and therefore it is not seen as being reproducible by another. But in science the possibility of an experiment's being reproduced by another experimenter with the same results is considered a condition of its being valid.

One thing Merton did not sufficiently realize is just how ideal rather than real the norm of scientific communalism is. The fact is that in science, as in business and other professions, the ideal of community is contradicted by a reality in which vital information is kept secret, social networks are formed, membership in which is a requirement for advancement or just plain survival, but from which certain people tend to be excluded on principle, and so on. For example, women scientists are "kept out of the loop" in many cases, guaranteeing a second-class status for them in the scientific occupational hierarchy.

Disinterestedness

This norm comes closest to approximating the popular image of the open-endedness of scientific inquiry. It means that scientists must not be interested in their research yielding any particular conclusions; instead, they should be interested only in obtaining valid results, or drawing valid conclusions, whatever these may be (although we have already seen that "valid" has a particular meaning within the world of science). Scientists do not do research in order to prove as true what they believe or hope is true; rather, they are interested in discovering the truth even if that truth turns out to be disappointing or even disturbing. In recent years various cases have been brought to light in which this norm has been violated—instances in which, typically, a scientist eager to climb to the top in a narrowly defined, and for that reason among others highly competitive, field of specialization, is found out to have distorted his research data in order to come up with more noteworthy findings than the data actually justify. Science is not only a vocation but a career; its practitioners are devoted not only to science but to themselves—unless it can be shown that only peculiarly selfless, saintly individuals are drawn to science. So far there is no evidence to suggest that. While according to the norms of science there is nothing in principle wrong with a new study that turns out to merely confirm something already borne out by a dozen previous studies, the fact is that such work is not going to lead to high honors or wealth for its author.

However, if lying in science is deviant, while zealous devotion to advancing one's career is not, **then there must be normal scientific practices which, like lying, are not governed by the spirit of pure disinterestedness** (since pure disinterestedness doesn't help advance one's career) **yet, unlike lying, do not constitute norm-violations.** And these could then be seen as instances of the limits of scientific open-endedness.

We have encountered the notion of a limit to scientific open-endedness before—in Max Weber's concept of **value-relevance**. Weber pointed out, you will recall, that, while scientific research can and should be carried out objectively, this cannot be expected of the initial decision to do the research. Instead, he argued that the choice of research topic invariably calls into play the scientist's "values." What we notice, find interesting, find worthy of study, consider questionable—all of that may give rise to objective scientific inquiry while itself arising out of our own scientifically inexplicable subjectivity. Whether and how the transition actually takes place between the subjective origins of research and the objectivity of the research act is a complicated and controversial issue. Is it conceivable that a sociologist who believes that racism remains a serious problem in American society, and who therefore sets out to explore the reasons for this, will end up discovering that racism is not a problem in American society after all? On the other hand it is quite conceivable that the sociologist will be surprised by the results of his research—regarding which groups are most likely to be prejudiced, the role of various factors such as income and education in encouraging or inhibiting ethnic animosity, and so on. But the research depends on the presupposition that racism exists; otherwise racism could not and would not be studied. The research, then, is not "open" to the possibility that racism is a figment of the imaginations of oversensitive minority members; nor is it even open to the less radical assumption that racism is in sharp decline and is mainly a thing of the past.

Value relevance in scientific research places limits on what can be called into question. Such limits exist in every form of inquiry, indeed in every type of conversation, scientific or otherwise. In practical terms, this means that our hypothetical study of racism has nothing to say to someone who denies the existence of racism. It cannot, for example, convince such a person that racism exists, since its existence is one of the presuppositions of the study, not one of its results. And there is nothing that sociology, or any other science, can do about this: when Weber spoke about the relevance of values, he meant it. If you look, for instance, at a typical textbook for a course in Social Problems, you will see that the chapter headings reflect a decision as to what constitutes a major social problem in contemporary society. If the text is the work of a mainstream author and is published by a mainstream company, this decision will reflect the present consensus among sociologists. Typical headings in our day include Racism, Sexism, and Poverty. Every decision implies a limitation; every act of inclusion is also an act of exclusion. The spread of AIDS is considered a social problem; the spread of homosexuality is not. And this is true in the natural sciences as well. Biology texts describe the theory of evolution, and do not feel obliged to give equal time (or any time) to "creationism." It is normal for sociologists to speak about gender inequality, just as it is normal for physicists to speak about electrons. Here again we see the **normal limits to disinterestedness within the sciences.**

But we could also imagine a normal case in which personal ambition rather than value relevance is the driving force that initiates inquiry. The problem is that, in reality, the motivation behind scientific inquiry, like motivation in all areas of life, is usually mixed, and it is impossible to clearly separate one from another in any actual case. In deciding to write a book on AIDS, for example, am I motivated by compassion for AIDS sufferers or by my knowledge that AIDS is a hot topic and that the book is likely to be a bestseller? Probably both; and, equally probably, I myself am not completely aware of the role played by normal human venality in my own decision-making process.

Organized Skepticism

Within the limits just described, scientists maintain an attitude of organized skepticism towards all theories and other statements made by fellow practitioners—that is, a suspension of belief in the absence of sufficient evidence. This is the "nothing is sacred" aspect of science that is part of its popular image as well as its own normative structure—a source of pride among scientists, and, often enough, contempt among the general public (since scientific skepticism is supposed to apply to all beliefs, no matter how cherished). As to the question how this skepticism relates to science's own cherished belief in itself, Merton seems to recognize the problem but not what to do about it:

> Most institutions demand unqualified faith; but the institution of science makes skepticism a virtue. Every institution involves, in this sense, a sacred area that is resistant to profane

examination in terms of scientific observation and logic. The institution of science itself involves emotional adherence to certain values. But whether it be the sacred sphere of political convictions or religious faith or economic rights, the scientific investigator does not conduct himself in the prescribed uncritical and ritualistic fashion (Merton, 1973).

Putting this seeming contradiction aside for the moment, it is undoubtedly true that scientific skepticism, even today, has the power to enrage people. Naturally, the violence of the reaction against scientific inquiry will be greatest where the beliefs science is perceived as threatening are considered most sacred—as in the case of religious doctrines, for example. Thus the modern scientific study of the Bible, which goes back at least 200 years, was officially resisted by the Catholic Church until the middle of the last century. It would be interesting to investigate the extent to which, even today, the masses of Catholics and Protestants, in the U.S. and elsewhere, are willing to accept the consensus views of New Testament scholars and historians of early Christianity on a variety of topics. To give just two examples of such consensus views (in case you want to test yourself): (1) the "virgin birth" stories in the gospels (they appear, in contradictory versions, in Matthew and Luke; the other gospels and Paul apparently know nothing about a virgin birth) belong to the realm of myth rather than history; the plain truth, from which such legends attempt to distract the reader's attention, probably is that Jesus was born out of wedlock (Ranke-Heinemann, 1994; Schaberg, 1987); (2) most of the statements attributed to Jesus in the gospels were never spoken by him; they are put into his mouth by the early church to serve its missionary purpose (Sanders, 1985).

Merton makes the important point that scientific inquiry—e.g., the historical study of religion—does not invalidate religious belief (since religious belief is not based on scientific evidence in the first place), and that therefore the religious rejection of science, while psychologically understandable, is illogical. Historians are more likely to respect the difference between history and faith than believers are. For example, historians of early Christianity can show that there is no historical basis for regarding Jesus' teachings as different in any fundamental way from the teachings of many of his fellow Jews; but they don't thereby claim to have invalidated the Christian's (or Jew's) claim that Christianity and Judaism are essentially different faiths. What the historians do claim about their work, though, is that it shows that the authority of the **historical Jesus**—or Paul or any of their fellow Jews—cannot be invoked as the grounds for such affirmations of faith. As long as Christianity claims scientific status for its affirmations of faith, then, the tension between science and Christianity will remain unresolved.

KUHN'S THEORY

Without scientific skepticism no uncomfortable truths could ever have been discovered. We noted that that skepticism is limited by science's own belief in itself; however, this doesn't mean that science necessarily and always regards itself as sacred. The postmodern condition is one in which modern scientific skepticism has begun to be applied to modernity itself, including the institution of modern science. (Since our modern commitment to thinking skeptically has led us to stop believing in modernity—i.e., since we have applied our modern way of thinking to modernity itself—the question arises: are we still to be considered modern? For the time being, then, our condition is called "postmodern.") For example, modern social science introduced the idea that beliefs no matter how sacred are merely products of human society (i.e., of culture): if we adhere to certain moral beliefs, that is merely because we have been taught to believe them. This way of thinking arose as an antidote to ethnocentrism: if we believe in x because we have been taught to, then that is also true of "those" people who believe in y; therefore we should not consider ourselves superior to them. And there is no reason why this attitude shouldn't be applied to sociology itself—in which case sociology would be seen simply as an artifact of modern Western culture, no more or less ultimately true than other cultural products, such as Western religion, morality, and political belief. While this step has not yet been taken, a similar one has. An example of it is Thomas Kuhn's **paradigm theory** of science (Kuhn, 1962). We spoke above (see "Communalism") of science as a progressive, continuous development in which each scientist builds on the work of previous ones. Then in the section on "Disinterestedness," we noted that science fixes limits to what counts as a legitimate question, topic, and so on. Both these aspects describe scientists as forming a community; and the second one clearly implies (what is also true in the first example but less obviously) that science by nature excludes as well as includes. So, for example, a consensus reigns at any given point in each science. The existence of this consensus makes further research possible (our example was that research on racism is inspired by the belief that racism is still a problem in American society). But where does a consensus come from? That is the subject of Kuhn's work. Every science, he argues, is governed at any given time by a particular **paradigm**—an image of the field's object of inquiry and the proper way of approaching it, i.e., a definition of subject-matter and of method. The paradigm makes **normal science** possible—research that addresses the subject-matter of the field according to the correct methods and in collaboration with other legitimate practitioners, all as defined by the paradigm. Yet scientific advances are not the result of the accomplishments of normal science but of paradigm shifts in science. In other words, scientific development is not evolutionary but **revolutionary.** Astronomy advanced from the view that the earth is the center of the universe (in accordance with which paradigm, countless observations could be and were made) to the view that the earth is but one body among others in the solar system (a new paradigm giving rise to new "normal" observations). A similar shift may be underway in history and the social sciences today: instead of seeing European culture as the norm for all cultures, a new multicultural paradigm is emerging; or, if a new paradigm is not yet emerging, criticism of the reigning one ("Eurocentrism") is nevertheless widespread, so that the development of a new one is obviously just a matter of time.

Because he was dealing with the physical rather than the social sciences, Kuhn overlooked the role that politics, broadly speaking, plays in motivating paradigm shifts. Obviously the call for a multicultural approach in the social sciences and history reflects the declining influence of Europe in the world (e.g., the growing proportion of the non-European population in the U.S.). Similarly there is today a "political" debate over methodology in the social sciences, in which feminists and others argue that women's experiences and perspectives have been consistently ignored by theorists and researchers alike. Kuhn, on the other hand, claimed that a new paradigm emerges when the reigning paradigm is revealed as useless in explaining certain phenomena—e.g., pre-Freudian psychology could not explain unconscious motivation. But these "certain phenomena" only exist, and exist as relevant, in the eyes of the advocates of the new paradigm, so the question how the new paradigm comes to be the dominant one is still unanswered. We know from history that advocates of a new paradigm will be scorned by the establishment: Freud was jeered in his day as feminism is in ours. But how, and under what circumstances, the despised minority is transformed into the establishment, seems to be a question about contingent social, political, cultural, and historical factors that differ from one case to another.

After this lengthy discussion of the nature of science, let us now return to the quote from Nietzsche with which we began this chapter. If a method is a means to an end, then "the victory of scientific method over science" implies that the means has become an end in itself. Science, beginning with Francis Bacon, promised a better world. It may have given us that; what it has given us without a doubt is a scientized world—a world in which everything is seen the way science sees things, i.e., as objects to be manipulated. Many twentieth century thinkers have criticized the scientific devotion to technical utilizability as an unnecessary narrowing of the human capacity to experience and learn about the world around us. What Nietzsche is getting at includes that criticism but a deeper one as well: the scientific mentality makes us notice things only in their manipulability, their usefulness to us, and this means—despite the claims of science to the contrary—that the modern viewpoint under the influence of modern science is a fundamentally subjectivistic one. That is, everything is seen from the point of view of the thinking, speaking, inquiring subject, i.e., us (Heidegger, 1967). Thus, the modern scientific world is not only one in which people are seen as "human resources" in the same way as we speak of "natural resources"—as raw material to be exploited: people are "personnel" as other things are "material." The amazing thing is that science for centuries has understood itself as an antidote to subjectivism as represented by religion, which transforms a vast impersonal universe in which the human is merely one being among countless others—although a highly adaptable one due to its possession of an oversized cerebral cortex—into a meaningful cosmos created and governed by a just and loving god who has a special affection for, and enters into a covenant of promise with, his children. (Once we have examined the meaning of religion from the sociological point of view, we will address the question of the relation between religion and science in the modern world.)

CONCLUSION

So much for scientific "objectivity." But does the foregoing mean that objectivity is impossible to achieve, and that therefore we should abandon it as a goal? Or does it simply mean that we need to be more honest, and recognize that objectivity, though worthy as a goal, is just that— a goal, something not yet arrived at? Science may not have to be "biased" to be non-objective. (It is interesting to note how the words "objective" and "biased" are played off against each other; each term seems to give meaning to the other: a clear case of what postmodernists call *binary opposition.*) It merely has to be selective in choosing what is scientifically apprehensible. In fact, if we examine the meaning of some basic modern scientific terms, we will see the extent to which science is "subjective"—that, as postmodernists contend, it is simply a *discourse,* albeit a very (understandably) powerful and prestigious one. *All of the basic terms by which science defines and certifies itself bear the mark of a process of selectivity.* The point to analyzing scientific technology is not to debunk science but only to debunk the claim that scientific speech—speech, that is, that occurs under the auspices of scientific method—is alone (potentially) valid, i.e., knowledgeable, speech. Think of some of these key scientific words: proof, evidence, correlation, research, observation, data, knowledge, certainty, validity, and on and on. Each of these has a *particular* meaning and reference *within* the world of scientific method. But even to grant this is not to suggest that science is "merely" one discourse among others (e.g., religious, philosophical, historical, commonsensical, etc.). If, however, it is deservedly pre-eminent, it must argue the case for its pre-eminence, and such an argument cannot take place using words whose meaning is derived from their use in the world of science. In other words, the use of reason— for we were thinking, of course, of rational argumentation—must transcend the scientific use of it. So the question—which we will leave as a question, partly because it is exceedingly difficult to pursue, and partly because its pursuit is not necessary to undertake in a book of this kind—is this: if "reason" means something different, something more, than what science means by it, then what is reason?

RELIGION

One could say of religion what is said of many other things: it is impossible to define, but we know one when we see one. "Impossible" may be an exaggeration, but there certainly are some serious obstacles that any satisfactory definition of religion must overcome. The principal one is that the various entities we usually call "religions" differ so widely from one another that a definition in terms of their common characteristics is too general to be of much use. The sociological definition of religion, at any rate, is as follows: **religion** is a collection of socially shared beliefs and socially organized practices oriented towards the sacred, where the sacred means that which commands our absolute respect or is the object of ultimate veneration. Thus for some religions the sacred refers to a personal god, while for others it refers to impersonal principles, cosmic laws, etc. But once we admit principles as well as god(s) as legitimate candidates for the role of "the sacred," how do we know when to stop? Isn't socio-economic equality a sacred principle to a socialist, and knowledge a sacred principle to a scientist? Aren't socialism and science therefore religions just as much as, say, Buddhism and Christianity are? This question can't be dismissed with the assertion that for genuine religions the sacred is supernatural. For one thing, those who revere the principles of freedom or justice don't necessarily regard them as implied in the human being's biological nature, or any other fact of nature; rather, the imperative to realize conditions of freedom and justice is ordinarily defended in terms of some conception of human dignity or destiny that isn't derived from "the facts" and is impossible to distinguish from what we usually call a "religious" point of view—unless we invoke superficial criteria, e.g. that certain key words, such as "god," aren't used by such people.

Instead of trying to solve this semantic problem at the outset, we will begin by simply looking at some of the basic characteristics of the major world religions. (One thing they have in common, incidentally, is that they all think of themselves as religions). Once we have done that we will perhaps be in a better position to understand why some other candidates do not qualify as religions in the full sense of the word.

THEISM AND ETHICALISM

As we've said, some religions—and for those brought up in Western cultures, the most familiar ones—are organized around the concept of god. Such religions are called **theistic.** They may be of two types: **monotheistic** (belief in one god) or **polytheistic** (belief in a plurality of gods). The three monotheistic religions in the modern world are Judaism, Christianity, and Islam. Examples of polytheistic religion are the pagan religions of ancient Greece and Rome, and Hinduism in India.

While to modern Westerners polytheism may seem somewhat bizarre, that is merely due to overfamiliarity with our own monotheistic tradition. Taken on its own terms, polytheism makes perfect sense. After all, if religion is an attempt to make sense out of human experience, polytheism succeeds abundantly. Given the mixture of pleasure and pain, success and failure, happiness and disappointment in every life, what could be more sensible than to attribute all this to the machinations of a disparate collection of equally supreme authorities? If you are doing quite well in business but suffer from poor health, what could be more reasonable than to assume that different gods are in control of different domains of existence? The fact is that the monotheistic view that we have learned to take for granted was originally—that is, when the ancient Israelites came up with the idea—a quite radical departure from common sense. (When we add on the fact that this monotheism includes the idea that the one God, creator of the universe, is to be worshipped but cannot be placated, bargained with, bribed, and so on, and that "his ways are not our ways," i.e., we cannot know with assurance what god has in store or why he acts as he does—so that, in short, religion here is, for the first time, sharply distinguished from magical thinking—we could say that monotheism is still a radical departure from common sense). That the same God makes possible both love and cancer strains the imagination. To give up polytheism, then, means in a sense to give up the possibility of complete human comprehension of the ambiguities of existence.

The three monotheistic religions have a great deal in common. This is especially true of Judaism and Christianity. Historically, Christianity emerged out of Second Temple Judaism. The "founder" of Christianity was himself Jewish ("Jesus" is a Latinized form of the Hebrew "Yeshua," a variant of the Biblical name "Joshua"); all of his original disciples were Jewish; and the collection of writings we are accustomed to calling the "Old Testament" was to them simply the Bible, or Holy Scripture. The earliest "New Testament" writings—the letters of Paul—were composed between 50 and 60 C.E.; the Gospels were written somewhat later—between 70 and 100 C.E. These writings were only collected together with similar Christian testimonies and called the "New Testament" towards the end of the second century. Modern scholarship has shown that Jesus of Nazareth was a devout and loyal Palestinian Jew; it is no accident that he is often addressed in the Gospels as "Rabbi," the Jewish name for teacher. Yet for various social, political, and religious reasons the "Jesus movement" began to diverge more and more from mainstream synagogue Judaism in the decades after Jesus' death so that by the end of the first century it was composed largely of non-Jews ("Gentiles"). But scholars today are at pains to point out that the final separation between Judaism and Christianity did not really occur until well into the fourth century; up to that time the boundaries between the two were quite fluid: it was still common in the fourth century, for example, for Christians to celebrate Jewish holidays, to worship in the synagogue, and so forth (Gager, 1993). And even despite the fact that there was an ultimate "parting of the ways," Judaism and Christianity always have had much in common with each other. Some of the basic beliefs they share are as follows: there is one god, creator of the universe; creation is therefore good; humans are made in the image of god, and as such are endowed with powers and responsibilities, including moral obligations, that other creatures are not; while god transcends the human realm, he has revealed to us the moral rules we are to live by (esp., the Ten Commandments); while god will ultimately judge us (i.e., judge the extent of our obedience to his commands), his judgment will be tempered by his mercy and his love for his children (i.e., us); and thus, while there is no guarantee, still there is good reason to hope that we will all enjoy eternal peace and eternal bliss in the "afterlife," when we "return to god" after our earthly pilgrimage is completed. These postulates are a lot for two faith communities to hold in common; and they are only the beginning (Casey, 1991).

Meanwhile Islam, the youngest of the three monotheistic religions, identifies its God, named Allah, as the same omnipotent creator worshippped by Judaism and Christianity. But it claims to have a clearer insight into the nature of this God, and specifically into the kinds of behavior he requires of us. This claim is based on the belief that the prophet Mohammed, the founder of Islam, received his revelation from God (recorded in the Koran, Islam's Holy Scripture) much more recently (about 600 C.E.) than the revelation in Christ, or the revelations to Moses and the other Biblical prophets. Islam regards Judaism and Christianity, therefore, as honorable but immature, i.e. incomplete, attempts to define and embody God's will.

The major religions originating in Asia stand in sharp contrast to the three Western monotheisms. In these **ethicalist** religions the emphasis is not on a divinity or divinities so much as on sacred principles of thought and action. Of course if the principles are sacred the question arises what difference it makes whether they come from a god or not. The answer is that the Western monotheistic concept of God—in Judaism, Christianity, and Islam alike—simultaneously highlights **humanity's greatness and smallness.** We are god's beloved creature, made in his image, yet we are, for all that, **merely creatures**—and as such, continuously threatened by temptations of all kinds, both moral and intellectual. (That is why these religions emphasize the need to rely on God's love and mercy as well as his explicit instructions.) This radical difference between the human and divine is absent from the great Eastern ethical religions. In other words, the ethicalist divine principles are principles that we not only should aspire to (as in Western monotheistic morality); they are principles that we can perfectly embody if we are sufficiently disciplined. For this reason the Eastern religions are sometimes called "transcendental"—meaning that they are religions in which the human being can rise above (=transcend) the earthly, creaturely state of existence and experience a God-like wisdom and serenity. Buddhism, which originated in India in the 6th century B.C.E., is the largest ethicalist religion in the world. The founder of Buddhism was an Indian prince named Siddhartha Gautama; "Buddhism" is an honorific title meaning "enlightened." Buddhism holds that unhappiness exists because we perceive a gap between what we desire and what we have. But this gap only exists because of our desires: it is in terms of what we want that we decide whether we have enough. Thus, to overcome our desires, to detach ourselves from worldly concerns, is to experience bliss or salvation ("Nirvana"). While Western monotheism conceives of an inner peace and even joy in the face of life's sorrows that can be experienced by the believer, it really has no conception of a life that would be free from sorrow as such. The most dramatic proof of this is that in the Hebrew Bible god himself suffers because of Israel's disobedience, while in the New Testament His son suffers a torturous death at the hands of the Roman occupying force in Judea. As one scholar has put it, "For Buddhism, suffering is unreal; for Judaism and Christianity, it is real—but it is not final" (White, 1985).

SOCIOLOGICAL PERSPECTIVES ON RELIGION

The three principal founders of modern sociology—Durkheim, Marx, and Weber—each believed that religion is an institution of fundamental significance in all societies, and much of their work (especially Durkheim's and Weber's) was devoted to explaining what that significance is. We will look briefly at the basic conclusions they reached.

Durkheim: Religion in the Service of Social Order

The functionalist approach to religion, deriving from the work of Durkheim, sees it as contributing to the maintenance of social order. How exactly does religion do this? We will identify four basic functions of religion.

Psychological Support

Religion helps individuals cope with stressful situations in life. It can help alleviate our anxieties, put our disappointments in perspective, console us in our sorrows, and compensate for our loneliness. Whether we are experiencing problems at work, with our health, or in our personal relationships, religion can help us live with them. This is a functionalist point insofar as it means that religion is serving the interests of society when it helps keep us going: it is in society's interest, and not just our own, that we be able to return to work (i.e., become functional again) within days of sustaining the shock of the death of a loved one. Religious services at funerals are designed to provide a setting for controlled mourning: we express our grief, yet at the same time are reminded—for example, by a reading from the Biblical book of Psalms—that death is after all a part of life, that it awaits all of us, that it is part of god's plan that we have no right to question, that to brood over death is therefore to condemn life, that the deceased has gone on to a better or at any rate more restful place, etc. If we were not encouraged to mourn, we would have to go crazy. But if we were encouraged only to mourn, we would have to go crazy as well, and probably sooner than in the first case. So instead we mourn within socially defined limits and in a formalized or structured setting. That way we can return to our roles as productive citizens within a reasonably short period of time.

The example of death raises an interesting point. While there are some catastrophes which many people successfully avoid in the course of their lives—e.g., unemployment, poverty, debilitating illness and injury—there are other ones that are a part of life itself, problems which no one escapes because **they belong to the nature of life.** These are the problems of death and evil. Not only does everyone die but everyone experiences mild or harsh mistreatment, either occasionally or continuously, as a result of the insensitivity or greed or meanness of others (just as others suffer mistreatment by us). **It is the task of religion to reconcile us to these facts of life.** This does not mean that it is the task of religion to impede efforts to cure disease or combat racism; rather its purpose is to enable believers to **accept a life in which death and evil, in one form or another, are basic ingredients. In this sense the religious view differs fundamentally from the scientific.**

Social Control

As bad as people's behavior is, chances are it would have been even worse through history without the influence of religious teachings. When a criminal statute defines homicide as a capital offense, that may act as a deterrent against killing; but a scriptural passage, commanding that "Thou shalt not kill," accepted as divinely inspired or even as the word of God itself, is an even greater deterrent. This is one reason why the decline of religious authority in the modern world can be seen as a problem. The question is whether any similarly effective authority has come along to replace the old one. It is common in modern Western cultures to consider the traditional Christian doctrine of hell as an outmoded superstition—a cruel hoax that had been perpetrated on humankind, but from which we have now been liberated. But, on the other hand, it is difficult to imagine a more effective deterrent against crime than the belief that the eternal flames of hell await the perpetrator in the next life.

Of course the meaning of the moral injunctions found in the Bible, like the meaning of the rest of the Bible and of texts generally, is not literally given by the text; the text contains only words, and these have to be interpreted. And indeed the Bible, like all other texts of significance, has given rise to a variety of differing interpretations. "Thou shalt not kill" sounds pretty clear, yet it implies different things to different readers. To some it means "don't kill under any circumstances." To a considerably greater number of people, adherence to the spirit of the Ten Commandments is said not to cover such things as killing in wartime, legal executions, homicide in self-defense, and so on.

One sociological issue in this is that, while there may exist a variety of interpretations of religious teachings, **some tend to be more influential than others—namely, those that interpret religious teachings as supportive of the status quo.** The reason for this is that the more powerful groups in society have a greater influence in shaping public opinion than others do, and so their interpretation of religion as supportive of the established order carries more weight than other interpretations do. Thus the social control function of religion means in reality that religious belief will tend to correlate with political and moral conservatism, since that is the kind of religiosity preached by politicians and mainstream churches. We will come back to this in our discussion of the Marxian theory of religion.

Identity and Solidarity

Like ethnicity, religion is a source of both individual and group pride. The individual's sense of self-worth is often based in part on identification with a particular religious tradition or membership in a particular religious congregation. Some sociologists maintain that, under the highly competitive, anonymous, bureaucratized conditions of modern society, the sense of community that religious affiliation offers may be more necessary to the individual than ever before. This would explain a basic paradox of American society: as developments in science and technology have accelerated in the last third of the 20th century, so has a "religious revival" taken place.

Marx: Religion in the Service of Oppressive Social Order

Marx was a bitter enemy of religion—because he saw it as an enemy of humankind. Not just an enemy of humankind but the most destructive enemy in history. Why? Because, according to Marx, religion is the most effective **ideological weapon** ever devised. Human beings—unlike animals, who kill only when they are hungry or literally threatened—have invented innumerable good reasons for killing each other; and religious beliefs have enabled more people to feel justified in killing their neighbors than any comparable set of ideas. It is one thing to go to war because you believe your neighbors are encroaching on territory that rightfully belongs to you; it is another thing to go to war because your neighbors are heathens or infidels or agents of the devil and that to kill them is therefore to do God's will. Whether or not a particular war gets described explicitly as a contest between godly and satanic forces, there is a tendency for armies to assume that their side is the righteous one and that their military initiatives are sanctioned by God.

But Marx was not concerned simply with the connection between religion and warfare. He believed that throughout history unjust social arrangements of various kinds have been able to sustain themselves because of the legitimacy conferred upon them by religious beliefs. His theory of religion encompasses two basic ideas:

a. Religious beliefs are interpreted by those in power in such a way as to justify and solidify their power. History is filled with examples of rulers justifying their domination of others by appeals to religion. In England and France during the Middle Ages, kings and bishops alike professed and promoted belief in the "divine right" of kings to rule. Both religious and civil authorities in the pre-Civil War American South professed and promoted the belief that slavery is an institution decreed by God. The white Dutch minority that ruled South Africa under the apartheid system professed and promoted the belief that God sent them to South Africa on a mission to rule over the native African population.

b. If religious beliefs are endorsed by the powerful because such beliefs serve their interests, what motivates the religiosity of the poor? It is easy to understand why the king might believe that he rules by divine right; but why do his oppressed subjects believe it too? Marx's answer is contained in his famous phrase, "Religion is the opium of the people." That is, religion acts as a drug, a pain-killer, a tranquilizer. Instead of feeling the pain of oppression, the poor person's thoughts drift, under the influence of religious belief, to an imaginary afterlife in which eternal rewards are distributed in direct proportion to one's prior sufferings on earth. Fantasies of future gratification distract us from the reality of present frustration. According to Marx, the poor are glad, or at least relieved, to find this distraction. Constant awareness of oppression is itself oppressive; and struggle against the forces of oppression is something that only exceptionally strong individuals are capable of. For most people it is easier to believe that their suffering is an expression of God's will than that it is due to the unjust policies of the powerful. Thus subjects as well as rulers find the idea of the divine right of kings appealing.

But for all its historical and logical cogency, there is a basic weakness in Marx's approach: it seems to be attacking, not religion itself, but the uses to which religion has been put. If religion can be used to justify inequality or distract attention from injustice, does that mean it is of the essence of religion to be used in these ways? In other words, does Marx's theory criticze religion, as it claims to do, or only the misuse of religion by oppressive and oppressed peoples? There are, after all, many historical instances of religious belief heightening people's awareness of injustice and strengthening their resolve to overcome it; the most famous recent example would be the civil rights movement: Martin Luther King's politics was inseparable from his Christianity. When King found inspiration for his struggle for racial equality in the Bible, was he misreading it? The role of religious beliefs in history is not as unambiguous as Marx thought.

Weber: Religion and the Formation of Social Order

Where Marx viewed religion as maintaining the status quo, Weber saw it as actively shaping and transforming it. And while Marx, and even more Durkheim, analyzed the impact of religious belief on society (and vice versa), Weber's profound and voluminous writings analyze in detail the content of various religious systems, in order to show how specific sets of beliefs have influenced society in specific ways. In his most famous work, **The Protestant Ethic and the Spirit of Capitalism,** he attempts to show that early Protestantism helped shape a new attitude towards work and material success that eventually led to modern capitalism. In order to understand his thesis we must briefly examine the meaning of its two basic terms, "Capitalism" and "Protestantism."

Capitalism

A capitalist economic system, such as we have in the United States, is based on private property, the profit motive, and free competition. It could seem that a nation committed to capitalism must be especially materialistic or greedy. Weber forces us to look more deeply into the matter. The desire for profit, as well as competition and private ownership, existed in pre-capitalist economies also. What makes capitalism different, according to Weber, is that it **views all these things as good**—rather than as necessary evils to be tolerated at best. Capitalism regards the competitive spirit as a sign of moral health, competition brings out the best in individuals as well as nations. The desire for gain is seen as the greatest incentive to hard work known to humankind. In short, capitalism is that economic system which **spiritualizes the drive towards**

the accumulation of wealth. It does so by emphasizing the process of accumulation—namely, hard work; wealth as such is only assigned a positive moral value insofar as it symbolizes effective hard work. Commitment to the process means that the ideal-typical capitalist is one who not only works hard but develops rational methods and procedures for ensuring the effectiveness of his efforts. Accumulation, if it symbolizes effective hard work, must not ensue haphazardly; accumulation is not a game but a **vocation** in which the capitalist specializes. One must be dedicated to it.

Now what has all this to do with religion?

Protestantism

What we know today as Protestantism began as a protest movement within the Roman Catholic Church in the early decades of the 16th century, led by an Augustinian monk named Martin Luther. At first, Luther did not intend to establish a new church but simply to revitalize the already existing one. In any case, to understand Protestantism in its original form we must understand the nature of Luther's dissatisfaction with the church of his day. Basically, Luther objected to the fact that, as he perceived it, the church placed itself in an intermediate position between God and humanity. While he explicitly attacked the church's practice of selling indulgences—remittances of punishment for sin—the deeper corruption detected by Luther was the church's assumption that it had the power to cancel such debts at all. In general, whether on particular occasions it acted corruptly—e.g., for financial gain—or out of pure spiritual motives, the church was committed to the view that it held the "keys to the kingdom." A specific religious regimen, it taught, would, if followed, ensure the believer's place in heaven; and the regimen consisted of a set of ritual and other prescriptions of the church. According to Luther both of these assumptions—that there are keys to the kingdom and that the church possesses them—are false. Luther understood the New Testament teachings on sin to mean that no human works could ever merit salvation, since even good works are infected by sin (e.g., they may be infected by pride at having done good; they may be motivated in part by the desire for future rewards—such as are promised for the virtuous by Jesus himself, etc.). Salvation, then, cannot be earned but only freely given by the "grace of God."

At this point the teachings of John Calvin, a younger French contemporary of Luther's and equally radical critic of Catholicism, become more directly relevant to Weber's theme. Calvin expresssed the idea that salvation cannot be earned by declaring that one's ultimate destiny (salvation or damnation) is predetermined by god—i.e., it is decided prior to and independent of one's life. While this doctrine of **predestination** meant that individuals cannot secure their fate through righteous behaviors, Calvin taught that people nevertheless had an obligation to act righteously, and that the epitome of righteousness was the act of having faith in god.

According to Weber, Calvinist teaching generated a tremendous amount of anxiety, since it appeared to sever the causal connection people were led to believe existed between behavior and fate. That connection had been perceived as most direct and most assured in the case of the ritual behaviors prescribed by the church. But for Calvin, as for Luther, the church had no power to effect an individual's salvation; the sacraments, such as the Eucharist (Lord's Supper) and confession, could perform no magic; Sunday could no longer compensate for the sinner's Monday-through-Saturday existence.

How could average believers incorporate such teachings into their lives? **By re-conceiving their worldly** (Monday-through-Saturday) **existence as an existence worthy of salvation.** In other words, according to Weber, people began to convince themselves that a sober life of hard work was indicative of those who are elected by God, and that the surest measure of one's sobriety and diligence was the degree of success one enjoyed. Thus the "work ethic" was born, and riches honestly acquired were considered an earthly sign and seal of God's approval.

Weber's attempt to link capitalism and Calvinism is not as completely speculative as it may seem. He would not have pursued his strange thesis if he had not first observed that in all the major capitalist countries of his day Protestantism—and Protestantism in a distinctly Calvinist form (e.g., Puritanism in America)—was the dominant religion, and that even in non-Protestant countries, such as France, the leading capitalists were almost always Protestants. But further, once we appreciate the genuineness of the problem he set out to solve, the admitted unprovability of his hypothesis becomes less significant. The problem was to understand how Western culture, **in apparent opposition to the full weight of Biblical teaching on the subject,** could possibly have come to define material success as a sign of virtue. It may also help to note the plausibility of Weber's assumption that, in the absence of a salvation effected by the church, the early Calvinists did need assurances, or signs, that God had indeed elected them. **The Protestant anxiety**—of being left alone, as it were, to work out one's salvation and to reach moral, religious, and intellectual conclusions in life without the aid of an omnipotent church—is the same anxiety located by Durkheim in his study of suicide.

Finally, an interesting application of Weber's theory can be seen in the fact that throughout our history many Americans have tended to interpret our incredible national prosperity as a sign that God favors America; Robert Bellah calls this tendency the American **civil religion**—the belief that American institutions and values (democracy, individual freedom) are sacred: for example, the idea that we are a nation "under god," and that god blesses America. No wonder, then, that defacing the American flag could strike many Americans as sacrilegious (Bellah, 1970).

TRENDS IN RELIGION TODAY, SOCIOLOGICALLY VIEWED

Fundamentalism

This term is used today in two very different contexts. It is used to describe the religious orientation of certain Muslim groups in various countries—most notably Iran, where radical

Shiites took over the government in 1979. But the movement is strong in many other countries, e.g., Saudi Arabia, Egypt, Algeria, and others. And the same word is used to describe a particular brand of American Christianity, represented most prominently by televangelists such as Pat Robertson, Jerry Falwell, and others. What do these two apparently disparate movements have in common—aside from the fact that they have both enjoyed a steady surge in popularity over the past twenty years, while many of the more mainstream religious bodies have seen their membership rolls shrink? What do they share such that they are both referred to as "fundamentalist"? Here are some of the basic similarities:

Scriptural Literalism

This is the cornerstone of fundamentalist religion. Of course the Scripture in question is different depending on whether one is a Muslim or a Christian. Here we will use the Bible rather than the Koran as our example, with the proviso that what we say about the fundamentalist Christian's relation to the Bible applies equally to the fundamentalist Muslim's relation to the Koran. In both cases, the fundamentalist is committed to a **literal reading** of scripture. To read something literally means to read it strictly "word for word," without reading into it (i.e., without reading one's own interpretation into it); it means reading just what the words say without embellishing or in any other way changing them. That seems clear enough. The problem is how one could possibly read the Bible that way. Certainly the early Christians who composed the New Testament didn't read the Bible—which for them meant the Hebrew Bible, or what Christians later came to refer to as the "Old Testament"—that way. The Gospels of Matthew and Luke, for example, interpret certain passages in the book of Isaiah as foretelling the messiahship of Jesus of Nazareth, even though Isaiah was composed several centuries before Jesus' time and makes no explicit mention of him. But the real problem is not that the Bible hasn't been read literally but that it **can't** be. What is the "literal" meaning of Jesus' parables? What is the "literal" meaning of Paul's theology in his letter to the Romans? There is none. **To be understood at all the Biblical writings have to be interpreted.** And if they have to be interpreted, it inevitably follows—given our imperfect state as mere human beings, who seek the truth but do not possess it—that they will be interpreted differently by different individuals and groups of individuals. And that is precisely what has happened historically—witness the division of Christianity into innumerable denominations and sects. When a fundamentalist says, "read the Bible literally, without interpreting it," this can only mean, "read the Bible according to my (or my group's) interpretation."

There is, however, a second way in which "literal" is used that makes the concept of a literal reading more plausible—namely, to refer to **historical literalness.** That is, those parts of the Bible which describe events can be—and from the fundamentalist point of view, should be—read as though the events really happened. An historically literal reading of the Bible is not impossible, although for people raised in a modern scientific culture, it is difficult. If one were to accept as historical such events as Jesus' virgin birth, his resurrection, and his nature miracles—walking on water, changing water into wine, and so on—one would also have to accept as historical (or explain why not) the numerous conversations between God and Moses in the Old Testament, and God's original visitation to Moses in the form of a burning bush—not to mention the great Flood, the events in the Garden of Eden, and the mighty acts of creation which preceded them (in the day-by-day order recoreded in Genesis, of which there are two contradictory accounts in Chapters I and II).

But the real question is not whether such a reading is possible but whether it is necessary. Fundamentalism identifies religious truth with historicity. That is why it tends to reject any theory, such as the theory of evolution, which denies the historicity of the Biblical narrative: it thinks such a theory denies the Bible's truth. To those who read the Bible non-literally, this isn't a problem: the Bible can be true without being literally, historically true all the time. How can something be true without being literally true? Think of a well-known and loved children's story such as "The Three Little Pigs." This story has a "moral"—which is probably why it has lasted so long and is still read to children today—about the value of hard work, the difference between short-term pleasure and long-term happiness, etc. In other words, the story tells the truth (or a truth) about life. And yet those pigs, and their houses of straw, sticks, and bricks never existed. Is the truth of the story thereby negated? In the 20th century, mainstream—non-fundamentalist—theologians tend to read the Bible in this more "figurative" way

Political Conservatism

Fundamentalism, East and West, burst onto the political scene in a big way at about the same time: while the Muslim revolution was taking place in Iran, Jerry Falwell's "Moral Majority" and other groups of Christian fundamentalists in the United States were beginning to throw their support behind right-wing Republican political candidates. The fundamentalist agenda includes a radical conservatism on "social issues": opposition to abortion rights and homosexual rights, advocacy of prayer in the public schools, and opposition to feminism (e.g., advocacy of a traditional wife-homemaker role for women).

The Muslim regime in Iran is a **theocracy** (=political rule by religious authorities). As for American fundamentalists, while a theocratic—in this case, Christian—state would probably be to their liking, American tradition—and law—points away from it. The 1st Amendment to the U.S. Constitution stipulates that "Congress shall make no law respecting an establishment of religion, or prohibiting the free exercise thereof." The authors of the Constitution, having been attacked for being dissenters in England, tried to frame a document that would protect dissenters at home; the idea of making one's own religion the country's official one was therefore no more acceptable in principle than making someone else's. What the "separation of church and state" means in practice has not always been clear; indeed, it wasn't until 1962 that the Supreme Court decided that even "non-denominational" prayer in public (i.e., government financed) schools violates the establishment clause. In 1993 the Court decided that a public school that let community groups use its facilities after school hours could not forbid such use to a religious group. And in recent years the Court has taken varying positions on the question whether Christmas and Channukah displays in public buildings violate the 1st Amendment.

But however these and similar cases are decided, the principle of separation remains intact; the only question is whether that principle is being compromised by the practice the Court is asked to evaluate. The principle entails that it is no more acceptable for the U.S. to declare itself a "Christian nation"—despite the fact that 90% of its citizens are Christian—than to declare itself a "white nation," even though a majority of its citizens fit that description, too.

In general, fundamentalism attracts and speaks for those who find themselves confused or frightened or alienated as a result of the tremendous changes in social norms that occurred in the West beginning in the 1960s. (Similarly, Islamic fundamentalism, in Iran and elsewhere, is a reaction against the perceived threat posed by the growing influence of Western culture in the Muslim world.) Biblical literalism is seen as providing the grounds for a traditional morality: fundamentalism tends to identify "moral" with "traditional," just as it identifies "true" with "historical." Some Biblical norms, however, would presumably be either too conservative (e.g., slavery) or not conservative enough (e.g., polygamy) for the typical fundamentalist's tastes. And besides, many feminists, Marxists, and others are as deeply attached to the Bible as fundamentalists are yet find in it the basis for a left-wing approach to social change.

Fundamentalism as a Source of Community

Part of the attraction of fundamentalism is that it offers people a sense of community in an increasingly impersonal world. One might wonder how this could be given the fact that some of these groups have millions of members. The answer is that the fundamentalist's sense of community derives from the sectarian intensity of fundamentalist belief. A sect is a religious organization that has broken off from a larger one (called a **denomination**), usually because it regards the larger one as having lost its religious vitality by adapting to the surrounding secular culture (Niebuhr, 1929; Troeltsch, 1931). The sect, then, identifies itself through a double contrast: a contrast with the sinful secular culture and the deluded pro-secularist denomination.

It was Ernst Troeltsch who first distinguished between denominational and sectarian religious organizations. Denominations tend to emphasize an attitude of **inclusiveness**—i.e., an attitude of respect for and interest in other religious groups than one's own, and even other, non-religious belief systems (e.g., science); while the sect tends to believe that it represents an island of truth and goodness in a sea of iniquity (=the secular world around them, and the world of other religions). Some American denominations include: Lutheran, Methodist, Reform and Conservative Judaism, Roman Catholic, etc.; some sects include Seventh Day Adventist, Jehovah's Witnesses, and Assemblies of God. While fundamentalist-leaning **individuals** exist in most denominations, there is a much greater overlap between fundamentalist attitudes and sectarian membership.

It is interesting that Marx, who was so otherwise obsessed with social class, paid so little attention to class differences in type as well as **degree** of religiosity. As for degree, he indicated that the poor have a greater need for religion—for the escape from reality it provides—than more economically privileged groups. But it is also true that the poor are for the very same reasons more likely to be attracted to the kind of **intense, other-worldly**—or end-of-the-worldly—type of religious message more often found in sectarian theology and preaching than in the denominational varieties. If you are doing well in this world, you may not want to listen to thundering orations concerning its impending apocalyptic destruction; if your present life is miserable, you may welcome just such a message.

The distinction between denominations and sects has always existed, but today the divergence between the two types of group—between the fundamentalist sect, for example, that calls for the re-introduction of prayer in the public schools and the Lutheran church that insists on the right to distribute condoms in a public park—is greater than ever.

The sense of belonging to an elect group of true and pure believers gives the sectarian a sense of identity that outweighs even the advantages that small group size, for example, may also have in this respect (although often they enjoy that advantage too: many fundamentalist groups in this country today are small-town, tight-knit affairs; and sects always originate as small breakaway movements). Thus, many American fundamentalists grew up in one of the mainline Protestant denominations; others, however, stay on as an opposition minority within the denominations (fundamentalism is especially strong as a minority movement within the Baptist denomination). Of course, the sectarian sense of specialness is easier to sustain when the group is small, and members relate to each other personally; the smallness of a group also provides for cohesiveness because it makes "them" seem more threatening.

Religious elitists tend to regard themselves as a persecuted minority even when they are a majority. Long after Christianity became the dominant religion in the Western world, the Christian was encouraged to see himself as one who bears the cross of Christ, suffering for his Christianity in a heathen world. From the 4th century on, the idea that to be a Christian in the West means to suffer for your religiosity—in lands where Christmas and Easter are national holidays, celebrated in public by the highest elected officials—seems somewhat pretentious.

Liberation Theology

Strictly speaking, liberation theology refers to a Marxist interpretation of the Bible that emerged within Catholic theology, especially in Latin America, during the 1960s, and has grown in influence ever since. Liberation theology understands the gospel's "good news" for the poor as a message of social and political, and not merely personal, liberation—i.e., as liberation from oppressive social structures rather than merely the oppressiveness of one's own sinfulness. It believes that Jesus should be seen as a revolutionary in every sense of the word. As a result, advocates of this approach have themselves become political activists, fighting for land reform and other measures that would provide some measure of economic justice for the Latin American peasant. Some religious leaders have been jailed, and even killed, in the process. While the Catholic Church has officially criticized liberation theology for its insistence that authentic Christianity must express itself as a commitment to political change—and change of a specific type, which may necessitate the use of violence as a means of pursuing justice—it has by no means condemned it. Thus, while remaining highly conservative on social issues such as abortion, the Catholic Church has become quite liberal on questions of economics, war and peace, and social justice (e.g., questions of racial equality). The position outlined in the 1986 U.S. Catholic bishops' letter, **Economic Justice for All**, while more moderate than liberation theology, is still considerably to the left of the recent platforms of either the Republican or the Democratic party.

As for mainstream Christianity and Judaism, much the same can be seen: a growing tendency over the past 30 years to get involved in social and political questions, mainly from a liberal point of view. The civil rights movement of the 1960's, as well as the anti-Vietnam war movement, was widely and actively supported by a wide range of Protestant and Jewish groups. We have here a rather glaring refutation of Marx's view that the dominant religions in any society necessarily support and reinforce the status quo. We also notice here a growing polarization within Western religion: on the one hand an upsurge in fundamentalism, which identifies Biblical morality with political conservatism; and on the other hand, the exact opposite interpretation gathering steam among more mainstream groups. Sociologists are bound to note that in this religion is merely reflecting the tendency toward fragmentation to be found in the culture as a whole.

Feminism

The feminist movement has taken hold within religion, as can be seen in a number of developments in recent years. Women clergy are now admitted in most large denominations in this country; the Catholic Church remains the one major exception. Although in many denominations the vote to admit women clergy has been close, it is important to point out that for such motions to carry they have to be supported by men as well as women. "Feminist" is not a label that is exclusively applicable to women any more than "civil rights advocate" is a label that applies only to blacks.

Another major area where the interest in female equality has made itself felt is in reform of the liturgy (worship service). Standard prayers have been revised to expunge sexist language (references to God the father and to his kingdom being the most obvious examples of such language). New Bible translations have been undertaken with the same aim—most notably, the New Revised Standard Version, a major new Protestant translation (replacing the highly influential and widely-used Revised Standard Version), which has retained only very few uses of the "generic male" pronoun ("he," "him," and "his" used to refer to women as well as men). Perhaps more significantly a feminist theology has emerged, in which the female qualities of God (and, for Christian feminists, Christ) are emphasized along with the male ones. That God the perfect exemplar of wisdom, creativity, and love should be spoken of with the assumption that one were speaking of a man, is now being criticized by denominational theologians of all types—including many Catholic ones. (See, for example, Johnson, 1992, and Ruether, 1983).

General Increase in Religiosity

Religiosity is on the rise, much of it outside traditional boundaries. As in the case of the family, religious forms, as well as their meaning and function for the individual and society, have changed dramatically during the course of the 20th century. These changes are sometimes mistaken for signs of weakness or worse. By forecasts of death we refer to the highly esteemed sociological theory of secularization, according to which the process of modernization entails the progressive weakening of the institution of religion. Not only does this theory sound reasonable enough in the abstract but it arose as a modest effort to summarize some incontrovertible empirical developments with regard to the place of religion in society. Religion, for example, is not the major force in the education of children that it was in pre-modern societies; parents may arrange for their children to receive religious instruction, but such instruction is supplementary to their "real" education, which in our society is wholly secular in content. Since we understand the world largely in terms of the knowledge yielded by modern science, raising children to become competent adults means providing them with the tools necessary to master some small domain, at least, of scientific reality. In this context, religion no longer has any function—except in the sense captured by the popular bumper sticker that reads: "As long as there are tests, there will be prayer in the schools." Still, most people, even those who pray for a high grade, would probably concede that high grades tend to result from mastery of the (scientific) course material rather than divine inspiration, let alone intervention. In other words, just as **what** we learn is thoroughly secularized, the modern conception of **how** we learn is too. Our knowledge of the world and our knowledge of how to acquire that knowledge have been thoroughly secularized. The modern world prefers science to religion, if for no other reason than that it has proven its effectiveness. As we noted above, science is oriented toward technical applicability, and in what it has set out to achieve it has succeeded brilliantly. Religion counsels and consoles; medicine cures. For these and other reasons—the most important being the historical tendency of organized religion to support (if not to actually constitute) oppressive political regimes—it is fair to say that secularization is a basic feature of modernity, but much more so in the case of Europe than of America—for the obvious reason that organized Christianity was never the political force in America that it was in Europe, and therefore never a force to be overcome. The U.S., as we noted, was founded on the principle of separation of church and state—since the founders had been persecuted under regimes where that principle was not operative. While the U.S., by the 1st Amendment, is officially more secularized than the European democracies—where, for example, it is often the case that clergy are state employees—informally it is less so: more Americans than Europeans consider religion to be an important part of their lives, by far. This has long perplexed secularization theorists. If modernization entails the decline of religious influence, why is it that the world's most modern—i.e., most technologically advanced—society is at the same time one of the most religious? In England and France about 10–15% of the population in an average week attend religious services of some kind; in the U.S. the figure is closer to 40%. The mystery is resolved when we take into account two aspects of American life which together have minimized the spread of religious indifference here.

First, as we've already noted, fundamentalism is on the rise. The irony of fundamentalism is that it thrives on modernization, since it is a reaction against it. Thus, the more indifferent society as a whole becomes to religion—or, in the eyes of fundamentalists, not indifferent but hostile, persecutory, etc.—the more zealous the religious response to it. (By way of analogy, consider the question: is the racial climate better or worse in the U.S. today than, say, thirty years ago? The answer is undoubtedly: both. On the one hand, minorities are obviously more a part of the American mainstream than ever before—e.g., about ⅓ of black households are middle-class; and yet, precisely on account of this progress, people who oppose minority advancement feel more bitterness towards minorities than they may have felt in the past, and so things are now in a sense worse than they were: more inter-ethnic tension, violence, and the rest. So, too, American society today is both more and less religious than it once was.)

Secondly, denominational religion has tried to cope with the threat of obsolescence by making appeals to the public's increasingly secularized consciousness—for example, **by emphasizing the ethical rather than dogmatic aspects of religion.** Throughout much of the 20th century, mainstream Christian churches have preached a distinctively 20th century Jesus—Jesus the moral paragon, the embodiment of our highest ideals, as against the more traditional Jesus the Son of God, begotten but not made, who will return to judge the quick and the dead in the last days, etc. The purpose of the switch is to prevent alienating people who feel that religious thinking is primitive and barbaric. Banished, for the most part, is not only the supernatural Jesus but the condemnatory, fanatical one—the one who had come to set parent against child, the one who foresaw wailing and gnashing of teeth for those who fail to follow him (and even the destruction of whole towns and villages), and so on. (The modern Jesus of peace and love—i.e., the one who fits in perfectly with our modern conceptions of moral goodness—is the Jesus of "liberal theology" (Moltmann, 1973).) In addition to focusing on moral rather than dogmatic teachings, the modern American mainstream church often appeals to its secularized constituents through an emphasis on social and political questions. A secularized public is impatient with those who don't "practice what they preach"—after all, science has proven itself to the general public not by its theories but by their practical applications. The Jesus who preached love is only adequately represented by a church that emphasizes works of love. We have already noted the involvement of the mainstream churches (and synagogues) in the struggle for civil rights for minorities; there is no major social or political question of our time that denominational Christianity and Judaism in this country has not spoken out on, usually from a more or less liberal perspective.

RELIGION AND POST-MODERN SOCIETY

Both fundamentalism and secularized denominationalism can be described as modern forms of religiosity: the one, a passionate reaction against modernity, the other an attempt to adjust to it. They are, in different ways, both subject to modernity, i.e., to the modern tension between religious faith and scientific skepticism. They are "symptoms" of modernity; they have not transcended or overcome modernity. Neither of them, therefore, represents a genuinely post-modern religiosity.

The weakness of secularization theory is that it stops with the modern period. If modernization implies secularization, does that mean that post-modernity implies an acceleration of the secularization process? Not necessarily. The signs are, in fact, that **increased interest in religion will prove to be a basic feature of post-modern culture.** This makes sense, since the crisis of modernity is in part a crisis of confidence in science—that science which had supposedly refuted religion once and for all. The crisis of modernity is a negative expression of a yearning for the things modernity is now viewed as having deprived us of—including the sense of the ultimate meaningfulness of life. Increased religiosity in a post- modern world, therefore, is hardly **paradoxical.** What are its features? They include the following:

(a) a yearning for spiritual fulfillment precisely among those who are materially fulfilled. Yuppies, in other words, have found God—having abandoned him in droves on their way to the top. The reason why we emphasize the religious enthusiasm of the middle classes is that such enthusiasm raises more interesting questions than the religiosity of the poor does. That is, **middle class religiosity can't be readily explained as a symptom of resentment.** Those who feel left out, abandoned, cheated, or humiliated by modernity—whether we think of modern sexual permissiveness or the modern scientific achievement ethic—understandably turn to religion for consolation; but what sense are we to make of religious enthusiasm on the part of "the best and the brightest"? It cannot be an attempt to escape from, or to wreak vengeance upon, modernity, but rather to somehow move beyond it. Some would argue that this is to be expected: according to Jurgen Habermas' evolutionary theory of society, for example, the basic need for physical security, once satisfied, gives rise to a demand for material comfort; and once we have achieved a comfortable life, the next step is to seek a meaningful one (Habermas, 1979). But the search for meaning is not necessarily a religious or spiritual quest; Habermas's model doesn't explain why so many people seem interested in precisely that version of reality that, a mere generation ago, had fallen so out of favor with the middle classes. Is the religious search for meaning the fulfillment of modernity (the icing on the cake of modern affluence) or a rejection of it? We mentioned in an earlier chapter the Yuppie spiritual crisis films of the early 1990s. Films about super-achievers who find their lives empty obviously struck a chord. We also mentioned in our Yuppie-analysis that the Yuppie ethic is one of hyper-autonomy. This is clearer than anywhere else in the case of Yuppie religiosity (especially because religion is supposedly one area where people are asked to forfeit their autonomy, i.e., to recognize their need to submit, pray, confess, and so on). The affluent want religion, but they want it their way: hence, "New Age" spirituality, outside all the traditional boundaries, and, in other cases, a return to the mainstream church combined with a rejection of traditional mainstream doctrine. Of course, the U.S., with its individualist ethic and its capitalist spirit, has always had a genius for creating new products to cater to individual tastes: just as we have over fifty brands of cigarettes—subdivided into lights, mediums, ultra-lights, menthols, recessed and non-recessed filters, non-filters, 100s, 120s, etc.—so we have a long-standing tradition of religious diversity: over one thousand Protestant sects and denominations, for example. The question is whether the new religiosity of the affluent represents anything really new in American religion. It may: for one thing, there is a **syncretism**—an eclectic blending of various styles and contents— to it that, in other areas of culture, has been identified as a distinctive feature of the post-modern.

(b) Secondly, we should say a word about the **ecumenical spirit of much of contemporary religiosity** (among other things, it makes the syncretism we just alluded to possible). Ecumenical means "universal": within Christianity the ecumenical movement refers to the organized attempt to unify the Christian churches—a movement that accelerated greatly as a result of the new era of openness and reform in the Catholic church, inaugurated at the Second Vatican Council of 1962–65. Since then, interfaith conferences and other collaborative projects have become common within denominational Christianity. But using the word in a broader sense we can say that a spirit of ecumenism characterizes much of American religion today. Jewish and Christian congregations hold joint Thanksgiving services, meeting one year at a church, the next year at a synagogue.

Christian theologians increasingly insist upon the Jewishness of Christianity, including the Jewishness of Jesus (Yehoshua) and Paul (Saul). Just as secular post-modernist thought attempts to transcend what it sees as the arrogant, imperialistic notion that Western civilization equals civilization as such, so post-modern religious thinking criticizes the (Western Christian) tendency to equate Christianity with religion itself (i.e., with advanced, noble, high religion). The "wider ecumenism," as it has been called, envisions a reconciliation of Christianity, not only with Judaism, the religion from which it broke away over 1,500 years ago, but with all the world's religions; Christian-Buddhist and Christian-Muslim dialogue have taken their places alongside the Christian-Jewish dialogue (Phan, 1991). And thus the reality of ecumenism takes its place alongside the reality of the global economy and the multicultural society.

CONCLUSION

In our discussion of the structure of modern society in Chapter V, we noted the paradoxical impact modernity has had on the family, and on intimate relations in general. The modern world, in which secondary groups proliferate and people are identified by their achievements, is precisely one in which the need for intimacy becomes acute. Thus, far from creating an environment in which family is irrelevant, modernity does just the reverse. Similarly, the modern scientization of the world, which originally implied the overcoming of religion as a worldly power, eventually created a new need for religion—but a more intimate, less worldly form of religion: religion as a source of a sense of personal identity, the meaningfulness of life, etc. Now one of the most profound questions in the history of ideas is that of the relation between religion and the world; but for sociologists that question is posed too abstractly. Everything depends on what kind of world, and what kind of religion, we're talking about. **The famous tension between religion and the world is a feature of modern society, but certainly not of society as such.** No such tension existed, for example, in Europe during the high Middle Ages: the Catholic church and the worldly "powers-that-be" worked in harmony with each other (by contrast, think of today's battles between church and state over sex education in the schools). That religion is important to many people in our society—important precisely because of the impersonality and scientization of modern society—hardly means that the tension between a modern scientific understanding of the world and a religious understanding ceases to exist for them. **Secularized religion tries to handle this tension by ignoring it, fundamentalism by exaggerating it.** As a result, secularized religion blends into modernity (so that it tends not to make a difference), while fundamentalism withdraws from it or attacks it (so that the difference it makes is divisive). In other words, neither movement helps promote dialogue between religion and secularism. Clearly fundamentalists wish to return to a pre-modern situation, before the rise of Darwinian theory, the modern historical criticism of the Bible, and the rest (that's going back a long ways: saying fundamentalism wants to return to a pre-1960s culture is a major under-statement). Secularized religion ignores the tension between religion and modernity by discreetly overlooking those basic elements of Western religiosity that are irreconcilable with a modern scientific view of the world. We already mentioned the denominational modernization of Jesus—his transformation from the god-man depicted in Christological dogma to the ideal human who can serve all people of good will as their ethical model. But more than just specific church teachings are at stake; Christianity, Judaism, and Islam all understand them-selves as **religions of revelation,** and how knowledge gained by revelation can be squared with knowledge gained by the use of scientific method is a serious and difficult problem. The truths of religion are **revealed rather than proved;** from a modern standpoint, what those truths are (e.g., the particular dogmas of Christianity) is less problematic than **how** they were arrived at.

Now the question we need to raise is whether this inherent tension between religious knowl-edge and scientific knowledge will necessarily characterize a post-modern culture the way it has characterized modern culture. On the one hand, the tension seems unavoidable as long as post-modernity doesn't imply a rejection of the scientific point of view—and, since nobody really wants to give up all the wondrous products of modern science, it would be hypocritical to renounce the attitudes and theories and procedures that made them possible. Obviously many people today want to tap into spiritual reality—often of a very mystical, supernatural kind—without sacrificing their ties to material reality. New Age religiosity exemplifies this tendency in two respects: its adherents embrace scientific (or pseudo-scientific) theories and technical gad-gets of all kinds; and they are, for the most part, middle-class achievers who seem to have no problem accepting the various material benefits society confers on them (that comes as a result of **their mastery, in most cases, of some domain of scientific-technical knowledge).** The problem with such people is that they seem to think that the scientific attitude—perhaps because it induces a sense of awe at the vastness and orderliness of the cosmos—is inherently consistent with spirituality. Of course a feeling for the awesomeness of the universe is one likely source for the insight into the existence of God (i.e., God the omnipotent creator). **But science is based, not on awe, but the desire to control,** which requires overcoming awe; and New Age religion seems to share this desire (e.g., to control one's life), and in that sense is **closer to the spirit of science than religion.**

By contrast the God of monotheism is not at our disposal; we are at "his" disposal. Is it possible to imagine a truly post-modern religiosity—one that would accept the world-view of modern science (as fundamentalism fails to do) without having to reject traditional religious teach-ings (as secularist denominationalism does)? The numerous recent works on "post-modern the-ology" suggests that this question is treated by many as being of great importance; how far these works succeed in actually constructing a post-modern theology is another question (see, for example, Bellah, et al, 1989). "Accepting the world-view of science" must include accepting the results yielded by the scientific study of religion; this an impressive number of contemporary theologians do. As applied to Christianity this means (just for starters): accepting the fact that much of the material in the Gospels is unhistorical (i.e., invented by the Gospel writers); that Paul only wrote six, or possibly seven, of the fourteen New Testament documents attributed to him; that Jesus's execution had little or nothing to do with religious disputes between him and his fellow Jews (since such disputes were commonplace among Jews, and could never have gotten any of them so angry as to want to kill him); that the only reason either the Romans, or the pro-Roman Jewish leadership, would want to do away with him is the same reason they wanted to (and did) do away with many other first century miracle workers: such characters presented a threat to public order, since anticipation of the arrival of the "kingdom of God" meant, for all normal first century Jews, anticipation of the downfall of Rome; and there was always the chance (indeed, it had happened) that those swept away by hopes that God was about to remove the Roman yoke would try to help him along. There is at present a vast literature—by historians, Bible scholars, and theologians—on these and related themes (see the bibliography in Sanders, 1985). Post-modern theology would be a theology that accepted all these scientifically verified findings, yet not as though they invalidated the religious truth of the New Testament (for Christians): only fundamentalism requires that religious truth rest on scientific foundations (hence, "creationism").

But nor would post-modern theology take the opposite view: that modern thought has successfully invalidated traditional religious thought. Where the fundamentalist has to reject the scientific finding that the virgin birth story is mythological, and the modern secularized denominationalist rejects the story of the virgin birth (or accepts it without knowing what to do with it), the post-modern theologian will ask how these two facts—that the virgin birth story is both a myth and, for Christian faith, "true"—can co-exist. Fundamentalists and secularized denominationlists alike assume that they cannot; in that sense both camps adhere to the (modern) **dichotomy between religion and science.** But the virgin birth can be seen as a metaphor for sinlessness; or, as one Catholic theologian has attempted, Jesus's (in fact) birth out of wedlock can be admitted and affirmed by Christianity: if Jesus's friendship with the outcast is symbolic of "Christian ethics," why be afraid to admit that Jesus himself, as an "illegitimate" child, was an outcast? (Schaberg, 1990)

Similarly, the fact that the resurrection event is **unverifiable** does not mean it is not meaningful but that its **meaning is not a literal one:** the "resurrection of Christ" refers to the belief that Jesus's cause triumphed in and through his death, a death that apparently proved that he had ultimately failed. For years this metaphorical reading has been a staple of normal theology, both Protestant and Catholic. (Similar metaphorical readings of such "events" as the Exodus of the Israelites, the expulsion from paradise, the flood, etc., are typical features of 20th century Jewish and Christian theology.)

What's sociologically interesting here is that, while modern science has been accused of destroying religion, **it is the spirit of modern science that has in fact provoked a revitaliza-**

tion of religion by encouraging such de-literalizations. Religion can appeal to educated people today precisely because it can be understood at the level of meaning rather than literally; facilitating that can be called a latent function of science.

4

CULTURE

The sociological study of culture is the study of the *attitudes and beliefs*, and consequently the *behavior*, that members of a society share (more or less) in common. To speak of culture is to speak of common culture. Even when we study the actual, tangible objects produced by a particular society (its *material culture*), we are led back to its *nonmaterial culture*: the discovery of a tool leads to an analysis of its use, and such an analysis inevitably involves thinking about a society's attitudes and beliefs. There is no getting around the fact that material culture is a consequence of nonmaterial culture, that church buildings are a reflection of religious beliefs. Thus sociologists are ultimately concerned with the nonmaterial culture of a society. The relation between attitudes and artifacts can be thought of as similar to the relation between attitudes and behaviors—especially since the production of an artifact *is* a behavior. But there is no behavior that is not based on a prior thought: going to school presupposes thinking it is necessary and/or desirable to do so.

One way of demonstrating the powerful influence of society on its members is to study culture, since, as we suggested, the study of culture is the study of what society leads us to have in common. The shared character of (certain) opinions among vast and apparently varied members of society is, to a sociologist, simply astounding. The average person complains about having to go to work but not about having to inhabit a body. ("Average" is not a synonym of "normal," but a result of it. Typical behaviors are typical because it is normal to behave in such-and-such a way; therefore most people do so.) There are not only normal things to do, there are normal thoughts to think, and normal feelings to feel. Does this mean that the "polarization" of which experts speak (and which was supposedly exemplified by red and blue states in the 2004 presidential election) is a fantasy? We will only be in a position to address this question seriously *after* we have examined what "common culture" involves. (The term "common culture" should seem redundant by now, since we know that culture *means* what is held in common.)

Norms of Society. "Norms" mean societal rules that prescribe and proscribe attitudes and behaviors. "Rules" is just as accurate a word as "norms" but it is not as useful, since it does not beget the telling adjective "normal." What the norms are, or at least some of them, can be specified by examining normal attitudes and behaviors, which, in the sociological view, exhibit them. So there is no need here for speculation—only observation. Of course *what* is being observed—how to articulate what is in front of our eyes—is always problematic, always open to dispute, and the reader should keep this in mind as we proceed. But, granting the possibility of disagreement, we must insist at the outset that our depiction of norms is driven not by any agenda but by the act of observation. The innumerable norms that pervade our lives have been broken down by sociologists into two main categories: *folkways* and *mores*.

Folkways, as the word implies, simply means the ways of the people: namely, customs and habits. By themselves they might not seem terribly important. They include rules of etiquette, appropriate gestures to use on specific occasions (handshakes when greeting new people, waves of the hand to signify hellos and goodbyes), etc. The rules that ethnomethodologists study are folkways. And the point we wish to make here is the same point that ethnomethodologists make: folkways are of interest because they illustrate that even our most trivial public behavior is governed by *rules*, and that—for some reason—people (including ourselves) get upset when they see violations of them. *Mores*, by contrast, are norms that are considered vitally important to the very existence of society: it is against the norms to murder people because society would break down if it were allowed. *Laws*—formal, officially enforceable norms—exist in order to support or uphold mores. The existence of laws, therefore, shows how important society takes mores to be. (The difference between mores and laws can be seen in the difference between the words "moral" and "legal." If you refrain from committing murder, it is probably because you are afraid of offending your *conscience*, in addition to your fear of what the criminal justice system might do. That conscience, one's moral sense, is itself a social product—that it represents the *internalization* of external demands—has long been postulated by sociologists. Most of us know people who we would prefer were dead but we do not even *think* of killing them—nor do we even imagine accidents killing them.) Where there is no law against moral offenses it is probably due to the fact that society believes that transgressions would occur anyway (think of the case of adultery). And so it is to protect the reputation of the law (its reputation for being effective) that there is no law against it. Finally, *taboos* are norms covering the most strongly prohibited acts—so strongly prohibited that, again, most of us *prohibit ourselves* from even conceiving of doing them. (Since this prohibition of thinking characterizes our reactions both to violations of mores as well as violations of taboos, it cannot be the feature that distinguishes the two concepts.) Incest and cannibalism are the best examples of tabooed acts. Violations of taboos are indeed violations of mores but they are considered much worse—hence, the separate word "taboo." It is a matter of interpretation which acts are tabooed and which "merely" violate mores. One way of distinguishing between them is that, although both are forbidden, we readily *understand* adultery and murder (as a cursory look at TV and movie listings indicates), even if we do not approve of them, while, as for tabooed acts, we simply "don't go there."

The discussion of norms leads to the topic of *sanctions*—rewards and punishments that society uses to motivate acceptable behavior. We say "leads to" for the following reason: it is one thing to specify what the norms are; it is another thing to specify how society induces us to follow them. The basic mechanism at work is fear—fear lest we lose what we have, fear lest we fail to gain what we want, and so on. (Most of us seem to be, not pursuing the American Dream, but trying to avoid the American nightmare—of constant financial worry, if not outright poverty.) This is where the concept of sanctions comes in. "Positive sanctions" are rewards; "negative sanctions" are punishments. In addition, positive sanctions and negative sanctions may both be formal or informal. At any given point in time, then, we are motivated by some combination of sanctions. Examples of each type would be as follows: (a) negative formal sanctions: the threat of being arrested, or of being fired; (b) negative informal sanctions: the fear of being embarrassed (we not only fear that the police will come to our door; we do not want to be known as the people in the building to whose door the police came: we are constantly guarding our reputation); (c) positive formal sanctions: the desire to be promoted or to get a raise; (d) positive informal sanctions (probably the rarest of all): the desire to receive a compliment, "pat on the back," etc. (We say rarest because a lot of people complain that they are only noticed at work, for example, when they do something wrong.)

Finally, in this brief survey of cultural concepts, we must say a word about *values*—ideas about what is desirable in life. The concept of *values* offers an alternative explanation to the concept of *sanctions* as to why we tend to behave normally. (Values are to sanctions as mores are to laws.) The alternative explanation is: because we *believe in* the norms. Thus, sociologists ask: what is the basis of our belief in the norms, and the general answer is because we value them. For example, we work hard (an example of normal behavior) because we believe in the value of *achievement*. Even in our "free time," we are active (we go to the gym, rebuild our homes, go to museums, etc.). Therefore, sociologists claim that Americans value achievement and activity. (These two are sometimes placed together and called the "work ethic": even if we are unsuccessful, or supposedly at leisure, it is normal to be busy. This may seem odd to people who know that Americans are also known as "couch potatoes"—incessant TV viewers, etc. But this may just be an expression of *exhaustion*, and so it may be symptomatic of our work ethic.) For most sociologists, these two—achievement and activity—head the list of American values. Also on the list would be the value of: *efficiency* (as evidenced by students who grow impatient when teachers stray from the curriculum, or by health insurance plans that prefer that patients take psychotropic drugs rather than engage in long-term therapy); *material comfort* (Americans are notorious for "needing" a lot more than people of other cultures need); and *individualism* (we believe in choosing our own careers and marital partners, and not to give in to parental pressures). Closely connected to these is the emerging value of *consumerism*, which should not be underestimated: it allows us to do disagreeable work. When students pick majors, they are already thinking about how much a job in that field pays, i.e., what one can buy with the educational credentials required to land the job.

Also as an expression of our belief in individualism, we are expected to belong to *subcultures*—groups that are different from but not opposed to the dominant culture of achievement, activity, and the rest, to which we also belong. If you identify with the particular ethnic group that you come from, and especially enjoy its cuisine, holidays, and other traditions, that would be a subcultural interest. Or, if you are a hobbyist of some sort, your hobby would be your subculture (we live in a society of *collectors*: of dolls, bottlecaps, etc.). Or, you may belong to both; a person may belong to more than one subculture. As against this, there is the concept of *countercultures*—groups formed *in opposition to* the dominant culture. In the United States today, it is very abstract to speak of countercultures, since none exist, except on the very fringes of society (for example, the KKK, or the American Nazi Party). But once upon a time—e.g., the student culture of the 1960s, which forced an end to U.S. involvement in Vietnam, or the civil rights movement of the 1950s, which fought for African-American freedom from discrimination—they thrived.

Ethnocentrism and Cultural Relativism. Being realistic includes acknowledging the fat that different cultures exist—across the globe, certainly, but even within our own society. The problem of the co-existence of different cultures raises the question of *ethnocentrism*—the belief that one's own culture ought to be the standard by which all cultures are evaluated. It is often said, for example, that Americans are especially ethnocentric, that we simply do not understand how others could not want to be like us if they only had the opportunity. Now, according to sociologists, everyone is somewhat ethnocentric: we exist on a continuum, from mildly ethnocentric to rabidly so; we are not either ethnocentric or non-ethnocentric. The reason is as follows: because everyone is raised according to one set of norms and values, so that by the time one is old enough to notice differences (in styles of dress, for example) the normal has already been defined as the natural. So, although we are taught to tolerate and even respect differences, we harbor the feeling that differences are "strange"—which, indeed, they may be, but "strange" now bears the negative connotation of "odd" or "weird." The sociological concept of the universal tendency toward ethnocentrism strains our belief in sociological disbelief in human nature. Humans seem—naturally—to have problems with what is different. But having problems and having insurmountable problems (because it is our nature to have them) are two different things. At any rate, the official antidote of the social sciences—where ethnocentrism can wreak havoc (think of anthropological studies of "savage" or "primitive" societies)—is called *cultural relativism*, the attempt to understand other cultures the way they understand themselves. No culture thinks of itself as savage or primitive. To sum up: ethnocentrism means judging without understanding (prejudice), while cultural relativism means understanding, and therefore not judging. Cultural relativism is certainly an improvement upon ethnocentrism but it contains problems of its own. The idea of not judging other cultures may appear problematic when they are engaged in what we consider to be awful behavior. So, for example, we can judge female genital mutilation as people but not as sociologists. The concept of cultural relativism thus reveals the *limits* of social science: it cannot speak morally.

RACE

To sociologists the meaning of "race" is more complex and ambiguous than it is to the general public. A **race** can be defined as a group of people regarded as distinct because they share certain distinct, visible, inborn physical characteristics. (The most salient of these characteristics is of course skin color, but other features are also involved, such as the size and shape of the eyes, lips, and nose.) This definition sounds sufficiently scientific and sufficiently commonsensical to please everybody. But sociologists believe that, defined in the above way, the term race is a misleading one for the following reasons:

(1) It implies that groups are fundamentally distinct when in fact human history is a history of interbreeding. Most people, if they could trace their family tree into the remote past, would be quite surprised to find out who they are related to.

(2) It ignores the fact that race categories are defined and established by societies rather than rooted in nature. Our society has created the categories "white" and "black," but this doesn't necessarily correspond to a real genetic distinction, since in our history—and especially during the period of slavery—these groups have cross-bred. In other words, if our race categories were based on biological fact, being "black" would be understood as describing a relative difference from being "white" rather than an absolute one.

Of course when we talk about "interbreeding" we seem to be talking about distinct groups reproducing over time until we arrive at the complex mixture that is us. Yet our criticism of the concept of "race" seemed to deny the existence of distinct groups. Don't groups have to be recognizably different in order for them to have come together? Sociologists do not deny group distinctions; they only deny that they are rooted in nature. Instead of race, sociologists prefer the term **ethnic group.** An ethnic group can be defined as a group of people regarded as distinct because they share a **common culture** as a result of a **shared geographical origin and a shared history.** The differences between one group and another, then, are significant—since "different culture" may refer to different values, religious beliefs, and language—but circumstantial. That is, they are rooted not in different "natures" but in different experiences.

Sociologists continue to use the word race (as we will do in this chapter) because it is so widely used in everyday life—used because it is so significant to so many people. Consciousness of race, of racial difference and the difference it makes, is itself a major feature of our society; it is because of what society has made of race that race has earned a separate section in this book, as it has in all introductory sociology textbooks. The physical difference called "race" has no significance until society confers significance upon it. Height and weight are visible features just as much as skin color is; yet you would be quite surprised to see a section on height or weight in this book. And the reason is that, with some exceptions, society doesn't make a big deal about such differences. So we use the word "race" the way we use the word "deviant": to describe a **socially constructed reality.**

As for the real differences, these are, as we have said, cultural-historical not biological. It should be understood, then, that black Americans, for example, are an ethnic group just as, say, Polish-Americans are: their geographical origins and history, and the cultural patterns that developed in the course of that history, are what makes them a distinct social group (more precisely, a collection of distinct groups). In this context we can understand the effort to replace the term "black" with the term "African-American" as an expression of dissatisfaction with the tendency to understand "black" as referring to a racial difference, and thus to regard black Americans as racially distinct from other Americans, instead of seeing them as belonging to an ethnic group just like everybody else. The term "African-American" accomplishes the latter; like "Italian-American," it refers to ethnicity not race; it describes a group of Americans in terms of their shared geographical origin and history. (Although it does so somewhat abstractly: like the terms Hispanic-American and Asian-American, the term African-American lumps together a number of distinct cultural groups—as, of course, the designation "black" did before it. This raises the question how to define "distinct." While this is a difficult question to answer, we should not overlook how much has been gained merely by raising the question: we know that the fact that group A is different from group B is a matter of definition. Which means that to raise the question of group distinctions is in part to ask who decides—the Census Bureau; the group members themselves; society as a whole—whether and how one group is distinct from another.)

Race is an important sociological topic because many people treat racial (biological) differences as more significant than ethnic (cultural) differences, and popular definitions of reality have real consequences. Thus, for example, to a white person the cultural characteristics that distinguish, say, a Haitian from a Nigerian are less significant than the racial characteristics they share; to such a person these two people are simply "black." Now to the Haitian and the Nigerian, their cultural particularity may be more significant than their common racial make-up; nevertheless, the fact that they are perceived—perhaps by the majority of their fellow citizens, if they are American— as "black" is going to have a major impact on their lives— not only in the sense that people have to take into account, and deal with, the reactions of others, but in the deeper sense that that need (especially when we are talking about the negative reactions of others) becomes a part of one's history, and therefore of one's identity. Included in the history of all the groups in this country collectively known as "black" is a history of suffering on account of being black. Therefore that history also includes a history of pride in black people's endurance, in their maintenance of dignity, and in their preservation of basic institutions (e.g., the family; see Gutman, 1976), in the face of overwhelming odds. Group pride, then, may here take the form of loyalty to one's blackness, to one's membership in a collective racial entity whose members have suffered and struggled collectively—a loyalty above and beyond, or at least in addition to, loyalty to one's particular cultural/ethnic history.

If significant group differences are cultural rather than biological, the problem of "racism" logically belongs under the heading of "ethnocentrism"—cultural superiority feelings. Those feelings, as we saw, are practically inevitable to some extent given the way individuals are socialized exclusively in terms of the norms and values of their own culture. At the same time, this tendency is mitigated somewhat in modern societies by the individual's increased exposure to members of different groups (beginning often as early as in day care) and by the school systems' attempts to teach children about the history and culture of various groups. But while serious religious and other cultural differences may understandably cause conflict, confusion and distrust, why mere physical differences become grounds for hostility seems more mysterious. Thus the question of racism is not simply identical with the question of ethnocentrism. It demands separate treatment because society has made it a separate question by singling people out for differential treatment on account of their "race."

One other frequently used term should be clarified before we go further: **minority group. Minority group** refers to any group which is placed in a subordinate or disadvantaged position in society on account of its distinctive physical or cultural characteristics. Typically these disadvantages include limited educational and job opportunities, restricted access to political power, discriminatory treatment in housing, and many others. "Minority group," therefore, refers to **the way a group is treated, not to the fact that it is a numerical minority.** In fact it may or may not be a numerical minority: blacks in South Africa constitute about 80% of the population yet, under apartheid, they clearly fit the definition of a minority group. While blacks most obviously fit the definition of minority group in our society, the term is generally applied also to Hispanics, Asians, and Native Americans.

When we say that minority group refers to how a group is treated rather than to numbers, the question arises: treated by whom? The concept of minority group, in other words, implies the existence of a majority group whose physical and cultural characteristics are held up—openly in places such as South Africa and more subtly and even unconsciously in places like the U.S.— as the standard or norm against which others are measured. In innumerable ways American culture daily reflects and reinforces the idea that the "average American" is white—and not just white but WASP. The characters companies place before the cameras to sell products are overwhelmingly white. They rarely have "foreign" accents, unless they happen to be promoting an "ethnic" item (e.g., an Italian food product). Characters on sitcoms and soaps usually have WASP-sounding names—unless, again, their ethnicity (i.e., their being different from the norm) is part of the story line. Thus, sitcoms about blacks or Jews are typically about being black or Jewish. The fact that programs with white leads are not about being white shows that whiteness is understood as the norm. It should be noted also that it is only in very recent years that nonwhites and non-WASPs on TV have ceased being the rare exception. And in commercials, where it is a matter of putting forward an image Americans can "trust," the WASP image still predominates. (The same can be said of the other programming area where trust is all-important: the news.

Notice the white faces and WASP-sounding names that dominate network news coverage. The tendency is less pronounced on the entertainment side—perhaps reflecting the fact that whites are less reluctant to be entertained by minorities than to be instructed by them.)

Finally, in sociology the term "minority group" need not refer to an ethnic or racial group at all, although that is how it is used in everyday speech. The most obvious case in point is women: they fit the definition of minority group regardless of their ethnicity. The same is true of gays and lesbians. Bearing in mind, then, that ethnic differences are not the only source of differential treatment in society, we turn our attention in this chapter to the problems faced by ethnic minorities.

PREJUDICE AND DISCRIMINATION

Here are two terms which, because of the tragic history of intergroup relations in our society and elsewhere, have become familiar terms in everyday as well as academic language use. While the sociological definitions of these terms reflect the way they are used in everyday life, the sociological view of the relation between prejudice and discrimination diverges, as we shall see, from the common-sense one.

For sociology as for common sense, **prejudice** refers to an attitude and **discrimination** to a behavior. **Prejudice** can be defined as a rigidly negative attitude towards an entire group of people; **discrimination** refers to the denial of opportunities to people on the basis of their group membership. The common-sense view is that prejudice and discrimination are causally related; that is, it is assumed that discrimination is caused by prejudice. A corollary assumption is that the way to reduce discrimination is to combat prejudice, since ultimately discrimination is nothing more or less than a symptom of prejudice. (Indeed, to say that common sense believes that prejudice and discrimination are "causally related" is an understatement; common sense sees prejudice and discrimination as two sides of the same coin—the attitudinal side and the behavioral side.) This also entails the view, finally, that a decrease in prejudice will necessarily result in a decrease in discrimination.

Sociology disputes all these assumptions. To understand why we must look at the way prejudice and discrimination operate in reality. Think of the following example: A white man owns a bar in a white working-class neighborhood; "the guys" who stop in for a beer afterwork are his principal customers. Occasionally a black person stops in for a drink. The owner doesn't exactly refuse to serve him (that would be a violation of the law); instead, he makes him feel unwelcome by ignoring him. Under these circumstances, such would-be customers normally leave after a few minutes. Why does the owner behave this way? Not, he explains, because he has anything against blacks, but because his regular customers do. His discriminatory treatment, then, is the result not of prejudice but of economic necessity. In other words, in contradiction to the common-sense claim that prejudice and discrimination go together, we seem to have a case here of discrimination without prejudice.

But do we? There are good reasons for discounting the bar owner's version of events—and, for that matter, the similar excuse we might hear from a real-estate agent who shows a black couple a house in an all-black neighborhood rather than the white one they asked to see a house in: I am not prejudiced but the white homeowners are, and I have to stay on good terms with them. The bar owner claims he is not prejudiced. But if you are the target of his act of discrimination, what difference does it make to learn that he really likes you? To victims of discrimination, at least, the alleged difference between prejudice and discrimination is non-existent, since prejudiced and non-prejudiced discrimination amount to the same thing.

Furthermore, for the owner's statement that he is not prejudiced to mean anything, mustn't his lack of prejudice have some concrete manifestation? Think of a husband who, to appease his wife's anger, declares "I love you!" If the only evidence that this is true is his saying it, if there is no loving behavior he can point to, why should he be believed? At best he means he **wants** to love her, or **wants to think of himself** as one who loves her, etc. So in the case of the bar owner, his declaration without action remains suspect: perhaps he just doesn't want to feel guilty about his actions, or be blamed for them. If persons are truly not prejudiced, shouldn't we expect them to not discriminate, rather than give new and improved reasons for continued discrimination?

The problem is that our justified anger over discrimination, coupled with the assumption that discrimination must be based on prejudice, keeps us from seeing that discrimination exists today for many reasons. The point of admitting these reasons is not to exculpate the discriminator but to realize that **discrimination may be a serious problem even in a society where prejudice is in decline** (or even absent altogether). Certainly prejudice has declined in American society over the last several decades: there is more amicable intergroup interaction, at work and elsewhere, than ever before in our history. Because of this many people—especially white people—assume that discrimination against minorities is no longer widespread in the U.S., despite the continued complaints of minorities, and figures that show persisitent gaps in education and income between minorities and whites. To recognize that discrimination against minorities persists in American society it is necessary to abandon the belief that discrimination is invariably caused by prejudice. That is why the bar owner example is important. If it is possible for the bar owner to discriminate without being prejudiced, then it is possible for a whole society to do so.

The question whether the bar owner's discrimination is or is not ultimately an expression of prejudice must remain unanswered, at least in the present context. What is clear is that he discriminates against minorities. The difficult question whether he is prejudiced distracts us from focusing on the discrimination—especially if we require proof of prejudice before we treat discrimination seriously because we have decided that discrimination, in the sense of a social problem to be combatted, only exists where prejudice exists.

Consider the variety of possible motives for discrimination—each of which may, ultimately, be connected to prejudice but are, regardless of such connections, sufficient to cause discrimination.

'Business necessity,' of course, heads the list, but there are others. A white child decides not to pursue a friendship with a black schoolmate outisde the classroom. We could think of this as a matter of cowardice rather than prejudice. Or, a white voter is turned off by a politician who advocates passage of a new civil rights bill to protect minorities. "I'm tired of hearing about their problems." Is this **indifference** to the suffering of others the same as **prejudice** against them? Or does it merely reflect an almost universal tendency to care more about one's own problems than about somebody else's?

Cowardice, indifference, a need to conform, anxieties over money—all these and more lead to acts of discrimination; and these things are certainly more common than outright hatred and bigotry. They are customary, habitual reactions of people who do not feel the pain of discrimination (at least discrimination against "them")—certainly more customary and habitual than risking one's social standing for the sake of friendship, or choosing to do what's right even despite the fear that it may bankrupt your business, or spending your precious free time studying the history of an ethnic group other than your own. In light of this, sociologists have come up with the concept of **institutional discrimination—the denial of opportunities due not to prejudice but to the customary, habitual, "normal" operations of society.** Here is an example of how institutional discrimination works. Suppose in a large corporation a recruitment committee is set up to find a replacement for a recently retired senior manager. The retiree—we'll call him Harry—is a white male: he was with the company for forty years, and forty years ago only white males were hired. The recruitment committee consists of high-ranking personnel who have also been with the company for many years—in other words, it consists of white males. Everybody liked Harry; he was not only a highly competent manager but an easy fellow to get along with. The committee, naturally, hopes to recruit someone like him. After interviewing a number of applicants—including not only white men but women, blacks, Hispanics, and Asians—the committee settles on a white man. In making their decision the recruiters might have said things to each other like, "There's something about Bob that I like" or "I think he'd fit in well," etc. And of course he would: he's more likely to be a sports fan than the Chinese candidiate, so that there would be plenty to talk about with him (Harry was a big sports fan); he's more likely not to be offended by "locker room talk" than the woman candidate, so that one wouldn't have to be constantly watching what one says (Harry appreciated dirty jokes); he's more likely to make a good drinking buddy than the Pakistani, who probably doesn't drink at all (Harry had a weakness for dry martinis). In short, the white male is more likely to fit in because he is being asked to fit in with other white males.

Now does this mean the recruiters are racist or sexist? Does it mean they think women and minorities are inferior to them? Does it mean they despise women and minorities and want to keep them out of high-paying jobs? No! Not only don't they say such things, there is no reason to think that they think them. Yet it is clear that in this situation **women and minorities do not have the same chance of being hired as a white man does, i.e., they do not enjoy equal**

opportunity. The bottom line is that the committee went with "what works"—what's been tried before and found satisfactory. The committee's motto could very well be, "If it ain't broke, don't fix it." The problem is that for women and minorities it is "broke" and therefore needs fixing.

Here are some other examples of institutional discrimination:

(a) "Legacies": Many Ivy League universities set aside admissions for the children of alumni. But alumni of elite universities tend to be white. Therefore without intending it—i.e., without acting on the basis of prejudice against minorities—the legacy system discriminates in favor of whites (Karabel and Karen, 1990).

(b) Factory relocations. Over the past thirty years, many industrial plants have moved from the cities to the suburbs—not out of racial prejudice but for economic reasons. However, due to discrimination in housing, minorities tend to be under-represented in the suburbs. Thus, factory re-locations make it harder for minorities than for whites to take jobs in the factories because for minorities taking the job is more likely to involve a long and expensive commute to work.

(c) "Last hired, first fired." Seniority rules sound completely fair—until you realize that, because of past discrimination in education as well as employment, minorities (and women) are, in many industries, more likely than whites to be among the last hired. Therefore layoffs based on seniority are discriminatory.

(d) Club membership requirements. A private club admits new members only if they are rcommended for admission by a present member. But as a result of overt discrimination in the past, all the present menbers are white. If you are a minority candidate, you are less likely than a white candidate to have a personal friend who belongs to the club. Thus, the club's admissions policy discriminates against minorities.

In most of these examples the fact of present discrimination can be explained as an effect of past history. "Legacies" are white because minorities couldn't get into the Ivy League in the past; women and minorities are laid off first because past discrimination means they've only been hired recently; and, similarly, our hypothetical recruitment committee composed of senior officials is white and male because of past discriminatory policies. Many if not most examples of institutional discrimination show **the effects of history—and of our present tendency not to consider or try to remedy the effects of history.** This is a major part of what is meant when we speak of institutional discrimination as "custom," "habit," and "norm." It is customary, habitual, and normal for an employer not to take into account the effects of past discriminatory burdens imposed on a candidate when judging his or her qualifications in the present.

This leads us to the most controversial example of all: institutional discrimination in the use of credentials in hiring. People often say they want a "color-blind" society, in which people are judged on the basis of "qualifications"—school records, civil service exam scores, job histories, and a whole range of similar "objective" criteria. But what if these criteria are not as objective as they seem? What if a background of poverty and substandard schooling make the 3.0 grade point average of a minority student a more impressive achievement than somebody else's 3.5? Doesn't this mean that the person with a slightly lower score, with slightly less "impressive" credentials, is not necessarily less qualified for the job? The irony is that everyone seems to agree that high grades, for example, do not necessarily translate into greater job competence—that, while decent grades are a reliable indication that a person possesses the basic knowledge necessary to do a job competently, and so are relevant criteria in hiring, only on the job do we discover whether the person "has what it takes." People constantly compare "real knowledge" to "book knowledge." They assail knowledge that is "merely academic." Yet when a white candidate who, let's say, scores 89 on a civil service exam, is passed over in favor of a minority candidate who scored 82 we cry "reverse discrimination"—as if we had claimed all along that grades and scores were exact measures of quality.

Here we are taking up the controversial topic of **affirmative action. Affirmative action** refers to **any program or policy that attempts to combat institutional discrimination and bring about equal employment opportunities for minorities (and women).** Affirmative action, then, includes the effort to take past history into account—for example, by putting less emphasis on certain credentials in cases where sole reliance on them would perpetuate the disproportionate hiring of whites. Affirmative action **usually does not** take the form of establishing different standards (e.g., test scores) for white and minority applicants; instead, it simply refers to a general commitment on the part of an employer to recruiting minorities and women. Whether or not this can be construed as "reverse discrimination," one thing should be made clear: there is no evidence to support the belief that affirmative action policies typically have the effect of placing unqualified or less qualified people in jobs than would be placed in the absence of such policies. To assume that is to assume that qualified minorities and women are either non-existent or in short supply: an assumption that is uninformed at best and racist and sexist at worst. (A more reasonable assumption is that we are producing many more qualified individuals of all kinds than good jobs, and that that is the real reason why affirmative action hurts whites.) That white males may occasionally suffer as a result of affirmative action is unfortunately true; but, while their suffering may make their claim that unqualified minorities and women are being hired in their place understandable, it doesn't make it true. Affirmative action policies may indeed be flawed, but evaluating them rationally requires that we appreciate the real social problem they are trying to solve: the problem of discrimination against minorities and women. If we try to evaluate them apart from that context, they are bound to seem unnecessary and unfair—reverse discrimination pure and simple.

The concept of institutional discrimination helps explain why, 30 years after passage of the most comprehensive civil rights legislation in U.S. history, minorities still do not enjoy full equality with whites. The fact that discrimination violates the law—like the relative decline in prejudice among whites—encourages the impression that discrimination is in decline, or is even a thing of the past. The problem is that the civil rights laws are only effective against the most overt, flagrant forms of discrimination. If you are an employer you can't lie to a minority applicant by saying a position has been filled when in fact it hasn't; but the civil rights laws don't require that you seriously consider hiring the person. Affirmative action does. Because of the relative laxity of civil rights laws, then, the federal government over the last 20 years has taken this further step to encourage equal opportunity. Is affirmative action coercive? Yes (although only in rare court cases against particular companies with flagrant histories of discrimination has it lead to mandating precise quotas in hiring); but American history teaches with stark clarity that, **in the absence of government coercion, the white majority cannot be expected to go out of its way to extend opportunities to blacks or other minorities.** For example, the Supreme Court decreed an end to segregated schools in its 1954 decision in *Brown v. Board of Education*, and subsequent rulings; Congress imposed desegregated public facilities beginning with the Civil Rights Acts of 1964. Unlike many white ethnic groups—Irish, Italian, Polish, and so on—blacks have not enjoyed gradual, step-by-step acceptance into the system over the course of their history: doors to opportunity were virtually as closed in 1963 (the year before passage of the civil rights laws) as in 1863 (the year of the Emancipation Proclamation). This was the same century during which the white ethnics experienced slow but steady growth in opportunity without Federal intervention. This answers the question—often asked rhetorically, by people who wish not to learn the answer but to make an accusation—"Why do blacks need special favors that my people never got?"

THEORIES OF RACISM

If, as the concept of institutional discrimination suggests, racial discrimination is a normal feature of society—normal in the sense that it can be expected to occur routinely unless extraordinary measures, such as Affirmative Action, are taken to combat it—the question arises: how did it get to be this way? Current acts of discrimination, as we have seen, may not be motivated by prejudice. Yet in every case we can see that it is prejudice after all—the prejudice of other people, or in another area of society, or in a previous period of history—that makes non-prejudiced discrimination possible. For example:

- The bar owner who refuses to serve blacks does so out of business necessity; but it is a business necessity because of his customers' prejudice;
- Factory re-locations discriminate against minorities because housing segregation exists; but housing segregation exists because of white suburbanites' prejudice;
- Seniority rules discriminate because minorities are more likely than whites to be "last hired"; but they are more likely to be last hired because of prejudiced hiring practices in the past.

Where, then, did all this prejudice come from? Is it the result of the "normal" tendency towards ethnocentrism that we desribed earlier? But that would mean that officially restricting people to a subordinate status in society, ensuring their unequal treatment under the law, enslaving them and committing genocide against them—all of which have occurred, in our society and in others—could be seen as logical expressions, or extensions, of the "natural" tendency to think more highly of one's own group than of others. Obviously "normal" group pride and genocide are not the same. Yet, just as obviously, they are not unconnected either, for genocide would be unimaginable in the absence of group superiority feelings. It seems that we need to look more closely at a question that was only hinted at in our earlier discussion of ethnocentrism: Under what circumstances does pride in self become contempt for others? In this section, then, we examine theories that try to explain the **origins of racism. Racism** can be defined as belief in the racial inferiority of a particular group that serves the purpose of justifying the unequal treatment of that group.

There are various theories of the origins of racism in both psychology and sociology. We will discuss both types of theory because, as we shall see, neither type makes much sense without the other.

PSYCHOLOGICAL THEORIES OF RACISM

In the psychological view, racist sentiments fulfill certain needs that particular individuals have: the need for an enemy, the need to dispel guilt, or the need to identify with authority. These needs can be satisfied in a pathological and destructive manner—that is, by the individual becoming a racist. We will briefly describe how each of these needs may be expressed through racism:

a. The need for an enemy. In this context the technical term used by social scientists for "enemy" would be **scapegoat.** A **scapegoat** is an innocent group on whom people blame their troubles because it is psychologically rewarding to do so. This concept was originally used in studies of antisemitism after World War II and has since been applied to anti-black hostility. While it is intended as a psychological contribution to the study of racism, the concept of scapegoating necessarily includes a sociological dimension, since the "troubles" that, historically, have actually led to outbreaks of racism (whether against blacks or Jews or others) are social, political, and especially economic in nature. Germans blamed "the Jews" for the political and economic crisis in which the nation was sunk between the two world wars; white racists today blame their economic plight on "welfare" spending (meaning programs that aid minorities).

Finding a scapegoat is psychologically useful because it reduces complex problems to simple terms. Instead of studying what really has been happening to our economy in recent years, we can simply blame "welfare" (or the Japanese). In the best of times, the complexity of reality, and the particularity of our own needs and interests, makes us reluctant to study the world around us thoroughly and dispassionately; but this is even more likely to be the case when we are under economic stress. Our patience wears thin; our frustration turns into aggression.

The scapegoat concept tries to explain not only the motive for hostility (the need to blame someone) but the reason why particular groups are chosen as targets. First of all, a scapegoated group must make a **safe target.** That is, it must be more or less incapable of fighting back. Otherwise attacking the group would cause more problems than it would solve: we would have added on to our original anxiety (over our economic situation) new anxiety (over the threats of retaliation by our newly-created enemy). Specifically, scapegoated groups tend to be small in number; "different" (either racially or religiously or both) and so somewhat distrusted and disliked by the normally ethnocentric majority to begin with; and without significant political power. At some level, then, white racists in America must know that minorities have not "taken over" the country, for they wouldn't have the nerve to attack them if they had. When spokesmen for the Nation of Islam blame black suffering on "the Jews," they are relying on the fact that attacking Jews is safer than attacking whites in general—and doing so may even gain them some allies among antisemitic whites.

b. The need to relieve guilt. Racism, in this account, is the result of **projection**—the attribution to others of one's own unwanted characteristics. We accuse others of what we ourselves (fear we) are guilty of. This may seem to be a bizarre kind of behavior but psychologists believe it is quite common. In many intimate relationships, for example, one of the partners may be habitually jealous even when it is obvious to both partners that there is nothing to be jealous about. How do we explain such irrational behavior? Psychologists would view it as a projection: my bad conscience is relieved by imagining that **you** are the unfaithful one. Projection can also explain the phenomenon of homophobia among men. To a psychologist nothing better demonstrates latent homosexual tendencies than exaggerated contempt for homosexuality. How better convince people— and especially myself—that I am 100% heterosexual than by hating those who aren't? With regard to blacks and Jews, the claim has been made that, historically, majority groups have projected a particular, distinct set of unwanted characteristics onto each (characteristics which then form into stereotypes with which the two groups are burdened in society). Basically, unwanted "id" characteristics have been projected onto blacks—so that they are viewed as lazy, oversexed, and careless (sometimes sentimentalized as carefree)—while unwanted "superego" characteristics have been projected onto Jews— so that they are viewed as overly rational, controlling, and obsessed with achievement and power. As in the case of homophobia, the fact that these traits are hated suggests to the psychologist that the hater knows them from within—and needs desperately to be convinced that it is not so, that the other (the black, the Jew) is the guilty one.

    c. The need to identify with authority. This theory was developed in the massive study, **The Authoritarian Personality,** (Adorno, **et al,** 1950) conducted after World War II in an attempt to explain the psychology of Nazism. The study concluded that race hatred is the result of a troubled childhood, in which the child is convinced by overly strict, emotionally aloof parents that to disobey their wishes is to risk losing their love. The child therefore learns to suppress any impulse that indicates a difference from what the parents want the child to be. The child grows into an adult who fears all people who are different because they function as **reminders of the child's suppressed difference from the parents.** Racial minorities, religious minorities, homosexuals—all of them threaten the individual's fragile sense of being accepted by the parents (who are now represented in the individual's unconscious by a variety of authority figures in the environment— teachers, employers, political leaders, etc.). The authoritarian personality thus identifies with those in power and cultivates a blind submissiveness to authority, from which vantage point he views all outsiders with fear and loathing.

SOCIOLOGICAL THEORIES OF RACISM

The sociological approach to racism is based on the idea that persons do not have to have disturbed minds in order to develop racist attitudes. It may seem shocking to conclude that, under certain conditions, hatred is "normal," but a sober look at human history appears to leave no alternative. The task of the sociologist, then, is to pursue this question: what are the specific conditions under which racism is most likely to develop? There are three main answers to this question in sociology today: those given by socialization theory, functionalist theory, and conflict theory.

    a. Socialization theory. Like the cultural transmission theory of deviance, this approach emphasizes the importance of human learning via imitation. Thus, according to socialization theory, an individual raised in an environment in which prejudice is a norm, is likely to become prejudiced as a result. There is no theory which suggests as clearly and consistently as this one does that individual pathology is completely irrelevant to the development of racism in society.

        Socialization theory does not attempt to explain how racism originates but only how it is transmitted (again like the cultural transmission theory of deviance). But rather than criticize it for what it does not do, let us look at what it does.

        For one thing, socialization theory draws our attention to the crucial importance of family and community in transmitting prejudice. Unlike the cultural transmission theory of deviance, this theory stresses the role, not of "bad companions," but of good ones. Some of the most notorious racists of the century simply reflected in exaggerated form the attitudes and values of the institutions that nurtured them. For the most part, though, socialization theory focuses not on instances of notoriety but on average, everyday, typical behaviors. And with good reason: Just as racism could not remain effective in any society if only those with emotional disturbances were tempted by it, so too it could not survive if it depended on the fervent animosity of the "true believer." The possibility of the Nazi Holocaust cannot be derived from an analysis of the deranged personality of Hitler, although many historians of World War II proceeded as if it could. Adorno's approach, described above, was basically the same: instead of diagnosing Hitler's sickness, he diagnosed the sickness of his followers. But Hitler rose and was sustained in power by means of the support, or at least acquiescence, of millions of people beyond his inner circle of fellow fanatics. Within this larger group the degree of active support for the regime of course varied; with regard to antisemitism, the differences ranged from outright hatred and contempt for Jews to a more passive attitude of mere insensitivity to their fate conditioned by centuries of Christian church teachings which treated the Jews as a reprobate people destined for misery. How do people without any special psychological motive for hating come to view the attempted annihilation of a minority group by one's own political leadership and in the name of one's own country with total indifference (if not enthusiasm)?

Part of the answer, we have suggested, is that the average German may have come to regard the suffering of the Jews as to-be-expected, since "the Jews" were responsible for Jesus' death and as a result have been replaced as God's people by the church. This church teaching, by which so many millions have been socialized, de-sensitized people to Jewish suffering (by "normalizing" it) and thus served as a presupposition for the rise of Nazism. Traditional Christian anti-Judaism provided the normal backdrop for the complicity of millions of normal people in a policy of systematic mass murder.

Since, according to socialization theory, racism spreads the more it is defined and perceived as normal—that is, the more it is accepted or encouraged by the institutions that shape and transmit societal norms—it follows that racism would decline if our institutions were to discourage it. A generation of children raised in an environment in which minorities occupy positions of authority—as doctors, school principals, elected and appointed officials, and so on—is likely to be less prejudiced than people raised in a society where they learn from experience to expect all authority figures to be white. As we shall see in discussing ethnocentrism, people tend to equate "normal" with "natural," "proper," and "right"; what typically happens is regarded as the way things are "supposed to be." (A non-racist society, then, is one in which people really do not assume that whites are supposed to be in charge.) Socialization theory thus has quite practical implications, for it suggests how socio-economic advances made by minorities not only improve the lives of those who are advancing but can actually, in the long run, bring about an overall decrease in prejudice among whites. In other words, socialization theory implies that **by eliminating discrimination we effectively combat prejudice as well,** since prejudice simply means regarding dicrimination as the way things are supposed to be because that is the way things have always been (in our experience). Thus socialization theory answers those critics of civil rights legislation who argue that changing behavior won't change people's hearts (and that therefore it is a waste of time to change people's behavior).

Our society at present seems to be in a transitional stage: there are a sufficient number of minorities in positions of authority to have reduced the general level of prejudice (in the sense that most people eventually "accept" and "adjust to" reality); yet they are sufficiently few in number to allow whites to view them as exceptional cases rather than as evidence that minoritiy groups are truly equal to whites in talent, intelligence, or whatever other qualities are assumed to be necessary to exercise authority competently and responsibly.

b. Functionalism. The functionalist theory of racism is simply an extension of the functionalist theory of ethnocentrism. Functionalists view ethnocentrism as a tendency that exists among all peoples because it is useful—functional—in promoting group solidarity. Where solidarity is weak or threatened for whatever reason, normal ethnocentrism is liable to spill over into racism. This is because a sense of "team spirit" is easily aroused by the thought of an enemy that must be defended against; the sense of "us" becomes sharper as we sharpen our image of "them." But this formula raises more questions than it answers. What factors tend to undermine social solidarity in the first place, and so encourage outbreaks of racism? Since we can define people as different, even as our enemies, in terms of any number of differntiating characteristics, how does it happen that the 'us' vs. 'them' mentality so often takes the form of race prejudice? And why are some groups singled out rather than others?

These questions don't arise for socialization theory, since that theory begins with racism already entrenched and then describes the process by which it is transmitted from one generation to the next. But for the functionalist such questions would seem to be central, since functionalism purportedly explains how racism comes about in the first place—i.e., how ethnocentrism intensifies under certain circumstances and is transformed into racism. Yet only the first of these questions has received much attention from functionalists. The reason is that functionalists believe in the overriding importance of social solidarity (as a condition of societal stability and efficiency) and so consider breakdowns in solidarity to be the only real social problems. Racism, from the functionalist point of view, is a social problem for precisely that reason (and only that reason): a racist society is the epitome of a society in which solidarity is threatened. While racism is perhaps functional in temporarily boosting the morale of the dominant group, it tends nevertheless to be dysfunctional for society in the long run. For widespread racism poses a threat both to societal **stability** and **efficiency.** Let us look briefly at each of these dangers.

1. The threat to stability. Consistent mistreatment can produce despair or a sense of resignation in its victims; but it can also produce anger and rage. A society which does not make serious attempts to eliminate discrimination can never be secure against outbreaks of violence by the oppressed. That a particular event may trigger the explosion (the assassination of Martin Luther King in 1968; the first Rodney King verdict in 1992) does not detract from the fact that a history of racism was the real "cause" of the rioting in both cases.

2. The threat to efficiency. Discrimination in education and employment hurts not only the victimized group but society as a whole. Just as, from the functionalist point of view, it is in society's interest to have a well-educated, highly-skilled work force, it goes against society's interest to deny people the opportunity to obtain a quality education and to acquire a high level of skills. At some point in the not-too-distant future, white men will constitute a statistical minority of the work force. How can the U.S. remain a major economic power unless we can ensure that minorities and women are given the same opportunities to develop their talents as white men are?

Through discrimination, moreover, society deprives itself of the unique contributions particular groups could make in particular fields—for example, the contribution that minority police could make in fostering improved relations between police and community in minority neighborhoods. In keeping with the democratic political principle that the greater the variety of voices heard, the more balanced and reasonable the outcome of a debate will be, it seems likely that society would benefit from having more women and minorities in roles such as judge, political office-holder, and so on.

c. Conflict theory. According to conflict theorists, **racial conflicts are not really about race but about power**—especially economic power (and political power insofar as it is a requirement for exercising economic power). The hostility between different groups is real; but what it reflects is not ethnocentrism—an idea that seems to rely on a quite unsociological premise about "human nature"—but rather the fact that different groups are in competition with each other—for jobs, education, housing, and other vital social resources. Underlying conflict theory, then, is the assumption that if there were more than enough of these resources to go around, racial conflict would cease.

Does this mean that conflict theory—as opposed to functionalism and to the psychological theories of racism—doesn't believe that prejudice is real? Not at all. What conflict theory is saying is that prejudice only becomes an active, influential, negative force in society when a **motive** for making it so is introduced; and that history shows consistently that this motive tends to be above all economic. Attitudes of superiority among groups may be obnoxious, but what is savage about human groups is not their superiority feelings but their greed.

Prejudice makes the subjugation of minorities possible, but greed—together with the power to put one's greed into practice—makes it actual. Discrimination occurs not because one group doesn't like another but because it wants to, and is able to, keep another group from acquiring the jobs or other resources it has so far been able to reserve for itself. It is true that the enslavement of Africans by European settlers in North America, and the slaughter of Native Americans by them, would not have been thinkable without the existence of "Eurocentrism"; but it still would never have happened unless the Europeans had wanted to establish economic hegemony for themselves in the settled territories; the evacuation of the land's original inhabitants, and the procurement of an abundant supply of cheap labor, were the means by which they achieved their goal.

But prejudice does not merely provide a background condition for the exploitation of racial minorities. Once a group is subjugated, theories of racial inequality are used to justify, and thus help perpetuate, the subjugation. Racism, in other words, functions as an **ideology legitimating economic conquest.** Thus, British colonial rule over African territories in the 19th century was justified by the argument that it was the "white man's burden" to bring the blessings of Christianity and the Western European work ethic to the heathen peoples of Africa. In other words, according to this belief the British had conquered Africa for the sake of the Africans. The conflict theorist sees less selfless motives at work. For example, the work ethic to which the Africans were forcibly introduced enriched, not the Africans, but the British companies installed in Africa in the wake of the British imperial conquest.

How can we apply the conflict theory of racism to the contemporary situation? To use an earlier example, opposition to affirmative action obviously has to do with the fact that whites and minorities are in competition for quality education and jobs; yet, when this opposition leads people to declare that minority employees are less qualified than the white candidates they have beaten out for the job, and that their only "qualification" was their race, then we can say that a racist ideology is being used to justify an economic interest (the white person's interest in getting the job). Public opposition to affirmative action usually takes the form of expressing doubts about the competence of minority job-holders who their opponents usually know nothing about except that they are minorities. From the conflict point of view it is not accidental that hostility to affirmative action is greatest among the white lower middle class and working class, since these groups stand to lose the most from it: they are in direct competition with minorities for civil service jobs, small government contracts, etc. By contrast, upper middle class white professionals have little to fear from affirmative action, and so can afford to be more "enlightened"

(although the limits of their enlightened attitudes are often revealed when, as a result of affirmative action in college admissions, their children have to compete against minorities.)

Since minorities can't rationally be blamed for wanting real job opportunities—even if it means that a white candidate is not hired as a result—they must be accused of being unqualified. In other words, without the introduction of a racist argument, the anti-affirmative action position runs the risk of self-contradiction (denying to minorities in principle what I want for myself). Even the outcry against quotas relies on a racist presupposition, since racially representational hiring among qualified candidates in a society with a scarcity of desirable jobs and a surplus of job-seekers is not obviously unfair, as quotas allegedly are.

Conflict theory is like a situational version of the scapegoating theory in that it seeks to identify the (economic) circumstances in which one group becomes the target for another's aggression. The targeted group is still a scapegoat in the sense that it is not to blame for the troubles the scapegoating group is having (minorities competing for good jobs may make it harder for whites to get them, but this is not the fault of minorities—who are, after all, just trying to make a living like everybody else—but of a society which is not generating enough good jobs for all who need and want them). The difference is that, according to conflict theory, the hostility is never an end in itself but only a means to an end. Suppose you get into a heated argument with someone. The person happens to be overweight. As the argument escalates you shout an insult about the person's being "fat"—not because you believe that being overweight is bad, evil, wrong, or sinful, but simply because you know that this is a way of hurting, of weakening, your opponent. That is, roughly, how conflict theory views race hatred. Race hatred has no status, no meaning, in itself, i.e., independent of how it is **used to try to bring about a desired (economic) end.**

Perhaps, as functionalism claims, we are all more or less ethnocentric. The conflict theorist asks: so what? Ethnocentrism only makes a difference when it becomes discrimination, exploitation, enslavement, and so on; and for these to occur, economic motives are necessary.

But the fact that underlying ethnocentrism provides "only" for the "possibility" (rather than the actual occurrence) of racial conflict appears to make it more not less relevant historically, for it means that without it economic conflicts could not be concealed under the guise of racial antagonisms. We would then have to face the problem of job scarcity rather than the pseudo-problem that "they" are taking away jobs that belong to "us." But where did this "us-them" mentality come from in the first place? It is this, not economics, that appears, after all, to lie at the root of the problem.

Conflict theorists answer that those in power encourage "us-them" thinking because it serves their economic interests, for if the white working class recognized that its economic interests would best be served by joining ranks with minority workers to form a common front to demand decent jobs and education for all, the careers of many of our political leaders would be in jeopardy.

Then again, the powerful may encourage or exploit us-them thinking, but do they create it? If not, where does it come from? It seems conflict theory, like functionalism, assumes the existence of ethnocentrism without explaining it.

5

STRUCTURE

BASIC STRUCTURAL CONCEPTS

The power of society is so great that it can make a uniform collectivity out of the unique individuals that a society's population is comprised of; that, at least, is what we see when we study **culture:** all of us participate in the normative order of values, mores, and folkways. But at the same time the power of society expresses itself as the capacity to make individuals—who, after all, are ultimately alike insofar as we are all human beings—decisively different from one another in attitudes, beliefs, and behaviors, on account of the different statuses and roles society assigns us. And that is what we see when we study **social structure**. The sociology of culture has to do with the norms and values members of society (more or less) hold in common; but it does not describe how relations among these individuals are organized. It is one thing to analyze the American work ethic; it is another thing to describe the patterned ways in which particular types of workers—for example, supervisors and their subordinates—are expected to interact with one another. **Social structure** is the study of the patterned relations among individuals in society.

The study of social structure is organized around three core concepts: **status, role,** and **group**.

Status

Statuses are socially defined positions people occupy in society. As such, they are sources of public identity—that is, they serve as the basic means by which people are categorized, evaluated, rewarded (or denied rewards), and so on. While every individual occupies a number of statuses, for most adults in modern Western societies **occupational status** is their principal source of public identity—or, in other words, it is their **master status**. Your status as mother, wife, Roman Catholic, and Italian-American may also be of importance to you but to society these tend to be secondary sources of identification, or **subordinate statuses**. This means that an adult without an occupational status will tend to be regarded in our kind of society as a second-class citizen. (Thus, in the middle-class marriage based on the traditional sexual division of labor, the woman's public identity is non-existent; she is simply defined in terms of her relation to her husband: Mrs. Smith, a doctor's wife, etc.)

In some situations a person's desire to be defined by occupational status may be frustrated by people who instead perceive the individual in terms of supposedly subordinate statuses such as gender or race. Imagine a white person who visits a doctor for the first time and only discovers upon entering the consulting room that the doctor is black. Does this patient perceive the doctor as "a doctor (=master status) who happens to be black (=subordinate status)" or as "a black person (=master status) who happens to be a doctor (=subordinate status)"? The difference may appear to be subtle but it is not if you are the person being defined. The effect of expressions in which a master status is grammatically qualified by a subordinate one (e.g., "woman doctor" or "lady plumber")— thus robbing it of its supposedly exclusive significance in the situation—is to remind the listener that the individual described is to be regarded as an exception to the rule; it invites us to assume, for example, that doctors are supposed to be men. Current language norms seem to permit these usages in the case of gender but not of race, i.e., qualifying occupational status by referring to a person's gender is not considered sexist but qualifying it by referring to their race is considered racist. That is, the sex difference is considered a real, and therefore a relevant, difference; racial differences are not. This shows us that even so basic a thing as how words like "difference" (and "same," "similar," etc.) are defined, is a social product with real consequences.

Sociologists use the term **ascribed status** to refer to any status—the most socially significant ones are gender, race, and class of origin, but age would also be included—which is simply "given" to us, and the term **achieved status** for any status, such as occupation or level of education, which we have acquired through our own activity. One of the fundamental characteristics of a modern society is that in principle, if not always in practice, **persons are evaluated on the basis of their achieved rather than their ascribed statuses**. And certainly persons are more likely to **evaluate themselves** on this basis—feeling proud to be a high achiever, guilty or ashamed for being underemployed, and so on.

Ascribed statuses influence achieved statuses in two important ways. The first, more obvious way is that "circumstances beyond one's control" limit or guarantee access to various pathways to success. Think of the difference between being born poor (i.e., to a poor family) and being born wealthy, and the impact these different sets of circumstances **may** have on occupational achievement (because, for example, there will exist family "connections" in one case but not in the other). The second way is more subtle but equally powerful: the circumstances of birth and upbringing influences a person's **definition** of success. A child born to medical doctors may consider that becoming a nurse means to move downwards on the achievement scale, and so may not consider nursing as a potential occupation; a child born to poor or working-class parents may think otherwise. (In this sense structure influences culture—actual social circumstances influence how we think.)

Role

The various statuses we occupy—wife, doctor, child, etc.—lead people to expect us to behave "accordingly." A **role** is the expected behavior pattern associated with a particular status. As statuses are societally defined, so are roles. To be married—to occupy that socially recognized status—means to conform to society's definition of being married; being "married to your work" doesn't count. Of course society's definition is subject to change. For example, our society seems to be in the process of deciding whether the status of "married" ought to be applicable, under certain conditions, to homosexual as well as heterosexual partnerships. Similarly society defines what counts as living up to or failing to live up to the role of husband or wife. A husband's physical abuse of his wife constitutes one clear violation of the husband role—although this has only been true in recent decades; previously such behavior was either considered socially acceptable or, if not, at least none of society's business. On the other hand, many behavior patterns previously mandated by society are no longer required (and have become none of society's business)—for example, the requirement that a "normal" marriage be one where, if the economic circumstances of the family allow it, the husband earns a living and the wife stays at home as the homemaker and primary child-care provider. Another example of changing role definitions is that society no longer assumes that the "normal" marriage is going to be oriented towards procreation.

"Role" is an abstract concept; actual behavior rarely if ever embodies the expected patterns. And especially in modern individualistic society, people are given considerable leeway in deciding precisely how to fulfill their role obligations (e.g., how to be a 'good' parent). But regardless of how closely or remotely our behavior approximates the standard, **role expectations exert a powerful influence over our lives**. This is easiest to recognize in situations where the difficulty of meeting expectations create problems for us; if the expectations were irrelevant, our failure to live up to them would not matter to us. Sociologists speak of two such problems: **role strain** and **role conflict**.

Role strain refers to situations in which **adequate performance of a role seems to demand doing two contradictory things at the same time**. The role of office manager, for example, may be understood to include creating a friendly atmosphere in which employees are motivated to work because they feel management is "on their side"; yet it also includes the obligation to enforce regulations no matter how unpopular they may be with the workers. (It is interesting to ask how the **workers** adapt to this situation. Do they identify with management? Is such identification a coping mechanism? Do they thereby forfeit their selves to the company? What is left of their "real" selves as a result? Are there other ways to cope—such as to ritually express hatred for work, the ritual character of the expression making it harmless and socially acceptable?) Any role which involves a similar kind of delicate balancing act may be productive of strain. Perhaps the clearest and commonest example is the parenting role, in which the obligation to be simultaneously affectionate and strict are combined. Parenting would be a lot easier if these two obligations could be neatly separated, i.e., if one were allowed to be affectionate or strict depending on the child's behavior, one's own mood, and so on. But, especially in caring for very young children, this is not the way we are supposed to behave. The child's fragile ego (understandably fragile due to the overwhelming difference in power between itself and the parent—and the child's consequent dependency upon the parent) could be shattered by an overly punitive response to its misbehavior, no matter how justified such a response could seem under the circumstances. Thus we are expected to convey to children that we are correcting their behavior for their own good, out of love for them. (As children get older, and they are considered to be more responsible for their behavior—and less fragile—parental outbursts of unmitigated fury are considered more acceptable. Incidentally, we see in this example that society goes quite far in defining **normal and deviant expressions of emotion**, thus influencing their frequency of occurrence.) And, looking at the opposite extreme, parenting would be a lot easier if parents never felt any obligation to act the disciplinarian at all. (This may be one of the reasons grandparents enjoy doing child-care more than parents do.) Parental love involves a further strain in that it calls upon the parent to help the child—emotionally as well as practically—while at the same time encouraging it to become independent. It is no wonder, then, why good parenting is so hard to find (why so many people seem to come from "dysfunctional families," even when both parents are present and there is enough money to go around).

Many other occupational roles create similar strains for similar reasons—that is, they require the practitioner to balance compassion and professional objectivity in the performance of the role. The "helping professions" (medicine, psychotherapy) provide one obvious example. Teaching is another: teachers try to sympathize with their students' problems yet must grade them on the basis of their performance.

Role conflict refers to a situation in which **the adequate performance of a role requires that we perform other roles of ours less adequately**—a situation, then, in which there is a "conflict of interest" between two different roles. This is a problem experienced especially by women today, who must often juggle family and work (and/or school) responsibilities. All these responsibilities cannot be met simultaneously; priorities must be set. While successful time budgeting is a possibility, so are intermittent battles with uncooperative spouses and unsympathetic bosses, as well as a nagging sense of guilt. Of course, men are susceptible to this problem as well. The desire to spend time with one's family, for example, may require curbing career ambitions regardless of gender. The potential for role conflict among men can be expected to increase the more society expects fathers to play an active role in child-rearing and other domestic tasks. Previously, part of the wife's responsibility had been to ensure that her husband never had to experience role conflict—by ensuring, for example, that the children would not disturb him if he had important work to do, or that he wouldn't have to "waste" his time going food shopping or doing laundry or taking a sick child to the doctor. But even today—as time-budget studies of the typical work weeks of husbands and wives show—husbands are more likely than wives to be spared these sorts of conflicts between occupational and family roles. A woman has to be a superwoman to resolve potential role conflicts; a man doesn't have to be a superman because he is likely to be exempted from the situation that gives rise to conflict (screaming child demanding attention; open textbook demanding to be read) in the first place. To the extent that men do feel pressure to give up their privileged role in the household, they may respond by refusing to sign up in the first place. That is, men's contemporary "fear of commitment" may be in part a response to women's demands for equality in the household.

Role conflict occurs whenever we are required to choose between two different roles. Often, as we noted, the discrepancy is between professional and personal identity. You are on the admissions committee of the college to which your nephew has just applied; you are a judge about to hear a case involving a friend of yours. In these and similar cases the conflict is understood—is socially defined—as insoluble; it would be unethical to favor your family and friends but inhuman not to. Therefore, in such cases we are expected to spare ourselves (and others) a potentially tragic fate by removing ourselves from the case. The possibility of conflicts of interest, then, is taken into account by the norms. The norms simply **do not expect us to overcome certain prejudices; they do not, in other words, depict the ideal-typical member of society as a purely rational being**—with, for example, no "natural" tendency to favor family over non-family members. Notice, though, that if the person should somehow successfully "favor" someone they know personally, this favoritism must take place within certain legally prescribed limits—it is legal for a family friend to tell you about an available job he happens to know about before the ad hits the papers, but illegal for you to be paid more for doing the same job as the person at the desk next to yours. So, personal favors are done but they are not supposed to transgress the impersonal rules. And in that sense, impersonality rules. The question, of course, is how and where and by whom is the boundary set between acceptable favors and unacceptable favoritism.

Group

We occupy statuses and perform roles within groups. Sociologists distinguish between two main kinds of groups, membership in each of which is a basic part of our experience in society—and a requirement for certification as normal (which is itself a basic part of our experience in society): **primary groups**, such as family and friends; and **secondary groups**, such as classmates and co-workers. What is the difference between these two types of groups? An obvious response would be that primary groups are more important to the individual than secondary groups are. But that is too vague. After all, the loss of a job may be as devastating as the loss of a spouse—in which case membership in a secondary group turns out to be as important as membership in the most intimate of primary groups. (Since a typical feature of male socialization in our society is the identification of masculinity with competition and conquest, with special emphasis on competence in the breadwinning or moneymaking role, men are especially liable to measure self-worth in terms of occupational achievement, and so they are especially likely to feel devastated when they fail in this regard. Another aspect to this is that society teaches us that when a marriage fails, both parties are to blame; there is no corresponding reassurance offered in the case of failure to hold a job.) But even if our response were more specific, and we were to say that membership in primary groups is more important than membership in secondary groups in the sense that it is important to an individual's identity or sense of self, the response would be insufficient. Some psychologists would argue that a healthy relationship to the mother in early childhood is essential to the individual's development of a sense of self, and is thus more important than any other relationship—it is the foundation on which all the others are built. Yet everyone knows of examples that contradict that idea—instances of apparently "well-adjusted" adults, successful in their careers and happy in their homes, whose childhood was anything but serene. While much time has been spent—reasonably enough—arguing what "well-adjusted" means, we would want to raise the question what "apparently" means. Freud argued that the "repressed always returns," but the question is: can some memories be so deeply repressed that, given the brevity of a typical lifetime, some people are successful at keeping them hidden from oneself? Can some memories be so deeply repressed as to not interfere with, to not even influence, one's present adult experiences and activities? Are there degrees and levels of repression?

Nevertheless family relationships, no matter how relatively unimportant particular individuals may consider them, are considered by sociologists to be "primary." Why? The basic reasons are these:

(a) they are personal. No matter how significant secondary group relations may be, only in exceptional cases do they operate on a personal level; while family relations, no matter how routine and taken-for-granted they may become, always do. Your boss may appreciate your skills, and praise and promote you—all the while not having the slightest idea of, or interest in, who you are as a person. Similarly, you might make friends at school but it is not inevitable that you will; and certainly the school administration regards you as an ID number rather than the unique individual you think you are. One of the consequences of living in a world in which secondary groups are increasingly significant (as measured by the time spent in them—the time spent at school and work—if nothing else) is that individuals are tempted to define themselves the way these impersonal groups do: in terms of competence and performance rather than personal qualities.

A secondary group is a group in which members are valued not for what they are but for what they do. Thus, primary groups are important **to the extent that** being viewed and valued as a person is important.

(b) they are of indefinite duration. No matter how seriously involved we are in our secondary group relations, we have little difficulty severing them as soon as our needs change or new opportunities arise. Some secondary group situations—such as going to school— are temporary by definition; others, such as employment in a particular company, may last decades. But if a job lasts that long it is not because we made a commitment or took a vow to stay with the company; it is just a fortunate accident (or an unfortunate one—nothing better came along). Primary group relations, by contrast, are expected to endure indefinitely unless some negative circumstance occurs to disrupt them. No one cries when secondary group relations come to an end; or, as in the case of graduations, we may be saddened by the termination of our school career but are equally gladdened by the thought of what awaits us next. This sense of balance would be inappropriate in the case of divorce; new opportunities may to some extent compensate for the loss, but the sense of loss is supposed to be of overriding relevance (for a while, at least). Thus, primary group relations are important **to the extent that** experiences of permanence and mutuality of commitment are important.

(c) they are an end-in-themselves. No matter how satisfying secondary group memberships may be, they are always merely a means-to-an-end. They exist to serve a practical purpose: to make a living, earn a degree (so as to make a living), etc. You might love your job but probably you don't love it enough to be willing to do it for nothing. You might find sociology to be a fascinating subject; but probably you wouldn't be reading this book unless you were going to receive some college credits (and perhaps fulfill some requirement) as a result. It is likely that the friendships formed within secondary groups are necessary buffers against the stress induced by the merely instrumental character of the work or school routine itself. But now to take the opposite case: do you hang out with your friends because you think that one of them is going to get you a good job? Are you kind to your mother because you are looking forward to an inheritance? That would be to treat primary group ties as though they were secondary group ties. Primary group relations, then, are important **to the extent that** relationships that are viewed as meaningful in themselves, free from any calculation of the gain to be derived from them, are important.

A characteristic feature of modern society is the prevalence of secondary groups. From the time you leave your home in the morning to the time you return at night you are likely to go from one secondary group situation to another—interacting at work, at school, in stores, with people who basically don't know or care, and who would not be upset (or in some cases even notice) if they never saw you again, and who value you—although they are taught not to be able to make this admission—only for what they can get out of you. The acquaintances in your neighborhood—shopkeepers, the super of your building—are friendly because they know (it is in their blood, it is "second nature," they have known this since childhood) it is good business to be friendly.

By contrast primary group ties permeated traditional society. And they were not restricted to the private sphere. Shopkeepers waited on their friends and neighbors, whose families they may have known for generations (the geographical mobility of modern society has made that less and less likely). This is the world which we can occasionally glimpse from TV shows ("Little House on the Prairie") and movies ("It's a Wonderful Life")—although these too are dying out. The common-sense world tends to romanticize this bygone era, and to lament the emergence of an impersonal environment in which people "don't count" except as statistics. Sociology, however, views these changes as ambiguous. The world of mutual loyalties and personal bonds was one which one belonged to as a full and active and well-received member according to the luck of circumstances and personality. It was also a world of deeply entrenched prejudices: it may have felt good to be part of a community but it felt less good to be an outsider—by virtue, say, of belonging to a racial, national, linguistic, or religious minority. Today it is increasingly possible for outsiders to belong precisely because there is nothing to belong **to**: we have created an individualistic society, in which primary group memberships count for less and less. This tendency has been abetted by the rise of high technology, which has enabled many otherwise socially "challenged" individuals to fit in as a result of their expertise in some computer-related area. At any rate, an impersonal world is one in which the traditional bases for prejudice are lacking: to be treated as a number means to be treated the same as the next (non-) person. (We will develop this theme in our discussion of bureaucracy). But first we need to provide a fuller context for the discussion of this and other questions relating to the ambiguous character of modern society by describing in some detail the basic characteristics of the social structure of modern society as understood by sociology.

MODERN SOCIETY

While statuses, roles, and groups are basic elements of the structure of all societies, modern society is characterized by certain specific features: achieved statuses take precedence over ascribed statuses; role conflict is an ever-present reality, or potential reality, for many people; and interaction in secondary group situations becomes a central fact of social life.

Now we want to discuss some additional developments associated with the rise of modern society. These changes bring with them a changed understanding of what it means to be a person; people in modern societies understand themselves and others differently from the way people in pre-modern societies did. Accordingly, they interact with others differently—at home, at work, and elsewhere. Indeed, the sociological view is that **the modern world has created a new kind of person**. (One of the questions that we need to address is whether the post-modern world is also doing so.) This view is in accord with the basic sociological principle that society is not merely an external reality but something which becomes a part of—becomes "internalized" by—the individuals that compose it. With that in mind, here are the main substantive characteristics of modern society:

Division of Labor

Work in the modern world is characterized by an ever-increasing specialization of tasks. A well-known example is modern medical practice: the percentage of general practitioners is decreasing, as more and more doctors specialize in increasingly narrowly defined areas of expertise. Theoretically, the division of labor is a positive development: if services are provided by specialists, they are more likely to be performed competently. And medicine seems to be a case in point: if you had a heart condition, you would be more likely to seek the services of a heart specialist than of a family doctor. The same, of course, would apply in the case of legal advice. Our society is one in which people desire, seek, and expect the help of experts. (One could argue that the existence of experts is produced by the need for them, and that this need is based on the fact that knowledge has expanded in modern times. But which comes first, the expansion of knowledge which makes expertise seem necessary, or the idea that decisions should be placed in the hands of experts—which then leads to the expansion of knowledge which makes this idea seem rational?) Since expertise is thus perceived as vital, more and more people grow up desiring, seeking, and expecting to become experts. In this sense the division of labor has had a far-reaching impact on the nature and quality of life in modern society. For example, it has caused:

(a) fundamental changes in the educational system. In a world of specialization, specialized education becomes the norm. While at most colleges a certain number of core courses in the humanities and sciences are still required even of students enrolled in technical programs, students tend to view these requirements as obstacles to be overcome as quickly and effortlessly as possible so that one can concentrate on courses in the major field (which are also treated as obstacles to be overcome—as mere requirements that may have more, but only relatively more, to do with the job it is leading towards than the general core requirements). Students know—before they take any course—that society rewards people for their expertise, not their general knowledge; they dispense their respect accordingly. The consequence of all this is that the very meaning of "highly educated" has changed: it no longer has the connotation of "well-rounded." Until as recently as a generation ago, to be highly educated, and thus to be considered worthy of the respect and high status typically accorded to the highly educated, meant having a general knowledge of, and interest in, a wide variety of subjects. In a technologically advanced society general knowledge is no longer functional. This fact affects teachers as well as students; they, too, may lack a clear sense of the purpose of general education in a technological society. Many colleges, to judge by recent reforms in this area, seem to have serious doubts about the importance of maintaining the liberal arts core in the face of demands—by the tax-paying public in some cases as well as by tuition-paying students—to concentrate their efforts on building up only those programs that impart marketable skills. (One inevitable consequence of a commitment to liberal arts courses is commitment to the idea that such courses will represent a variety of points of view; the current trend towards curricular uniformity within particular disciplines—with buzz-words such as "accountability," "outcomes," "assessment," and the like used to rein in erring faculty members—expresses nothing so much as lack of commitment to the liberal arts.)

(b) the withering of community ties. Common interests draw individuals together, and having similar work means having common interests. Now in a modern society, we often do not know our neighbors for a variety of reasons: people spend more time away from the neighborhood—not only because they are at work but also because they are commuting longer distances to and from work; they relocate more often for the sake of career advancement, etc. But even if we are rooted in a particular neighborhood, and get to spend a lot of our time there, the modern division of labor creates a situation in which our neighbors not only do work that is different from ours but which may be totally incomprehensible to us. We may feel closer to certain TV characters than to our neighbors; how many conversations have been interrupted because it is time for "my show" to go on?

(c) a diminished sense of individual responsibility. The roles people are assigned within the division of labor are often so narrowly circumscribed—especially in large-scale bureaucratic organizations—that the refusal to take responsibility for anything that takes place beyond one's cubby hole is actually an index of job competence. And even within one's cubby hole, it is always "the rules," rather than the human beings who implement them, that are ultimately responsible. Or, those in charge of the whole operation are said to be responsible (think of examples of corruption within government agencies). But usually that doesn't help: those in charge ritually declare that, as those in charge (that is, according to "the rules") they of course take responsibility for, say, the misbehavior of their subordinates. Thus everyone escapes responsibility: the subordinates because they were answering to higher-ups, and the higher-ups because they were simply interpreting, and perhaps misinterpreting, "the rules"—and in any case their declaration of responsibility is merely a formality. In following the rules about how to admit to breaking the rules, they have again shown their loyalty to the rules—and so are spared punishment. We will return to this problem of passing the buck in our discussion of bureaucracy. It is a serious one; some sociologists argue that the logic of bureaucratic non-responsibility alone makes possible the participation of ordinary citizens in mass murder—a non-responsibility enshrined in the chilling phrase "I was just following orders."

Decline of the Family

The family was just as much affected by the industrial revolution as the "outside world" was. The form of the typical family, as well as its meaning for typical individuals and its functions for society, were all transformed as a result of industrialization. Most important among them was the emergence of the isolated nuclear family characterized by the sexual division of labor as the dominant family type (dominant as an ideal if not always a reality). But alongside the theme of the changing family and the changes continue today, at an accelerated pace; e.g., the tremendous increase in the percentage of single female-headed households—we must take up the theme of the declining significance of the family. In the first half of the twentieth century, many sociologists had about given up on the family, arguing that the separation of the occupational from the domestic spheres wrought by industrialization made the family less and less relevant to individuals and to society as a whole. Functionalists observed that not only the principal traditional function of the family—to serve as a unit of domestic production—but a variety of other functions had been transferred from the family to other institutions with the advent of modern industrial society. For example, modern medicine replaces grandma's home remedies; modern entertainment media (films, TV) replace family get-togethers; the fast-food and frozen-food industries put an end to the need for home-cooked meals, etc. This tendency for the family to become irrelevant has accelerated today, as people become more and more attached to the individualistic achievement ethic of a high-tech, post-industrial world.

To the extent that individuals in modern society feel less closely bound to their families it is because they **are** less bound to them, i.e., they are less in need of them. Conversely, the intense family devotion that is characteristic of individuals in traditional societies was a reflection of the individual's total dependence on the family: people tend to be sentimentally attached to their benefactors. (In a modern society it is normal for a child to make a career decision that goes against the parents' wishes—the only thing of questionable normality is the career itself; in a traditional society the mere fact of personal choice in such a case would render it deviant.) In societies where the skills children needed to master in order to be able to eventually survive as adults were handed down by the parents—e.g., how to run the farm—children understandably remained "close to" their parents as they grew up. And the fact that not only the work skills but the land to which the skills were going to be applied came from the parents, made reverence for the parents all that more inevitable and more complete. (The declining significance of the traditional "wisdom" possessed by older people in a fast-changing world, together with the declining importance of property ownership as a source of social status, are two of the basic causes of "ageism," or prejudice against the elderly.) Today the knowledge, or at least the credentials, individuals need comes from the school system; while the jobs they need are obtained from a variety of sources—employment agencies, connections made at school, etc.—but, in most cases, not directly from the family. Typical members of a modern society—and especially typical highly-educated ones—can understandably feel they have gotten where they are on their own, though they may, in addition, acknowledge that their parents helped them, especially through their earliest years (or they may regard them as impediments from the start). The fact that the occupational status of upper middle class professionals—doctors, lawyers, accountants—derives largely from educational achievement explains in part why they **tend to be less closely attached to their families of origin than the working class**. As more jobs—not just in the upper middle class, of course, but throughout the social class system—begin to be tied to greater and greater educational attainment, the individualistic ethic seems bound to grow, at the expense of traditional attachments to parents and other family members. But if this is so, the question arises:

Why do people who have no deep attachment to their families bother to marry and form new ones? The functionalist answer is that the same modern society that liberates individuals from the necessity of family loyalty liberates them from the idea of personal loyalty as such (hence, a secondary group world)—**but that this makes them, ironically, more than ever in need of the ultimate primary relationship: namely, intimacy.** Today, "intimate relationship" is a synonym for a regular sex partner, but that is not the point at issue here. Instead, we are pointing again to the theme of modern society as a world of achieved statuses and secondary group relations, in which individuals use one another (they hope) for their mutual socio-economic advantage, but where their attachment to each other goes no deeper than that. A setting apart from that—a "haven in a heartless world" (Lasch, 1977)—is, then, more necessary than ever before: a sphere in which people are committed to each other as persons; can trust and confide in each other (the occupational world is one which constantly requires saying the "right" thing, withholding information, exaggerating or simply lying, displaying the correct image, and so on); and can assume that they are valued as persons rather than as functionaries or some other type of utilizable object. Because the need is so great, the potential for disappointment is also great; hence, the astounding instability of contemporary relationships. But this may be a reflection of the (unreflective) use of occupational choice as a model for all other choices in life: just as we move from job to job as we grow tired of our current one, or other prospects arise, so, too, we shop from relationship to relationship. Employers want to encourage the idea that what we are seeing is not the instability of employment but a strengthening of the employee's sense of autonomy—a "smart employee is always looking." The insecurity produced by the market is touted as a desirable characteristic of the person. (Or one could argue that the idea that one shops for jobs and spouses, and so dispenses with them when that seems desirable, equally come from the use of shopping as a model for all significant social action. In a consumer-driven economy, such an idea is not at all far-fetched.)

Science Replaces Religion

In the modern world, religion has lost much of the influence it previously enjoyed; sociologists refer to this as the **secularization** process. Given the importance of religion to so many people today the statement that it is in decline may seem absurd. But all it takes is a brief look at the worldly power religion once had to recognize why we speak of secularization. Religious teachings not only served, in traditional societies, as the ultimate source of legitimation of political authority—as in the concept of the "divine right" of kings—and the ultimate ground of ethics and morality; it served as the source of the average person's knowledge of reality. The pre-modern understanding of the world and how it works is primarily a religious understanding. In such societies the institution of education is not different from the institution of religion; accordingly, all subjects are taught from a religious point of view. In the modern view religion may help people in various ways but it does not impart an objective knowledge of reality. Knowing is different from believing; and only science knows.

For most people this modern scientific view prevails in everyday life. When a grotesque crime is committed, newspapers consult psychiatric experts to help explain how the perpetrator could have done such a thing; they do not seek the opinions of exorcists. Readers expect as much: they expect to hear about the individual's troubled family background rather than about demonic possession. A rocket ship explosion is called a tragic "accident"—and possible technical and human flaws are investigated; the tsunami are referred to as "natural disasters." In neither case are we to examine the possibility of divine intervention or divine punishment as a rational explanation. One may at the same time pray for the earthquake victims and their families; there is no contradiction here. Even though the secularization thesis claims that scientific knowledge is more influential in the modern world than religious knowledge, the presupposition of this thesis is undeniable: that the two spheres are separate. **This** is the truth of secularization. In the Middle Ages, by contrast, everyday labor and serving God were not seen as distinct. Who today—other than religious officials and entrepreneurs—would have the ability to honestly say that their work was a religious enterprise?

As the knowledge society produces and distributes is secular knowledge, so too its morality is secular. We are exhorted to treat others kindly not because humans are "made in the image of God" but because such treatment is said to do justice to the dignity, equality, and unity of humanity—notions which one does not have to be religious to accept. (How many people today would say that we know murder is wrong because God speaks thus in the Hebrew Bible, and that otherwise we would not know?) Or we are urged to act humanely on more practical grounds—because only through co-operation can a nation survive, let alone thrive, economically and politically; or because violence breeds violence, so that no one is safe in a prejudiced society, etc? Of course spokespersons for religious organizations may think and speak otherwise, but the point, again, is that their influence is more limited than in the past. This is true despite the current popularity of fundamentalism.

While our knowledge and our values have thus become secularized, there is nothing paradoxical about the fact that religion remains an important force in many people's lives. We can think of the influence of religion today as analogous to the influnce of the family. We described the "decline of the family"—meaning its traditional functions have been taken over by other institutions (education, medicine, mass media, psychiatry, etc.)—while, at the same time, we noted that family relations are now more important than ever before: they provide individuals, thrown into an anonymous environment of secondary group relations, with their only source of unconditional emotional support. Religion in modern society serves much the same purpose; it **provides for the emotional needs of individuals.** Whether it functions more like the family or like psychotherapy—whether it seems to provide a natural shelter from the coldness of modern life or compensates for the absence of such a shelter—depends on the individual case: there is a difference between people who rely for support on the religion they've been brought up on and those who turn for support later in life in an act of conversion. But in either case the basic psychological function of religion remains the same. The upsurge in religious enthusiasm in the last twenty years or so represents a response to deprivations inherent in postmodern life. The postmodern world is characterized by a ceaseless production of information and an increased pluralism of values. As if this weren't enough to throw the average person into a frenzy of confusion, it is served up by mass media dependent for their existence on the ability to provide constant visual and aural stimulation. The result is a widespread sense of the ambiguity and contingency of all truth claims and the fragmentation of society into interest groups, and so an increased longing for stable, secure, absolute meaning as well as community. The postmodern world thus produces both relativism and fundamentalism. But this too is proof (unless you are a fundamentalist) that relativism rules, for how else can one describe a society that has room for both relativists and fundamentalists?

But there is more to religiosity than fundamentalism; to say that religious belief provides therapy is not to deny its more exalted function of providing a sense of ultimate meaning. Indeed, it could be argued that we can expect religious enthusiasm of all kinds to become more widespread under postmodern conditions than under modern ones. One reason, of course, is that, in a consumer society, where the customer is always right, religious belief requires less subjection and commitment than it used to: one can become a kabbalsitic Jew simply by reading a book or two and declaring one's kinship with it. But that is to address the **opportunity** for religious belief, where we want to address the **motive** behind it. And the motive is real: religious enthusiasm is fed by **disillusionment with the scientific ideal of continuous progress (in knowledge and material well-being) through technological mastery (of nature and humanity)**. For generations this illusion provided millions with a secular substitute for religious faith. The question is, where do people turn once that God has been repudiated? The answer, which includes fundamentalism but does not comprise it alone, is a complicated one. Religiosity lives on in many guises in a postmodern world.

BUREAUCRACY

In everyday discourse, the word bureaucracy has exclusively negative connotations. Commonsense associations with the term include: large and cumbersome government agencies; unhelpful, even rude, personnel; long lines; "red tape"; the "runaround," etc. The reality of bureaucracy is somewhat more complex and ambiguous.

We have already noted that modern life is characterized by the predominance of secondary groups—that is, by impersonal and instrumental relations among people in public settings. Bureaucracy is the logical extension of this modern tendency to eliminate personal sentiments and traditional loyalties as organizing principles of interaction. Thus the development of bureaucracy, though it occurred gradually, signifies a radical departure with the past, making demands on human beings that are violently at odds with the standard operating procedure that had been followed for centuries. Bureaucracy is a form of interaction from which, in the ideal case, all "irrational" traits—all emotions, for example—are purged, and the individual functions as a machine-like being oriented solely toward the goal of efficiency.

Max Weber, who pioneered the study of bureaucracy, considered the rise of bureaucracy to be the most disastrous feature of modernization, yet at the same time a necessary one; and, regardless of its pluses and minuses, certainly **the definitive characteristic of the modern age**. Since Weber's time, sociologists have linked the growth of bureaucracy to both the 20th century's unprecedented progress toward egalitarianism and its unprecedented outbursts of inhumanity (e.g., the Holocaust). To understand how this can be, we must begin at the beginning.

A **bureaucracy** is any type of large-scale organization—a business, a university, a government—that is governed by the principles of rationality and efficiency. Ironically, while we tend to think of bureaucracies as hopelessly inefficient, bureaucratic procedures are **expressly designed for the purpose of promoting efficiency** (and they often succeed).

The principles of rationality and efficiency underlie all the basic characteristics of bureaucratic organization outlined by Weber. In describing these features we want to keep in mind the ambiguous nature of bureaucracy—how it liberates human beings yet imprisons them; how it releases human potential yet crushes it.

Division of Labor

Bureaucratic employees are assigned a specified and limited set of duties. In theory this specialization of tasks should enhance organizational efficiency by enabling personnel to know exactly what they are supposed to do and to become expert in doing it. But even if everything works according to plan, a number of fresh problems are created by this arrangement. For example, the fact that duties are limited means responsibilities are limited, too. This is the source of the bureaucratic "runaround." For customers or clients to get effective service from a bureaucracy requires that they locate the particular department, and the particular office within the particular department, that is responsible for handling their particular kind of case. (In today's world we are more likely to be wasting our time holding on—going from office to office in virtual space—than literally running around. But it is still time wasted—despite companies distracting us from this hard fact by claiming that we are getting somewhere. The point is: where we need to be is always somewhere else.) Officials outside that particular office are not helpful because they are not supposed to be. Thus, the runaround is a consequence of bureaucratic structure—not of the meanness of the people who happen to work for bureaucracies (such as ourselves). But what about the frequent unhelpfulness of those who are supposed to help? Here we should keep in mind the **limited responsibility** which, more or less, characterizes all bureaucratic personnel. It means that bureaucracy tends to stifle creativity by discouraging any contributions from employees that go beyond the bounds of their job descriptions (and/or represent a usurpation of power). This leads to frustration, which may then be displaced onto the public: customers and clients often make safer targets than management, although the trend is to force employees to be pleasant to **them** as well.

Hierarchy of Offices

Hierarchy means an organized structure of authority—a pyramid of power. In a bureaucracy decision-making authority is specifically allocated, just as all tasks are. And, as in the assignment of tasks, the distribution of bureaucratic power is based on position (job title) rather than personality. The power of particular office-holders derives from the power of their office; the office-holder is not above the office. **Power that resides in the office, where the office is governed by rules, is not mere power in the sense of force: it is authority**. The President of the United States, as highest office-holder in the nation's largest bureaucratic organization, the federal government, wields considerable power; but to exercise power beyond the specified limits is to betray the office. In theory, and sometimes in practice, even a President can be held responsible for abuses of power: in 1974 Richard Nixon had to resign from the Presidency under pressure for just that reason. Hierarchy of offices, then, exists in part to protect against a tyranny by the powerful. In addition, it helps ensure bureaucratic continuity: if a President dies in office, that may be a national tragedy, but the Presidency itself survives, and arrangements are in place to install a successor.

Meritocratic Ethic

The relevance of personal characteristics is further offset by the bureaucratic emphasis on **qualifications** (although this is only true with certain—qualifications—when it comes to high office-holders, and especially the political ones discussed above. Popular appeal, as sold by the media, helps a great deal as well. But this is to talk about the power of the media, which in this context somewhat offsets the influence of bureaucratic norms). Hiring decisions are made on the basis of credentials; promotions are based on considerations of merit. But sociologists (as well as lay people) notice that bureaucracy is usually not as objective as it claims to be. This is true in two senses:

(a) personnel decisions are often based on subjective or at least unofficial criteria—having the "right look," seeming to "fit in" with the rest of the staff, and so on. According to many analysts, the persistence of gender and race discrimination is a consequence of the unquestioned or unacknowledged use of these seemingly innocent criteria. For example, looking for someone who will blend in may seem perfectly understandable; but if the present staff is all white male, minorities and women are less likely to be judged as meeting that criterion (hence the remedy of Affirmative Action).

(b) Employers are unlikely to recognize that objective criteria—e.g., credentials—fail to measure the impact discrimination has had on the individual's ability to acquire them. The "B" average of a student who has had to work full-time to get through college may be a greater achievement than the "A" average of a student who didn't have to work; but college transcripts are "objective" documents and therefore don't indicate that difference. (Insofar as the difference exists as a legacy of race and gender discrimination—of substandard schooling or of gender bias in the classroom—we are back to the issue of Affirmative Action.) Choosing the candidate with the most "impressive" resume may seem legitimate, but if an unequal opportunity system means that white males are more likely than others to have acquired good records, then white males will continue to enjoy unfair competitive advantages under the bureaucratic credentials system.

Rules and Regulations

Here is where we encounter the notorious "red tape" phenomenon. Not only are personnel told what to do but they are told explicitly how to do it. This form must be filled out; this number of copies made, to be distributed to these other departments as follows, etc. And all this applies, of course, to the public as well: you must fill out all the proper forms before the bureaucrats can help you. When people urge that we just somehow get rid of bureaucracies and bureaucrats, it is usually this aspect of it that they have in mind. Bureaucratic paperwork seems like a colossal waste of time as well as money (the taxpayers' money if the bureaucracy is a government agency). **But the paperwork exists for good reasons**. First of all, records are kept to ensure accountability. Professors have the power to grade but that power is limited by the requirement that the grade bear some resemblance to the student's performance (test scores, attendance, etc.), which is a matter of record. Written records thus protect against momentary whim; they also protect against the weakness of human memory. (And memory lapses may be intentional, or at least self-serving: few of us would want a world in which businesses never had to issue receipts upon payment.)

The commitment to record-keeping becomes a problem **when it is viewed not as a means to an end but as an end-in-itself**. The very complexity of bureaucracy, while repugnant to some, has a kind of hypnotic effect on others. To work within the vast bureaucratic maze of rules and procedures is to be tempted to think that complying with the rules and following the procedures is the purpose for which the bureaucracy exists. But the bureaucracy doesn't exist for the sake of following the rules, i.e., it doesn't exist to merely perpetuate itself but in order to fulfill some societal function efficiently—to educate if it is a school, to heal if it is a hospital, and so on. But if you were to visit the administrative offices of a school or hospital, you would probably not get the impression that teaching and healing were uppermost in the minds of the personnel. (This fixation on means rather than ends is called **ritualism** in Robert Merton's theory of deviance). In addition, the obsession with rules leads to indifference toward exceptional cases—another major source of public frustration with bureaucracy. If bureaucracy is dedicated to mechanically enforcing rules for the sake of bureaucratic efficiency (a circular kind of logic), then if through no fault of your own you cannot comply with the rules (you don't have the particular document they require of you), the bureaucracy may be unwilling to help ("process") you. (Thorstein Veblen referred to the bureaucrat's "trained incapacity" to handle exceptions.) Here again bureaucratic structure rather than the callousness of individual employees is at fault. Personnel are trained to enforce rules, not to bend them whenever they deem it appropriate.

Yet we want to emphasize again the positive side of bureaucracy—and in this case, the positive side of rules and regulations. Think of the criminal justice system. It is often attacked for making the prosecution, conviction, and imprisonment of criminal defendants an overly complicated process. But to a very great extent the justice system is **complicated on principle**; the process is elaborate because in our system it is **supposed to be** difficult for the state to imprison its citizens. The criminal justice bureaucracy exists to ensure that defendants are dealt with in accordance with rules rather than left to the mercies of public sentiment, which is often of the "string-'em-up" (and ask questions later) variety. In this context the impersonality of the bureaucrat is a virtue. The rules are indeed quite elaborate, involving a whole series of protections for the accused, including the right to legal representation, a jury trial, etc. But all you have to do is be accused of a crime you did not commit to recognize with absolute certainty that these elaborate arrangements—to weed out potentially biased jurors, for example—are by no means too elaborate. The bureaucratization of criminal justice signifies that, while criminals are to be treated as responsible for their behavior, society is also responsible for the way it treats criminals.

Bureaucracy is a major topic not only in modern sociology but in modern philosophy and literature as well. Various writers have suggested that the unparalleled brutality of the twentieth century occurred not despite but because of modern bureaucratic arrangements. For sociology in particular this theme is central because it illustrates dramatically the **power of social forces to shape the attitudes and behaviors of people**. Bureaucracy is a structure that produces a certain mindset. Human beings are no more unfeeling than in previous epochs; yet they may act more unfeelingly because responding on the basis of human sympathies violates the canons of secondary group behavior, especially in bureaucracies. Bureaucracy makes it not only possible but normal to hurt and reject people without feeling guilty about it. Think of that the next time a bank teller refuses to cash your check and then says, "Have a nice day." This artificial response—in most cases merely an example of mechanical obedience to explicit bureaucratic rules—is not only not an expression of compassion; it seems to make a mockery of compassion. As "Hello, and welcome to Blockbuster" makes a mockery of greeting acquaintances. People act like machines—and machines act like people (acting like machines): a soda machine "says" "Thank you" for dropping coins in the slot; a pre-recorded human voice "tells you" to remain on hold (as "all representatives"—meaning lowly workers—"are busy helping other customers"— a tricky way of dispelling the anger you may feel at having to wait: the bureaucracy produces the anger by making you wait yet suggests that the anger is unjustified because "other customers" means "people just like you"). Compassion means suffering along with; yet bureaucratic amiability is more an attempt to dissociate the bureaucracy from the sufferer—and thus from responsibility for the suffering—by smilingly ignoring the fact that anyone is suffering at all.

It may appear to be an exaggeration to refer to a frustrated customer on hold as "suffering." So, then, let us talk about more obvious cases of suffering.

Stanley Milgram's "obedience" experiments show how human beings under the spell of bureaucratic routine are capable of inflicting direct and intense physical suffering on complete strangers. Milgram, then a Yale psychology professor, recruited volunteers to participate in what they were told was going to be an experiment designed to test the effects of punishment on the learning process. A volunteer "learner" was asked to repeat word lists recited by a volunteer "teacher"; each time the learner failed to recall the words correctly, the teacher would punish the learner with an electric shock. Upon each subsequent wrong answer, increased voltages would be applied. Now the volunteer learner was actually Milgram's assistant; but the volunteer teacher didn't know this. Nor did the teacher know that the so-called "electric shock generator" was nothing of the kind, nor that the shrieks of agony coming from the learner each time he received a shock were also fake. Milgram was testing whether the volunteer teachers would be willing to give electric shocks to innocent strangers. In most cases they were—even when the learner disclosed he had a heart condition, even when he begged the teacher not to hurt him. (The actual rate of compliance depended on several factors that varied in different repetitions of the experiment. For example, when teacher and learner were placed in different rooms and the teacher conveyed the shocks by pressing a button, the obedience rate was about 70%; when teacher and learner were in the same room and the teacher conveyed the shock by forcing the learner's hand onto a metal plate, the obedience rate fell to about 30%.)

Why did the teachers co-operate to the extent that they did? Because Milgram **successfully acted the part of a typical bureaucratic authority figure**. He didn't grin at the sound of the learner's screams; he merely said, in calm rational tones, to the often perplexed teachers: "Please proceed; the experiment requires that we continue through the end of the word lists"; "The experiment will not be valid unless we continue"; etc. (Notice how the experiment—a means to an end—is transformed in such talk into an end in itself.) Milgram assured those teachers who were upset at the learner's cries that, while the learner was perhaps in pain, no real damage was being inflicted on him. Here Milgram was invoking **the authority of modern science**, which takes precedence over the evidence of the senses. Not only the emotions but even the sense-perceptions of the teachers could thus be nullified under the right circumstances.

Milgram deliberately constructed a situation in which human responses are defined as irrelevant or counterproductive or misleading—by a figure (Milgram) whose authority was assumed to be **merited**—because it is authority in a recognized **hierarchy of offices** (Professor, Yale University)—and who is himself following rules and procedures that we ordinarily do not question (because they are the rules and procedures of science). The point is not that science is evil but that by being bureaucratized it can do evil without the evil being seen as such, even by the perpetrators. Under the right circumstances, torture becomes "experimentation." Efficiency is so important to bureaucracy that the development of efficient means becomes self-justifying—regardless, that is, of the ends they are bringing about. In fact, the end that is brought about is re-defined in terms of the means: pain becomes the sign of a successfully conducted experiment. Now we move from the realm of simulated torture to the realm of real torture.

BUREAUCRACY AND THE HOLOCAUST

Zygmunt Bauman's analysis of the Holocuast—the organized mass murder of Jews by the Nazis during World War II—conatins an indictment not only of modern society but of modern sociology, which he accuses of indulging in the same illusions about the nature of evil that characterize modernity and which made the Holocaust, in his view, a peculiarly modern crime. What makes the Holocaust peculiarly modern? There is no doubt that a vast bureaucratic machinery was necessary to carry out the "Final Solution." What Bauman argues is that bureaucracy provided not just the technical means but the **rationale** for genocide, that a bureaucratic world-view alone could have made an attempted justification for genocide possible. **Only from within a bureaucratic world-view could traditional moral considerations become so irrelevant as to make genocide conceivable.** The starting point for understanding this view of the Holocaust is to recognize that the Holocaust was carried out by mostly **normal people acting in accordance with the norms of bureaucratic procedure**. Bauman quotes Raul Hilberg, the great historian of the Holocaust:

> The German perpetrator was not a special kind of German . . . We know that the very nature of administrative planning, of the jurisdictional structure and of the budgetary system precluded the special selection and special training of personnel. Any member of the Order Police could be a guard at a ghetto or on a train. Every lawyer in the Reich Security Main Office was presumed to be suitable for leadership in the mobile killing units; every finance expert to the Economic-Administrative Main Office was considered a natural choice for service in a death camp. In other words, all necessary operations were accomplished with whatever personnel were at hand. (Bauman, 1991, p. 21)

From the psychiatric point of view the conclusions are the same. Bauman quotes psychologists George M. Kren and Leon Rappoport:

> By conventional clinical criteria no more than 10 per cent of the SS could be considered "abnormal." This observation fits the general trend of testimony by survivors indicating that in most of the camps, there was usually one, or at most a few, SS men known for their intense outbursts of sadistic cruelty. The others were not always decent persons, but their behavior was at least considered comprehensible by the prisoners . . . Our judgement is that the overwhelming majority of SS men, leaders as well as rank and file, would have easily passed all the psychiatric tests ordinarily given to American army recruits or Kansas City policemen. (p. 19)

So far we seem to be faced with the same fundamental question posed by the Milgram experiments: How do ordinary people become capable of cruelty toward complete strangers—without, so to speak, being transformed out of their ordinariness (e.g., into a state of impassioned rage, wild paranoia, etc.—states that convicted murderers often cite in order to explain their crimes)? That is one question. But the fact that the Holocaust, unlike the Milgram experiments, was not make-believe, raises another question—a question not about ordinary people who obeyed orders to torture and murder but about the (mostly) ordinary people who—like Dr. Milgram but for real—**gave** the orders.

Now the practice of genocide presupposed a theory of genocide. Both these components, Bauman says, can be—and can only be—understood within the context of modern bureaucratic rationality. To begin with, the idea of killing the Jews evolved only gradually. Hitler's objective was to make the territory of the Third Reich "judenfrei," i.e., free of Jews. (How he could have come up with such an objective Bauman also explains in terms of modernity, as we shall see shortly.) What exactly that meant was not at all clear. Initially it meant forced emigration—indeed, evidence suggests that as late as July, 1941, the Germans were looking for a suitable place to dump their Jewish population. The problem of finding such a place grew as the Reich's territory grew by annexation and conquest. Nisko in central Poland; Madagascar, a remote colony of defeated France; somewhere in the vast expanse of Russia once it was defeated—all these areas were proposed and ultimately, on practical grounds, rejected. On practical grounds again the Nazis hit upon murder as the "final solution" to the "Jewish problem." According to Bauman:

> Once the objective (judenfrei) had been set, everything went on exactly as Weber, with his usual clarity, spelled out: "The 'political master' finds himself in the position of the 'dilettante' who stands opposite the 'expert,' facing the trained official who stands within the management of administration." The objective had to be implemented; how this was to be done depended on the circumstances, always judged by the "experts" from the point of view of feasibility and the costs of alternative opportunities of action. (p. 15)

Genocide as practical, feasible, do-able, less costly than the alternatives: these are the criteria by which the decision to implement the final solution was arrived at. Once that decision was made, implementation of it required the mobilization of a vast array of bureaucratic personnel. How could these functionaries torture and murder as they did? Bauman poses this key question more precisely; for him the question, "How could they do it?" means, quoting Hannah Arendt, how could they "overcome the animal pity by which all normal men are affected in the presence of physical suffering?" (p. 20) In other words, becoming inhuman, given that you are human to begin with, requires undergoing a process of de-humanization—which is what becoming part of a bureaucratic machine entails. Here Bauman cites Herbert C. Kelman's enumeration of the conditions necessary for individuals to commit atrocities without feeling any moral inhibitions: the actions must be expected and authorized; and the victims must be defined as sub-human by the organization. Bauman finds that the first condition is identified by Weber as a constituent feature of bureaucracy. We saw it at work in the Milgram experiments. An emphasis on legitimate orders—i.e., orders coming from recognized superiors in the chain of command (= "authorization")—together with impersonal, technical descriptions of the actions to be carried out (e.g., "After pulling lever A, proceed to lever B," as opposed to "Now kill the bastards") enables the individuals to displace responsibility for their actions onto those in authority and, less obviously, to re-define the nature of the action itself. Thus:

> At (an early stage), the rounded-up victims were brought in front of machine guns and killed at point-blank range. Though efforts were made to keep the weapons at the longest possible distance from the ditches into which the murdered were to fall, it was exceedingly difficult for the shooters to overlook the connection between shooting and killing. This is why the administrators of genocide found the method primitive and inefficient, as well as dangerous to the morale of the perpetrators. Other murder techniques were therefore sought—such as would optically separate the killers from their victims. The search was successful, and led to the invention of first the mobile, then the stationary gas chambers; the latter—the most perfect the Nazis had time to invent—reduced the role of the killer to that of the "sanitation officer" asked to empty a sack of "disinfecting chemicals" through an aperture in the roof of a building the interior of which he was not prompted to visit. (p. 26)

By its very complexity, furthermore, bureaucracy tends to increase the distance between actions and their consequences. On this point Bauman quotes Hilberg:

> "It must be kept in mind that most of the participants . . . did not fire rifles at Jewish children or pour gas into gas chambers . . . Most bureaucrats composed memoranda, drew up blueprints, talked on the telephone, and participated in conferences. They could destroy a whole people by sitting at their desk." (p. 24)

While the example here is that of physical distance, "routinization" basically implies a **psychological distance**: the neutrality of the words used to describe murder, and the technical ordinariness of the instructions as to how to commit it, draws the mind away from a direct relation to what is being done and replaces it with a fixation on how it is done. **The process becomes the reality; means render ends invisible.** This is more significant than the physical invisibility of the victims. For, just as Milgram showed that, to get people to act cruelly, physical distance from the victim is not always necessary, but emotional distance is, the Holocaust shows the same thing on an incomprehensibly grander scale.

Because of its emphasis on rationality and efficiency, bureaucracy creates the sense that it is self-justifying. Orders are legitimate because they come from legitimate authorities. What makes the authorities legitimate? The fact that they are designated as such by the bureaucracy! To acknowledge that legitimacy and to act on it is the definition of bureaucratic "morality." In practice it means distrusting and putting aside all merely personal reactions and motives—the "overcoming of animal pity." According to Weber:

> The honour of the civil servant is vested in his ability to execute conscientiously the order of superior authorities, exactly as if the order agreed with his own conviction. This holds even if the order seems wrong to him and if, despite the civil servant's remonstrances, the authority insists on the order. (p. 22)

Bauman notes what this means: "Through honour, discipline is substituted for moral responsibility." (ibid.)

The authority of bureaucracy is inseparable from the authority of scientific language and procedure. Milgram's experiments would surely have turned out differently if he hadn't tranquilized his subjects with an introductory technical discourse on the nature of his scientific "learning experiment." But the power of these "moral sleeping pills" (Bauman's phrase) goes beyond even their use in the Holocaust. The Holocaust, for Bauman, shows the unlimited hidden potential of modern society to make people morally blind. Questions of morality seem so pathetically simplistic, and therefore irrelevant, when contrasted with a discussion by experts of technical matters.

Modernity means **the victory of the technical over the ethical**; bureaucracy is the most visible symbol of this victory; and the Holocaust reveals the costs of victory. In this victory, according to Bauman, sociology has played a major role. For sociology not only describes the modernization process but endorses it; for "sociological common sense . . . includes among many others such articles of faith as the benefits of reason's rule over the emotions, the superiority of rationality over (what else?) irrational action, (and) the endemic clash between the demands of efficiency and the moral leanings with which 'personal relations' are so hopelessly infused." (p. 10) The result is that there is nothing in Weber's classic description of the ideal-typical bureaucracy "that would necessitate the description of the Nazi state as excessive." (ibid.) The death camps were normally functioning bureaucracies in Weber's terms. Just as bureaucracy severs technical from moral questions, to the detriment of the latter, sociology

> . . . promoted, as its own criteria of propriety, the same principles of rational action it visualized as constitutive of its object. It also promoted, as binding rules of its own discourse, the inadmissibility of ethical problematics . . . Phrases like "the sanctity of human life" or "moral duty" sound as alien in a sociology seminar as they do in the . . . sanitized rooms of a bureaucratic office. (p. 29)

If questioning of moral ends is out of place in sociology, it is impossible for sociology to distinguish between a hospital and a death camp. Bauman's view appears to be the opposite of Weber's: not only does he claim that questions of morality shouldn't be irrelevant, as bureaucracy intends; he suggests that bureaucracy itself makes questions of morality urgent—by creating evil on a new and grander scale. Here we come back to Hitler. Where did he get his antisemitism from? A combination of places, to be sure, including the negative stereotypes of Jews and Judaism produced and dispersed by Christian theologians and churchpeople for centuries. But the transformation of this prejudice into the idea that the Jews—or any people—can and should be gotten rid of is, according to Bauman, only possible in a modern context. Why? Because

> . . . from the Enlightenment on, the modern world was distinguished by its activist, engineering attitude toward nature and toward itself. Science was not to be conducted for its own sake; it was seen as, first and foremost, an instrument of awesome power allowing its holder to improve on reality, to re-shape it according to human plans and designs . . .

But, again, we think that the main point in what he is saying is that modernity seeks to "improve on reality" to make it more commensurate with science; it is science that is, if you will, both the means and the end.

Under the influence of modern rationality, antisemitism turned into a clinical diagnosis of Jews as unfit to live. This is the scientization of hatred. (Bauman points to the Nazis' attempts to "breed" a "superior" race, and to kill off mentally insane and physically disabled people, as similar phenomena.) By failing to acknowledge this modern form of evil, Bauman argues, sociology displays its general unwillingness to acknowledge that **evil can result from attachment to societal norms as well as alienation from them.** Bauman believes that "the process of socialization consists in the manipulation of moral capacity—not its production." By contrast, normal sociology, from the time of Durkheim on, has held that morality is the product of society (its norms). As Bauman says—and as Milgram's experiments implicitly suggest—this raises the question whether, and under what circumstances, acting morally can and must be said to consist in insubordination to legally constituted authority.

POST-INDUSTRIAL SOCIETY

Since the early 1970s, when Daniel Bell first introduced the term, sociologists have described our society, and those like it (i.e., the technically advanced nations of Western Europe) as having entered a "post-industrial" phase (Bell, 1973). This does not mean that the main sociological characteristics of industrial society have died out. Indeed, "post-industrial" refers in part to the fact that certain tendencies of industrial society—a complex division of labor, the proliferation of secondary groups, the emphasis on achieved status—have **greatly accelerated** (and in one of Marx's most brilliant formulations, quantity eventually changes into quality). In the process aspects of industrial society which were supposed to (and often did) solve problems have **created new problems of their own**. The division of labor was supposed to—and did—mean increased efficiency; yet today we are more likely to be aware of the inefficency it causes in the form of bureaucratic red tape, etc. And the image of trained specialists cheerfully performing well-defined tasks has turned into a nightmare of alienation: people who feel like mere cogs in a machine (because that is what they are), disconnected from any sense of the meaningfulness of their work, and who live only for their leisure time (where "meaningfulness" is provided by tranquilizing or stimulating mass media entertainments). Or—perhaps worse—workers may be people who don't know they are alienated (and in that sense are doubly alienated), who identify with the company as though their interests were identical. A world of secondary groups and achieved statuses was supposed to be one of increased freedom—the freedom to realize self-potential unfettered by traditional loyalties and their corresponding obligations. And so it has: but this increased freedom has also led to an increased sense of isolation, as relationships become defined as optional (free contracts), and interpersonal commitments, where they do occur, tend to be based mainly on calculations of mutual gain (including emotional gain: what once was described as intimacy is commonly described nowadays as co-dependency).

In part, then, "post-industrial society" refers to the crisis in industrial society, or to the exhaustion of its ideals. But in addition to the breakdown of the old, post-industrial refers to the emergence of something new. Structurally, what is new is the technology of the last several decades, creating societies that are post-industrial in the sense that the manufacturing sectors of their economies have declined in importance and been replaced by a whole new range of products and services. How has this change affected the lives of people in society as a whole? We will look briefly at some of the main sociological characteristics of the post-industrial age:

The **service sector of the economy has expanded** dramatically as technological innovations decrease the proportion of workers needed for industrial production. Millions of people who in previous generations would have grown up to become factory workers today find themselves in community colleges training to become service personnel (this may help explain the increase in the proportion of male nursing students). There is a greater emphasis on college education of all types than ever before, as the high-tech environment demands more sophisticated skills of even the average employee than industry did. The modern emphasis on scientific knowledge has become more pronounced in post-industrial society, as various traditional fields—again, think of nursing—are transformed into technical ones. Nursing students must study not only anatomy and physiology and microbiology but contemporary developments in medical technology as well; future teachers must learn the various techniques of computer-assisted instruction as well as the old-fashioned, human-assisted kind.

The rise of technology has not only led to a shift from the primary and secondary (agricultural and manufacturing) sectors to the tertiary (service) sector but a dramatic increase in the types of service occupations in society. The astounding technical success modern societies have had in feeding and clothing (most of) their people has led to **the discovery of other, less tangible needs** (and the creation of new ones) and to the belief that these too can be satisfied by technical means. The "need" for communication and friendship—to feel at home in an anonymous environment—is "satisfied" by the use of cell phones. As basic needs are fulfilled, "need" is redefined upward: the less anxious we are whether we can put food on the table, the more concerned we become that precisely the right foods be put there, whether we are talking about the psychological need for luxury or beauty (hence the Food Channel, well-known gourmet chefs, bookstores stocking their books) or the physiological need for a healthy diet (health-food stores, ingredient labeling, and, again, cookbooks galore).

The fact that more jobs than ever before involve dealing with people and promoting services rather than growing or making things means that **communication has become a vitally important survival skill**—as crucial for the competent performance of many typical service-sector jobs as physical dexterity was for many industrial jobs. (This is occurring at the same time that a decline in traditional literacy skills is occurring; this apparent paradox, however, can be overcome by recognizing that the communication skills called for—to, for example, competently promote a new long-distance call package—involve a type of technical mastery of the language and art of selling that is different from the acquisition of traditional literacy skills.) It also entails increased reliance on the use of images and other means of persuasion, since many jobs involve attempts to sell people things they don't need in the obvious sense that they need food and shelter: in post-industrial society, the need itself has to be sold. Thus, workers are trained in self-presentation—how to dress, act, and speak in order to produce the desired effect on the audience.

The shift from industrial to technological means a **greater degree of global interdependence** as the advanced nations produce less and less of what their populations need. The decline in the proportion of workers employed in industry in the U.S. is due not only to increased efficiency (automation, for example) but to a geographical transfer of manufacturing (and lower-level service) jobs to third-world countries where labor is cheaper. The more dependent we become on other nations the more dependent they become on us: they produce for us, but then we give them jobs. In some cases this does mean that amicable relations must prevail (some observers have suggested that war between India and Pakistan is inconceivable because it would disrupt American corporate interests too much: many Indians, for example, are in India working for American

Express) so that the image of a belligerent America that sets the terms all the time is at best exaggerated. In general it is safe to say that Western European ethnocentrism is no longer viable now that the West has lost its unquestioned dominance in the global marketplace. An additional factor to take into account is that American companies are constantly on the lookout for foreign markets; there is simply a limit to what the American consumer can (be motivated to) buy; this, too, may affect our relations with other countries—although presumably we don't have to show any more genuine respect to foreigners than telephone salespeople, for example, show their fellow citizens when interrupting the latter's dinner to make a pitch; it would be ironic if, in dealing with foreigners, we had to be more respectful because of their more exacting standards of politeness.

The emphasis on educational and occupational achievement leads to an **increased emphasis on individual freedom**, especially by those who have succeeded in achieving. The (illusory?) sense of independence—of having made it on one's own—leads to the feeling that I have the right to decide how I will live, without the "help" of family or community standards. This ethic is reinforced by the idea that individual freedom is a condition of achievement and not just a consequence of it—you must, for example, be free to enter the occupation of your choice. The post-industrial age, then, is an age of individual "lifestyle" decisions, an age where rights tend to be exalted above responsibilities. (This is not to say that the two are necessarily incompatible. A person may be committed both to exercising the right of free speech and the obligation to speak of others respectfully—or may not.) The problem is that a freedom granted by society has no meaning if society at the same time determines too strictly how one is going to be allowed to exercise it; the question, of course, is what "too strictly" means or should mean in particular cases. At any rate, it is clear that important decisions that used to be made **for** individuals are now made **by** them: whether, when, and who to marry; whether to believe in God, and which one(s). And the individual is also free to regard such decisions as unimportant: some gays and lesbians want to marry; others regard the whole issue of same-sex marriage as insignificant. Thus we decide not only what to do with our lives but the priority we give to the various things we do. Alongside people for whom "family" is the all-important social reality, however they define family, we have workaholics and chocaholics; one can be obsessed with Jesus, Satan, collectible dolls, or the Grateful Dead, and without ever having to give a reason why. Freedom of self-expression now includes the right of being unaccountable as to the reason or meaning of what one expresses (as long as it doesn't hurt anyone). Thus, instead of dialogue on talk shows, we have mutual monologue: two or more people expressing their views, each totally uninfluenced—except to be amused or outraged—by the views of the other. (One question is whether political "debate" has taken its cue from television.) While the trivialization of language that this implies alarms some critics, the fact that little of the talk is taken seriously may be the secret of our society's survival: if we took to heart the hateful things said on TV and radio, we would be killing each other. Fortunately, for the most part it is simply consumed as entertainment.

Finally, the growth in individual freedom, insofar as it has led to an increased sense of isolation, has had the paradoxical effect of producing a **new yearning for community**. A society in which people are simply given, as it were, marriage and family responsibilities may be an oppressive one but it is undoubtedly a meaningful one (even if the meaning is taken for granted). Signs of a search for community, as a search for meaning and purpose, are all around us: a renewal of religious enthusiasm among the unlikeliest population groups—e.g., high achievers who find that the fulfillment of their secular dreams for worldly success leaves them strangely unsatisfied; a trend toward big (traditional) weddings; a growth in ethnic pride among people who in the past would have been satisfied with calling themselves "American" (we should not be confused by the post-9/11 tendency to discard one's ethnic particularity in favor of the more general nationalistic self-identification—just as we should not be distracted by the display of American flags all over New York City!), etc. We live in a society in which news anchors in every region of the country have exactly the same accent; some people are understandably tired of that. Our society, however, has become expert at appearing to celebrate differences while in reality the differences are assimilated to a higher unity; a greater mixture of types is included in what turns out to be the same old thing (in the sense that it is not made new by the inclusion of new types): so intelligence has been added to the "talents" beauty contestants must display; and the contestants themselves may represent a wide range of ethnic types . . . but it is still a beauty pageant. A sense of community or solidarity is most typically achieved by identifying with TV shows and personalities; or by identifying oneself as a consumer (and so basically the same as others, who similarly identify themselves). After all, in our society who does not enjoy TV (or movies) and shopping?

CONCLUSION: ON STRUCTURE VS. CULTURE

The preceding pages have given us a very different picture of contemporary social reality from that provided by the Culture chapter. This may not be obvious to the reader; but, since the difference—some would say, opposition—between the "cultural" and "structural" approaches has become a major theme in sociology, we should try to spell out in conclusion what the difference is.

The basic question is **whether the elements of culture have a determining influence on social structure or vice versa**. In other words, **are norms the product of social circumstances (the structural view) or the cause of those circumstances (the cultural view)?** This sounds like a highly theoretical question but in fact it is debated daily by commentators in the press, on TV and radio, and among average people—most of whom, it seems, take the cultural view. A cultural view is being adopted whenever we explain social problems—crime, poverty, drugs—as the result of a change (breakdown) in values. The structural view, by contrast, would be that structural changes—high minority-male unemployment due to the decline of decent-paying low-skill labor, combined with substandard public schooling—leads to cultural changes (a lower marrying rate). Structuralists argue, for example, that the lower classes, while they are less likely to marry than members of the middle classes, are no less "committed" to the "value" of marriage; people marry when they can afford to. (Would you marry someone where there is mutual attraction but where the other person is at best marginally employable, where marriage, for whatever reason, would entail serious financial sacrifice?) In all social classes—and in the upper class most of all—considerations of economic and social status are a major if unspoken part of the marriage decision-making process.

People who marry often get divorced; it was not always so. Why the change? Because women on average have better jobs than they used to and so can afford to leave (the structural view) or because contemporary values emphasize self and happiness over family and sacrifice for others (the cultural view)? People who take a culturalist view often contradict themselves when they define reality in terms of what they can see and touch rather than "mere" ideas. (But it should be noted that structuralists contradict themselves too: structuralist sociology professors don't accept excuses for late term papers even when they (should) know that on structural grounds the student's excuse may well be valid: I have to work long hours; I was kept awake last night by the sound of gunfire, etc.)

It should be noted that public sympathy for the cultural view is abetted by the fact that it is less economically threatening: if the problems of minorities or the poor are due to their values rather than lack of available jobs or quality education—structural problems that cost money to solve—it is up to them to solve them. (Perhaps the most unsubtle attempt to absolve the public of responsibility for combating social problems by defining it as an attitude problem was former First Lady Nancy Reagan's anti-drug campaign in the 1980s. The diagnosis of the drug epidemic as a problem of individual self-discipline meant that the solution would cost the taxpayer no more than the cost of billboards bearing the message "Just Say No!") Notice that we are taking a structuralist view of the public's sympathy for culturalist explanations. Sociologists do tend to take the former position, but here we will present a case for it. And that case is focused on the following point: if the culturalist view wants to explain behaviors in terms of values, doesn't it have to deal with the fact that values themselves are socially produced and distributed? On sociological grounds differences in values cannot be explained, but differences in circumstances can be. And not only that: differences in values become harder and harder to explain the more everyone "learns" from the mass media. The **structure** of society is such that just about every household can afford a TV. What happens as a result of watching may be different in different cases but the condition—of TV watching—is the same in every case. The media have replaced science, which replaced religion, as the ultimate source of truth for most people; the media are to a postmodern world what science was to the modern world and what religion was to the premodern world. (Notice that each of these three sources of truth comes with its own definition of reality.) We live in a society in which, increasingly, something is considered to have happened if it was reported on TV or in the paper. Indeed, scientific findings may be reported on TV or in the paper, but the fact that they are reported on TV or in the paper is what makes them believable. The ascendancy of the media means the ascendancy of different viewpoints whose credibility depends on their popular appeal rather than technical scientific criteria: if modernity made the Holocaust possible, postmodernity makes Holocaust-denial possible.

Other areas where the culture/structure question arises are the sociology of race and the sociology of deviant behavior. For example: Is racism a product of ethnocentrism (cultural prejudice) or economic competition among different groups? Is gang membership the result of bad families or the fact that some people do not have an opportunity to excel in the marketplace? In any case, we will continue to examine the merits of both approaches in the following chapters.

6

SOCIALIZATION

Sociology considers the self to be a social product. Such a notion would explain, for example, why the typical self in our society is more committed to being an individual than the typical self in a pre-modern society.

If we claim that the self is social in origin, then we must confront these two basic questions: (1) precisely how do we go from being the unique beings we are as infants to being typical members of society? and (2) how does it happen that not everyone turns out to be typical? The second question is normally taken up under the heading of the sociology of deviance. The first question, which we will explore in the present chapter, is normally answered through a description of the **socialization** process—the process whereby individuals learn to adopt the attitudes and behaviors expected of them as members of a particular society.

BECOMING HUMAN

Empirical evidence as well as theoretical insight have led sociologists to conclude that human beings have to be socialized to become recognizably human. The evidence referred to is of children raised in isolation from other humans. For example, there is the case of Isabelle, a child kept locked up in a dark room for the first six years of her life by her grandparents, to protect them from the shame of her illegitimate birth; she eventually escaped with her mother, a deaf-mute, and thereupon became an object of scientific study. Two things about her behavior after her captivity stand out. First, it was infantile. She could not speak—at least not in words (she made some strange croaking sounds); and it was thought at first that she could not hear, since she showed no reaction to the sounds around her. Furthermore:

> When presented with a ball, she held it in the palm of her hand, then reached out and stroked my face with it. Such behavior is comparable to that of a child of six months. She made no attempt to squeeze it, to throw it, or bounce it. (Davis 1940)

Secondly, she made up for lost time: within a few months, she could speak in complete sentences, and by the age of nine she was able to attend school with other children. How to explain Isabelle's strange developmental history? Isabelle was deprived of almost all interactional models: she could not speak because she had never been around speech. Yet she had been around her mother, and had learned to communicate with her through gestures. Being with her mother meant not only that Isabelle was introduced to the practice of communication but, perhaps more fundamentally, to a positive image of other people. At first, Isabelle reacted with intense, wild distrust to the presence of stangers; this made sense, since the only people she was ever exposed to besides her mother were her captors. Yet she quickly overcame this fear. Thus, both Isabelle's problem and her ability to overcome it can be explained by the interactions she had in early childhood. The fact that she caught up so quickly suggests an innate potential among humans—to speak, read, write, etc.— and in that sense a "natural" rather than social-interactional factor. Even if all cognitive development in humans could be understood as a process of imitation, we would still have to explain how it is that humans are capable of such imitation. And that would seem to mean talking about human nature not just "nurture." However, what the Isabelle example shows is that we only know of the existence of this human nature, this potential for humanness, as a result of the individual's interaction with others—so that "human nature" even in light of the Isabelle study remains for sociologists merely an interesting philosophical hypothesis that can have no bearing on the actual study, the actual analysis, of human thought and behavior.

The sociological question is more mundane than the philosophical one. Instead of asking, how is it possible for us to become human beings?, the sociologist asks, how **do we** become human beings? There are several competing answers to this question.

THEORIES OF SOCIALIZATION

Since they are about the development of the individual, theories of socialization, like theories of deviant behavior, exist in psychology as well as in sociology. And we will argue here, as we will in the Deviance chapter, that, helpful as the psychological theories are, they present an incomplete and unrealistic image of human behavior that needs to be supplemented by sociology. We will also see that the differences among the major psychological theories, as well as among the major sociological theories, are as great as the differences between the psychological approach as a whole and the sociological.

PSYCHOLOGICAL THEORIES OF SOCIALIZATION

Behaviorism (B.F. Skinner)

Skinner's basic thesis is that behavior is motivated by some combination of the promise of reward and the threat of punishment. We learn to act a certain way because we learn to associate performing an act with either the attainment of something pleasurable or the avoidance of something painful or both. This is clearly true of the motivation of children and animals; the question is whether it is also true of human adults.

Children below a certain age have no awareness of the intrinsic meaning or value of behaviors but only of their consequences. So, for example, they are willing to go to sleep when their parents tell them to not because they appreciate the importance of sleep but because their parents—whose approval they seek and whose disapproval they seek to avoid—have ordered them to. They have not yet been taught about sleep but only trained to go to sleep. In other words, they have not been made to **understand** but only to **behave** a certain way. This is why it makes sense for Skinner's theory to be called behaviorism. Sometimes it is called **learning theory**—which could seem misleading to anyone who thinks there is a difference between learning and training. On the other hand, the name is apt insofar as it suggests the idea that human behavior is infinitely malleable. To say that human behavior is based on learning is to say it is **not** based on human nature. Behaviorism is an extreme version of the "nurture not nature" view. Skinner is more an agnostic than an atheist when it comes to the question of human nature; he doesn't deny its existence, he only denies that we can ever gain any knowledge of it. What we can have knowledge of is behavior, since it is observable; what we can also have knowledge of are the environments in which particular behaviors take place, since they too are observable. And we can observe that the relation between an environmental stimulus (e.g., a parent's command) and a behavioral response (a child's acquiescence) is a causal one. Thus we have the materials for a science, rather than merely a philosophy, of human behavior.

But what behaviorism most has in common with other instances of modern scientific theorizing may well be its **assumption**—a philosphical assumption—that human behavior is infinitely malleable. This assumption is basic to the spirit of modern science. Originally it was applied to the realm of nature. According to Enlightenment thought, nature behaves in accordance with laws that can be apprehended by human reason. To unlock the secrets of nature means to be able to control or modify natural phenomena—hence modern medicine, for example, which is inconceivable apart from knowledge of the laws of the behavior of organisms. Eventually this natural-scientific confidence in the ability of scientific reason to subdue nature was extended to the realm of human behavior. If the natural world can be made subject to human manipulation and control, why not the human world? But to go from control of the natural world to control of the human world requires regarding humanity as part of the natural world. In Skinner's case this concept of humanity is not based on any elaborate theory but rather on a confessed—or defiant—inability to know anything about the "internal" aspects of humans—the mind or soul of individuals—as opposed to the external, behavioral aspects. To treat human conduct merely as behavior, without attempting to see it as a reflection of some deep internal "state of mind" of the actor, in order to be in a position to describe the laws by which it is physically set in motion, is to treat humanity the way you would treat natural phenomena. After all, we don't, at least in the modern world, ask why heavy objects desire to fall to the earth faster than light objects; we only **observe that they do,** and the various natural factors—weight, volume, air pressure—that **cause** objects to fall at different velocities (Heidegger, 1967).

Did the belief that humanity is merely a part of nature lead to the development of the modern sciences of human behavior, and so eventually to attempts to control and modify behavior (attempts we will discuss shortly)? Or did the dream of controlling and modifying human behavior, the way the natural sciences master nature, lead to the decision to treat human behavior as merely a part of nature? Did the impetus for the development of modern natural science come simply from a widespread impatience with philosophical meditations on nature that, whether true or false, didn't "get anywhere"—didn't cure diseases, didn't build bridges, and in general didn't make the lives of average people any pleasanter or longer? Modern science intended to change all that—originally, modern natural science, but then, beginning in the latter part of the 19th century, modern social science as well.

At the basis of Skinner's behaviorism there is definitely an interest in the ability to control behavior. The idea of alterability implies manipulability. Indeed, Skinner first became famous outside of academic psychology with the publication of his novel, **Walden Two** (1947), which describes a utopian world where, thanks to the latest learning techniques, everybody behaves the way they are being asked to. Crime and deviance are things of the past. But a less utopian, and even more famous, appearance of Skinnerian theory in the everyday world has come in the form of behavior therapy (or behavior modification therapy, or behavior mod), which involves altering a patient's behavior patterns by altering his or her perceptions of the rewards and punishments consequent upon particular behaviors. This form of therapy is especially useful in the treatment of addictions. If people smoke because they associate it with something positive, such as relief from tension, then to cure them of smoking requires training them to associate it with something negative, such as disease or the alienation of family and friends. Both these negative consequences are played up in ads discouraging smoking. Thus we see how behaviorist-type techniques are used daily in the mass media, to get people to want to buy particular products, vote for particular political candidates (and/or against other ones), etc. There is no doubt as to the practical applicability of behaviorism. The theoretical problems with it seem to be these:

(a) It assumes that human beings are motivated exclusively by hedonistic considerations. Thus it is able to explain ordinary behaviors but not extraordinary behaviors—acts of self-sacrifice, heroism, and so on—in which persons deliberately do what they know will be painful for the sake of a "higher good," i.e., a good higher than pleasure. Of course a behaviorist could say that heroes act heroically because it is gratifying to their egos (= pleasurable). But if that were true, then there is no difference between a Hitler and a Mother Teresa: one kills people because he finds it pleasurable, the other saves lives for the same reason. A second behaviorist response could be to say that the heroes are only more far-sighted hedonists: they can see future pleasure (e.g., freedom for their people in the case of those who struggle for human rights) resulting from acceptance of short-term pain. But if their motivation is thus as hedonistic as ours, why is it so difficult for people to become willing to act heroically? Is it really because they don't recognize the pleasure they will get out of it?

(b) Behaviorism assumes that the proven alterability of human behavior closes the question whether there is a human nature, at least for all practical purposes. But that would be like saying that the ability of a totalitarian regime to make all citizens obey orders proves that there is no fundamental human desire for freedom. This is an important point because it shows how ultimately irrelevant Skinnerian psychology is to sociology. Superficially, their concerns appear similar. Sociology, too, deals with learned behavior and with reward and punishment: people learn normal behaviors and learn to do them by associating obedience with reward—e.g., being certified as "normal"—and disobedience with punishment—being labelled "deviant," i.e., suffering social ostracism. Sociologists commonly hold that in learning the rules—for example, learning to orient towards finding a career—social actors learn to see obedience as rewarding. In this respect, sociology is akin to behaviorism. But unlike behaviorists, most sociologists would argue that this learning process never occurs smoothly and mechanically, and is never perfectly completed—because human beings, in the sociological view, have to first **decide whether obeying the rules is worth it or not;** and, if they do decide to obey, they then have to **interpret what constitutes obedience** (they have to interpret the roles they are being asked to play).

This active relationship between individual and society is emphasized in most sociological theories of socialization, as we shall see below; and it implies that individuals, while formed by society, are still somehow not merely the sum total of the environmental influences that have acted upon them.

Developmental Theories (Piaget, Kohlberg)

These are almost the opposite of behaviorism—they describe the development of thought rather than the manipulation of behavior. And they tend to regard self-development as a natural process that follows a pre-defined pattern—instead of seeing the human being as a mass of aimless potential ready to be nurtured into anything the nurturer pleases. The most influential theory of this kind is Jean Piaget's **cognitive developmental psychology.** On the basis of empirical study of thousands of children, Piaget concluded that cognitive (mental) maturation follows a universal pattern comprising four stages of development beginning in infancy and culminating at about age 12, when the child achieves the ability to think as a mature adult. Briefly these stages are as follows:

(a) sensorimotor stage (0–2 yrs.). The infant relates to the world, and to itself, in sheerly sensual terms—through seeing, hearing, smelling, touching, tasting, and moving about rather than thinking. But the term "relates to" is misleading; the infant is thrown into, absorbed in, a world of objects—without yet being aware of itself as a subject. In the first four months of life the infant does not even perceive its body as a distinct entity separate from the rest of the environment. And, through the first year, it regards the immediate physical environment as the totality of the world—hence, it has no sense of "object permanence": if mommy leaves the room, the infant assumes mommy no longer exists. Therefore, if mommy doesn't return right away, the infant gets terribly upset.

(b) pre-operational stage (2–7). The child, having just discovered the separate existence of its self, now becomes fixated on it. This stage is also known, therefore, as the **egocentric** stage; me, myself, and I become the principal figures in the child's environment. Children at this stage can speak—which means they can think, i.e., use symbols, and so can achieve a relation to the environment rather than merely be absorbed in it. They can have ideas about reality; but these ideas are necessarily (1) concrete rather than abstract and (2) self-centered. A well-known experiment of Piaget's illustrates pre-operational thinking. He filled two glasses with equal amounts of water and asked several five- and six-year olds whether the amounts were the same. After they agreed that it was, he proceeded to empty the water from one of the glasses into a taller, thinner one and asked the children which of the two glasses now had more water—and they answered that the taller glass did. In other words, the children did not grasp the concept "more"; they had their own interpretation of it which was, apparently, tied to the greater impression made by the big glass, and in that sense is related to (2), the child's self-centeredness.

A typical illustration of pre-operational self-centeredness is the following. A child during the pre-operational stage is capable of telling a questioner that he has a brother, but if he is then asked, "Does your brother have a brother?," he will say "No." In other words, the child cannot see the world from his brother's point of view, only his own.

(c) concrete operational (7–11). Children at this stage can now use abstract concepts—but only to describe the concrete world. The symbolic worlds of mathematics and science are now accessible to them but not those of philosophy or morality. The "reality" of death exists for them only through their exposure to concrete examples in their immediate environment, such as the death of a pet. The abstract world of ideas is intelligible only in its direct connection to the world of tangible objects.

(d) formal operational (12–). The individual is now capable of a kind of thinking that is not dependent on the here and now. One can think about justice and equality even though surrounded by their opposites. And of course the reverse is true: one can be anxious about one's own future prospects even as one enjoys being well-fed in the present. This capacity for abstract thought is, for Piaget, the definitive mark of fully developed human cognitive capacity. Do we all reach this stage? Some have suggested that close to ⅓ of American thirty-year-olds have not reached it (Kohlberg and Gilligan, 1971). The tendency to base voting decisions on the current state of one's pocketbook— or on which candidate last visited your neighborhood; or worse, which candidate **looks** most like a leader to you—would seem to vindicate the most pessimistic assessments of the average American's ability (or willingness?) to engage in formal operational thinking.

The capacity for formal operational thought includes the ability to think in terms of moral ideals. But according to Lawrence Kohlberg, a student of Piaget's, there is a type of morality corresponding (more or less) to the earlier developmental stages as well. Kohlberg has identified **six stages of moral development,** culminating in mature, abstract moral reasoning. These stages are as follows:

I. Preconventional Level

Stage 1. The punishment and obedience orientation. The physical consequences of action determine its goodness or badness regardless of the human meaning or value of these consequences. Avoidance of punishment and unquestioning deference to power are valued in their own right, not in terms of respect for an underlying moral order supported by punishment and authority (the latter being stage 4).

Stage 2. The instrumental relativist orientation. Right action consists of that which instrumentally satisfies one's own needs and occasionally the needs of others. Human relations are viewed in terms like those of the marketplace. Elements of fairness, of reciprocity, and of equal sharing are present, but they are always interpreted in a physical pragmatic way. Reciprocity is a matter of "you scratch my back and I'll scratch yours," not of loyalty, gratitude, and justice.

II. Conventional level

Stage 3. The interpersonal concordance or "good boy–nice girl" orientation. Good behavior is that which pleases or helps others and is approved by them. There is much conformity to stereotypical images of what is majority or "natural" behavior. Behavior is frequently judged by intention—"he means well" becomes important for the first time. One earns approval by being "nice."

Stage 4. The "law and order" orientation. There is orientation toward authority, fixed rules, and the maintenance of the social order. Right behavior consists of doing one's duty, showing respect for authority, and maintaining the given social order for its own sake.

III. Postconventional, autonomous, or principled level

Stage 5. The social-contract legalistic orientation, generally with utlitarian overtones. Right action tends to be defined in terms of general individual rights, and standards which have been critically examined and agreed upon by the whole society. There is a clear awareness of the relativism of personal values and opinions and a corresponding emphasis upon procedural rules for reaching consensus. Aside from what is constitutionally and democratically agreed upon, the right is a matter of personal "values" and "opinion." The result is an emphasis upon the "legal point of view," but with an emphasis upon the possibility of changing law in terms of rational considerations of social utility (rather than freezing it in terms of stage 4 "law and order") . . .

Stage 6. The universal ethical principle orientation. Right is defined by the decision of conscience in accord with self-chosen ethical principles appealing to logical comprehensiveness, universality, and consistency. These principles are abstract and ethical (the Golden Rule, the categorical imperative) . . . At heart, these are universal principles of justice, of the reciprocity and equality of human rights, and of respect for the dignity of human beings as individual persons. (Kohlberg, 1971)

Some explanatory comments: It is helpful to see these six stages—as Kohlberg does—as three pairs (corresponding roughly to the pre-operational, concrete operational, and formal operational stages of cognitive development). In the first pair of stages, individuals—as in Skinner's theory—understand right or wrong "in terms of the physical or hedonistic consequences of action." In the second pair, right and wrong are defined as obedience or disobedience to conventional **authority figures**—parents, the nation, the law—with whom the individuals at this point **identify.** Only in the final two stages are individuals able to **commit themselves** to a morality that is abstract in the sense that it is **independent of considerations both of physical consequences and the weight of established authority.** This, for Kohlberg, is truly principled moral reasoning. It culminates in Stage 6 reasoning, where the individual is committed not merely to a morality of individual freedom and respect for differences guaranteed by law, but to **absolute, universal values**—i.e., to ideas rather than to persons (such as myself who I don't want to get hurt—stages 1 and 2—or my parents or teachers who I don't want to displease—stages 3 and 4), and to ultimate truths rather than merely to rules and procedures designed to help us get along with one another (stage 5).

Stage 6, according to Kohlberg, is not reached by everybody. Indeed it is characteristic only of exceptional individuals, who are willing to sacrifice comfort and convenience for the sake of principle. A poor man's wife lays dying because her husband cannot afford to buy the medicine that alone can save her. He respects the right of property, and the laws against theft that protect that right; yet, he believes, life is more important than laws and property rights; therefore, he feels that it is morally acceptable to steal a drug if it will save his wife's life. It is this reckless risk-taking morality—which sacrifices **rules for principles**—that Kohlberg regards as the supreme type of moral reasoning. In her highly influential work, **In A Different Voice,** Carol Gilligan, a student of Kohlberg's and a Harvard psychology professor, takes an opposing view. She points out that, by Kohlberg's definition of stage six as the highest stage of moral reasoning, not only do just a limited number of people reach it, but they are more likely to be males than females. She asks: does the fact that boys are more likely than girls to exemplify stage six reasoning mean that males are inherently more moral than females, or only that they tend to be more moral **in the stage six sense, which Kohlberg mistakenly regards as the ultimate?** It is from Gilligan's work that the example of the drugstore theft comes. She found that boys were more likely than girls to judge that theft under the circumstances was justified, on the principle of the sanctity of life—and in that sense more likely to qualify as stage six thinkers. But she found that the girls' response to this moral dilemma reflected not a lower form of moral reasoning—unless one assumes with Kohlberg that stage six as defined by him is the highest—but simply a **different** one. The girls typically **resisted treating the two principles involved (property and life) as opposed.** Instead of positing the dilemma in terms of "stealing" vs. "dying," they came up with other alternatives—such as convincing the druggist to loan the medication to the poor man. In other words, the girls (because they have been trained to think this way as girls) tended to think in terms of relating, communicating, creating consensus, bringing about the desired result in the most mutually acceptable way, etc., whereas the boys (because they have been trained to think this way as boys) tended to think in terms of what the desired result was, period ("a man's gotta do what he's gotta do"). From the vantage point of stage six, the girls' "different voice" could seem wimpy (or, more precisely, **conventional**—unwilling to flaunt rules and regulations for the sake of ideals, as in stage 4, the "law and order" orientation); from the vantage point of the girls, stage six reasoning could seem self-destructive: what's the use of stealing the drug if you then go to jail for it and thus make your wife not much better off than if she'd died? (Gilligan, 1982) Unlike Kohlberg and Piaget, who describe moral and cognitive development as though they occurred in a vacuum, Gilligan's theory is sociologically relevant because it raises the question of the influence of society in the development of the self, through the example of the differential development of boys and girls. We will return to this topic below.

Psychoanalytic Theory (Freud)

Of the three major psychological theories of socialization, Freud's psychoanalytic model without a doubt has the most in common with traditional sociological approaches. Most people who know only the popular stereotypes of Freud—as a sex-crazed cocaine addict, for example—tend to think of his theories as eccentric, bizarre, and self-evidently absurd. So let us begin by pointing out the following: in comparison to behaviorism (which treats the self as a passive recipient of external stimuli) and developmentalism (which treats external environmental influences with similar disdain), Freud's view seems wholesomely—and realistically—"middle-of-the-road": he sees the socialized self as a product of the interaction between the individual and society. What makes Freud seem so radical is his insistence that this interaction is a very **tense and difficult one; that it begins the moment of birth; and that it rarely culminates in the production of a truly healthy and happy individual** (i.e., it almost inevitably leaves scars). Freud saw life as essentially tragic—like the ancient Greek dramatists to which his work is allied in many ways. But to the Greeks, the idea that life is tragic was not scandalous. Modern science changed all that. Thus, Freud found himself strangely at variance with the scientific culture that formed him, and which he never ceased expressing devotion to.

Freud's image of the development of the self is, briefly, as follows:

The human personality consists of three parts—the **ego,** the **super-ego,** and the **id**—only the last of which is present at birth. The **id** refers to appetites, impulses. The infant is controlled by its id, and thus is more like an animal than what we think of as human: it is a collection of needs, and whatever it needs it needs now. So, the infant cries when it is hungry or wet, demanding immediate attention to its needs. Soon enough, however, the child learns to control itself, to suppress its impulses; and it learns through fear of punishment—which means it does not want to give up its desires, but feels forced to. In other words, the **superego** begins to develop. This is the sense of **conscience:** instead of "I want" and "I don't want," the child begins to think in terms of "I should" and "I shouldn't." The conscience is an **internalized version of external authority;** that is, the original fear of parental punishment is gradually **transformed into the sense of guilt.** Freud recognized that civilization requires a highly developed sense of guilt among individuals; in this his image of adult behavior is quite different from Skinner's hedonistic version. We (adults) obey the norms not because (or not only or principally because) we fear being punished but because we would feel too guilty if we disobeyed. On this Freud agrees with Durkheim, who argued that abolishing laws against homicide would not appreciably increase the homicide rate, since it is not fear of punishment but the influence of cultural norms that keep most people from committing homicide. But then Freud poses a question that Durkheim doesn't: how much guilt is too much? Freud felt that the major threat to civilization (or "social order" in Durkheimian terms) is not the undercontrolled id but the overcontrolled id. Guilt means self-denial, a certain amount of which, to repeat, is necessary for there to be civilization at all—as against a world in which people stole one another's food whenever they felt hungry, the only question being whether one was sufficiently bigger than one's intended victim to get away unscathed. However, if the self never gets to express itself at all—because it has learned to regard its desires as uncivilized or for some other reason evil—it is liable at some point to explode. Hence, Freud's famous expression "the repressed always returns"—or, in modern psychological terms, frustration leads to aggression. Thus, according to Freud, the preservation of civilization, and of the self, requires not just the development of the superego, then, but of the **ego**—the rational or realistic part of the personality that seeks a balance between the self-accusations of the superego and the self-indulgence of the id. The ego is the most vulnerable, most fragile and most important aspect of the personality. Freud's motto for the ideal outcome of psychoanalytic therapy was: "Where id was, there ego shall be": the deep, pre-civilizational impulses of the organism should not be destroyed but transformed under the guidance of the ego—in such a way as to become socially harmless, and, if possible, even useful. The useless urge to daydream can in some people be transformed into inspiring works of art and philosophy; the urge to dominate can turn into the capacity for political leadership. These transformations of impulses into socially useful traits are called **sublimations.**

But for the most part Freud emphasized the precariousness of the balance struck between society and the individual; he never abandoned the idea, present in his work from its beginnings when he was more under the influence of biology and the other natural sciences that the human being like other animals is largely governed by the urge to gratify its impulses. He later (in 1920) argued that the ultimate expression of that urge, ironically, is the **instinct towards death,** the permanent peace ultimate end of all tension (as sexual gratification is a temporary release). This means that not only the most obvious requirement of civilization—instinctual self-control—but all the other basic requirements—of patient planning, listening, compromising, etc.—are in fundamental opposition to the natural tendencies of the individual.

Yet, as we said, the opposite problem is more central to Freudian thinking: the problem of excessive self-control, excessive guilt. The fear of being oneself creates neuroses, in which individuals, fearful of recognizing, let alone seeking, what they want, find pathological yet socially harmless substitute gratifications for the forbidden (usually sexual) gratification they typically seek. These substitutes include: obsessive worrying, compulsive handwashing, paranoid fantasying, and so on. These were the symptoms Freud dealt with daily in his clinical practice.

What is the sociological significance of Freudian theory? Aside from the basic similarity between Freud and classical sociological (esp., Durkheimian) theory—with their shared emphasis on society as an external force imposing itself by necessity upon the otherwise unlimited selfishness (or animality) of individuals; and, consequently, an emphasis on socialization as progress from "lower" to "higher," e.g., from the expression of emotion to the exercise of reason—Freud's work is significant because of its recognition that the socialization process is interactional, and that its results, therefore, are always imperfect.

It can also be argued that Freud's emphasis on the fragility of civilization reveals a distinctly post-modern strain in his thinking—and that it is therefore no accident that, after a period during which his work was declared obsolete by many social scientists, it is being taken up again by post-modernists. And while Durkheim's name is almost synonymous with the sociological concept of order, he too, like Freud, was acutely aware of the precariousness of social order, and the self-destructive, irrational forces that lay beneath the thin veneer of civilization—he did, after all, write a book about suicide in an era when faith in the power of scientific reason to ensure human happiness had reached its peak (just as Freud was then theorizing about the ultimately irrepressible animal drives of human beings).

At the same time Freud, like Durkheim, is vulnerable to the charge of being **naively modern** in outlook; that is, both theorists, while acknowledging the impossibility of completely subduing the instinctual forces of individuals (Freud), or of guaranteeing social solidarity in the face of conflicting individual interests (Durkheim), presupposed the desirability of doing so. In other words, both Freud and Durkheim believed that all hope for human well-being resides in the power of society to mold humanity. All good comes from society, and all evil from the individual, according to them. This is the view criticized by Bauman, as we saw above—criticized on the grounds that it leaves out of account all the **evil created by society,** in many cases by legitimately constituted political authority, and by the forces not of instinct but of culture. For it is culture that shapes people's attitudes—of undying loyalty and commitment, in many cases—towards established authority. That is why Bauman finds the Holocaust so significant: as an event it represents the greatest crisis in the history of civilization; as an event that, for fifty years, has not been seriously studied, let alone understood, it represents the greatest crisis in the history of sociology. Bauman's critique of Durkheim—which, in our interpretation, could be applied equally to Freud—is stated in the following:

> Perhaps the most formidable of Durkheim's influences on social-scientific practice was the conception of society as, essentially, an actively moralizing force. "Man is a moral being only because he lives in society." "Morality, in all its forms, is never met with except in society." "The individual submits to society and this submission is the condition of his liberation. For man's freedom consists in deliverance from blind, unthinking physical forces; he achieves this by opposing against them the great and intelligent force of society, under whose protection he shelters . . ." These and similar memorable phrases of Durkheim reverberate to this day in sociological practice . . . The alternative to the moral grip of society is not human autonomy, but the rule of animal passions. It is because the pre-social drives of the human animal are selfish, cruel and threatening that they have to be tamed and subdued . . . Take away social coercion, and humans will relapse into the barbarity from which they had been but precariously lifted by the force of society. (Bauman, 1991, pp. 172–73)

The logical consequence of such thinking is that "rule-enforcement (is) viewed as the process of humanization, rather than of suppression of one form of humanity by another." As against this, Bauman claims that "the process of socialization consists in the manipulation of moral capacity—not in its production." This means that human beings not only have the capacity to be socially indoctrinated but also "the ability to resist, escape, and survive the processing, so that at the end of the day the authority and the responsibility for moral choice rests where they resided at the start—with the human person." Many people resisted Hitler—some to the point of martyrdom. What established categories of social-scientific reasoning cover such phenomena? For Freud, as for Durkheim, "resistance" to social order necessarily belongs under the heading of the return of the repressed; it is pathology, deviance. And that is because they have no conception of a pre-social morality (such as that referred to in Arendt's phrase, "animal pity," cited by Bauman).

In sum, we are suggesting two major problems with Freudian theory: an underestimation of the moral resources of the person and an overestimation of those of society. This has a doubly distorting effect on Freud's image of the individual in the socialization process. On the one hand the sheer animality of the pre-social self is exaggerated; on the other hand the "animality" of the so-called civilized behavior of socialized individuals goes unnoticed. What teaches us more about the terrifying unlimitedness of human greed—the wailing of a hungry infant or the civilized, rational behavior of corporate executives who raise their salaries while laying off workers in times of declining profits? Which is to be feared most—the "instinctual" aggressiveness of a toddler who picks a fight with a playmate, or the socially produced aggressiveness of soldiers eager to kill for God and country? Where is sexuality more out of control—in the polysexual fantasies of childhood or in the socially approved domination of women that characterizes normal adult male heterosexuality (in which traditionally, for example, sex has been understood as a husband's right, for which there is no corresponding right of a wife to refuse)? Since Freud spends so much time describing individual pathological behavior, it is only fair to criticize him for not recognizing the social origins of individual pathology. Rape, for example, has as much to do with norms of male heterosexual aggression, which it has taken beyond accepted limits— which are rather vague: is it rape when he "twists her arm" figuratively or only literally?—as it does with the idiosyncratic needs of particular individuals. (Rape is an apt example since few convicted rapists are psychologically disturbed.)

SOCIOLOGICAL THEORIES OF SOCIALIZATION

There are two classical sociological theories of socialization—G.H. Mead's and Charles Cooley's. We will briefly describe and evaluate each of them.

G. H. Mead

Mead regards the self as the product of a 3-stage process of development. In each of these stages interaction with others is the principal impetus to self-development, and a pre-requisite for progress to a higher level of maturity. The three stages are as follows: (a) imitation. In this stage, which lasts until about age 3, children express interest in the people around them by mimicking their behavior. What they don't imitate is the other's state of mind or feelings. As in Piaget's sensorimotor stage, children at this stage are only aware of externals; they inhabit a world of shadows rather than reality. But this primitive fascination with the behavior of others evolves into the (b) play stage, in which children not only imitate behavior but **identify with** their objects of imitation. As Mead puts it, they begin to **take the role of others**—by dressing up in grown-up clothes and pretending to be mommy, for example. Playing with dolls is an obvious example of role-taking: the child interacts with the doll **from the point of view of a parent.** This **ability to see the world from another's point of view** is a necessary condition for meaningful interaction, but not a sufficient condition. For, in the play stage, the child is limited to identification with particular others—parents, teachers, siblings, etc. For children to develop normal selves they must continue on to the (c) game stage, which becomes possible in the early school years. The basic difference between the game and play stages is that in the game stage children are able to see the world from the point of view of others regardless of whether they know them or not, sheerly on the basis of their knowledge of the position of the other(s) within the social context at hand. Games illustrate this clearly. In playing baseball, for example, you know what to expect the first baseman and the shortstop to do when a ground ball is hit to the latter regardless of whether you have any personal acquaintance with either of them. You know what to expect of them—you can see the game, so to speak, from their point of view—because you know the roles that have been assigned to them, and thus the behavior to be expected of them regardless of their particularity as individuals. This means knowing how "people in general" rather than how particular people are likely to act—because you know their social roles.

Society produces others-in-general: shortstops who in general (regardless of personal character traits) behave like this; store clerks who in general behave like that, etc. Because of our knowledge of the **generalized other**—the other produced by society's rules and role assignments—we are able to move through the world competently, knowing what to expect of others and what others expect of us on account of our positions in relation to one another in the social world. The socialized self, then, resembles a sociologist in that both of them understand individuals in terms of their social roles. The sociologist, of course, does so consciously and explicitly, and for the purpose of being able to explain the behavior; the everyday actor does so "naturally," without reflecting on it, and for the practical purpose of surviving in the world.

Organized social life for Mead is thus very much like a game: individuals called "parents" behave in certain ways just as individuals called "shortstops" do, all in accordance with the rules—which do, however, allow for some individual variation in how the role can be performed while still being considered competent, i.e., acceptable-under-the-rules.

What makes this model sociological is not only the emphasis on the socially produced self but on the overriding importance of the social context for determining what actors should and do expect of each other. We expect the first baseman and the shortstop to behave this or that way because they are now engaged in playing the game of baseball; but, more to the point, first basemen and shortstops **only exist within the game** of baseball. In the same way, parents only exist within the institution (the "game") called the "family." Thus, the social context doesn't merely constrain or mold us (as for Freud and Durkheim); it produces us.

As in the case of Freud, there is an emphasis in Mead on the incompleteness of the socialization process. But he conceives of this incompleteness differently. For him the self never becomes completely at one with its various social roles; there is always something left over, a remainder, an element of sheer individual impulsiveness and spontaneity. Mead calls this unsocialized aspect of the self the "I"; the sum of our social roles he calls the "me." What Mead has done here is quite profound: he has tried to describe socialization in such a way as to emphasize the power of society without forgetting that a pre-condition of the socialization process (which we saw in our description of the imitation and play stages) is **the individual's active, spontaneous, enthusiastic participation in the process of interaction. That enthusiasm is not itself a product of society**—yet, by the time of the game stage certainly, it is placed in the service of conformity to societal norms. This spontaneous spirit, this "I" which makes the "me" possible, is not a merely anti-social, destructive instinctual force like the Freudian id. Indeed, it itself has **led to** the development of the socialized self. The existence of the I means that in principle **individuals are never totally subject to the rules of the game;** they have the potential to evaluate, to resist, and to creatively transform the social environment to which they have subjected themselves. In this sense it would seem that Mead's analysis is not subject to the criticism that Bauman levels against modern sociology as represented by Durkheim.

Charles Cooley/Erving Goffman

Cooley depicts individuals as considerably more passive in the socialization process than Mead does. His basic contribution to the theory of socialization is his concept of the **looking-glass self,** according to which your self-concept is based on what you think others think of you. To appreciate this insight we have to appreciate the impact that self-concepts have on the real lives of individuals. A self-concept is the way you think about yourself. The fact is that long before you reach adulthood you have formed a comprehensive self-concept; you have assessed your strengths and weaknesses and basically graded yourself in all the socially relevant categories: attractiveness, intelligence, social skills, and the rest. How positively or negatively you judge yourself will influence not just your attitudes but your behavior: if you think you are not intelligent enough to become a doctor, you won't try to become one; if you define yourself as physically frail, you won't try out for sports, and so on. Now Cooley asks: where do these self-assessments come from? And his answer is, they come from (our perception of) others' assessments of us. Where did you learn that you are "cute" (or uncute) if not from other people's reactions to you? Where did you learn that you are bright if not from the comments of teachers and parents?

Would people ever think of judging themselves unless they were first judged? Obviously not: a baby waking up in its crib doesn't hide from mommy because he is afraid she will find his breath offensive. Being "self-conscious" in this way is definitely learned; society sets the standards for "pleasant-smelling," we learn those standards, and we learn how to live up to them. It is in terms of external standards, then, that we judge ourselves. That is why Cooley uses the metaphor of the looking-glass, the mirror. To look in a mirror—which every adult (i.e., every socialized self) does before leaving the house in the morning, even though it is not literally necessary (blind persons can dress, bathe, etc.)—is to see oneself as an object from the point of view of the outside world (the point of view we adopt when looking at ourselves). Consulting the mirror before leaving the house means that we need first to assure ourselves that "they" approve of us before we can approve of ourselves; when we see ourselves as acceptable in their eyes (the mirror's), we allow ourselves to leave—and not before. To the argument that the opinion of others is irrelevant ("I don't care what they think, I know I'm good"), Cooley responded:

> If failure or disgrace arrives, if one suddenly finds that the faces of men show coldness or contempt instead of the kindness and deference that he is used to, he will perceive from the shock, the fear, the sense of being outcast and helpless, that he was living in the minds of others without knowing it. (Cooley, 1902, p. 208)

When the discouragement of others becomes too consistent or too severe, a profound crisis in self-confidence can occur, and can lead to aggressive or self-destructive behavior. As we will see in Chapter VIII, one of the major contemporary sociological theories of deviant behavior— labeling theory—is based on the concept of the looking-glass self. In Cooley the emphasis is more on normal self-development—the way in which, for example, being treated with respect encourages us to continue behaving respectably. Labeling theory develops the other side of the story: if you are treated as though there were something wrong with you, the chances are good that eventually something **will** be wrong with you.

The weakness in Cooley's model lies in its **unrealistically passive image** of the individual. In this respect, an important modification of Cooley's insights is represented by Erving Goffman's theory of **impression management.** Goffman, like Cooley, treats individuals as virtually captive to the need for societal approval; the difference is that Goffman ascribes to people considerable ability to **manipulate the reactions of others** and thus win that approval. "Impression management" means managing, or controlling, the impressions that the individual makes on others in the course of interaction. Now there is one situation in life where everyone admits they are attempting to do impression management—a job interview. Far from being yourself, you attempt at a job interview to control the other's impression of you through a deliberate, sustained impersonation of the "right candidate" for the job. In effect what Goffman is saying is that all interactions are like that; we are always doing a self-presentation, i.e., presenting selected aspects of ourselves in order to be seen the way we wish to be seen. If we spend so much of our time trying to impress others, to avoid embarrassing performances, i.e., performances that discredit us in the eyes of others, to be seen favorably, or at least not unfavorably, to stand out from the crowd or melt into it, to be visible or invisible as the situation requires—if we work so hard at these things, it must be because the opinion of others is all-important to us. Goffman more or less assumes that; and his highly readable and entertaining works contain detailed descriptions of the various strategies people employ to evoke the desired audience reaction. How our ordinarily mean parents act nice in front of our friends; how they cheerfully invite company into the living room, even though the rest of the time no one is allowed to set foot in it—these are typically Goffmanesque phenomena. Part of the reason for Goffman's appeal is that he articulates the feeling people have of living in a world where images are more important than reality, where a President's credibility rating is more important than his actual record, and the ability to appear "tough" ranks high on the list of valued political character traits.

In Goffman's world people are "operators" with a pathetically modest goal—to be socially accepted. It is as though in Goffman's world the creative energies of Mead's "I" are totally at the service of enhancing the "me"—like a creative artist who goes into advertising. Goffman's account is undoubtedly realistic. But, while it has great descriptive force, it has little explanatory value. Is Goffman describing a process of self-alienation that is inherent in the socialization process? Or is he describing a peculiarly modern (or post-modern) social phenomenon? If so, what is it about modern society that has led to the self becoming an impression manager? Does it have to do, perhaps, with the modern rise of secondary groups—creating a situation in which people have neither the need nor the desire nor the time to really get to know us, but have the need to know just enough to know what to make of us? (Thus, if you are dressed a certain way, you can instantly "communicate" to someone that you are middle-class, respectable, trustworthy, etc.) But if it is a modern phenomenon, is there an underlying "real" self whose characteristics and potential can be analyzed once the peculiar conditions of modern society are theoretically put off to one side?

GENDER SOCIALIZATION

All the preceding theories are subject to the critique that they are too general. The psychological theories tend to be put forward as descriptions of universal law-like processes of development; but even the less scientific-sounding sociological accounts appear to make similar claims. Of the theories we've described, Giligan's alone raises the question of the social production of particular types of selves—i.e., a typical male self and a typical female self. In a sense sociologists have known about the gendered self all along; they have long spoken of **gender socialization**—how males and females are raised to adopt the attitudes and behaviors society considers appropriate for males and females. Society doesn't mold us simply with a view to making us into normal adults but into normal male and female adults. What Gilligan's work adds to the sociology of gender socialization is evidence of how deep the socially produced difference between male and female is—that it affects even our moral reasoning, our conceptions of right and wrong. In our culture, of course, we commonsensically allow for individual differences of opinion based on different values, beliefs, and so on; that is an expression of our commitment to individualism. And we even allow that such differences of opinion can and will exist on serious questions of morality. But that such differences are among other things "gendered"—that they are patterned, the product of typical socialization practices that are typically different for males and females—offends against our common-sense individualism. Common sense seemingly accepts the centrality of gender differences in every case—often exaggerating the differences and attributing them to nature (as in: men can do certain occupations better than women)—except that of moral reasoning, making value-judgments, etc. The latter are supposed to exemplify the free exercise of conscience rather than the non-rational workings of nature. What sociology does is see **all** differences between men and women (beyond the functional difference in reproduction) as the product of socialization.

Gender socialization is an important topic for two reasons. First, it can be used to supplement the general theories of socialization since it involves a discussion of how particular selves (in this case, the normal male and the normal female) are produced in particular societies (in this case, our own). Secondly, while common sense may disagree with sociology on the sources of the differences between men and women (common sense attributing most of them to nature and sociology attributing most of them to society), it is not a violation of common sense—even if it is not something everyday actors ordinarily reflect on—to assert that the experience of being male or female is practically inseparable from the experience of being a self at all. Whenever we encounter another human being we immediately encounter him—him? or should we say her?—as male or female; before we notice anything else about them, we take note of their gender. And we see ourselves reflected in his or her eyes as male or female; i.e., we are immediately conscious of ourselves as gendered persons. To what extent, and how, this influences our perception of, and behavior towards, the other, is too vast a topic to discuss here. In some cases the influence is obvious—as when a male encounters a female in a singles' bar. In other cases the influence may be less conscious—as when a male student encounters his female professor—but that doesn't mean it is non-existent. Is there any doubt that the content of same-sex conversations typically differs from that of cross-sex conversations, that men do "guys' talk" and women "girls' talk"—as they have been taught to do?

AGENTS OF GENDER SOCIALIZATION

People become male or female because that is what they have been taught to be, and because they have been given no choice in the matter, i.e., it was never suggested that they could be something else, or that they ought to first decide what they want to be with regard to gender before committing themselves to the process of becoming it. The gender socialization process, like all learning, begins at home; it is continued in school, where not only teachers but peers contribute to the process. And throughout, especially in our day, the mass media play a vital supporting role. The influence of these various agents of socialization will be described briefly in the following.

The Home

Parents treat sons and daughters differently from the earliest stages of infancy. For example, parents typically talk more to baby girls than baby boys and are more solicitous of them when they injure themselves. In these and other ways parents communicate their perception of their child to their child. And the perception they are communicating is that boys are more self-sufficient, and stronger, than girls. This message used to be reinforced quite concretely through the use of different dress codes for boys and girls: blue for boys and pink for girls, jeans for boys and dresses for girls, etc. The latter clearly exemplifies the interactionist concept of the **self-fulfilling prophecy:** girls were defined as more delicate, less physical creatures than boys; therefore they were given dresses rather than jeans to wear; therefore they couldn't play as roughly at the playground as boys; therefore they grew up to be more delicate. Dress codes for children have broken down: girls and boys both typically wear jeans, overalls, etc., and now meet, therefore, more as equals at the playground than they did in the past. But interestingly—and this is something we will see again in discussing peer group pressure—the breakdown of the dress code is incomplete; or, more precisely, dress codes have **half**-broken down: girls can now wear what used to be considered strictly boys' clothes, but boys cannot yet wear what are considered girls' clothes. A boy in a dress, or a pink outfit, is as subject to ridicule today as he would've been in the past. Why would this be? And if the ridicule is justified, why isn't similar treatment justified in the case of girls who have the nerve to wear overalls or wear blue?

Parents further influence their children's self-concepts through the toys they buy for them—which, traditionally, have been as gender-specific as clothing. Girls are still given dolls to play with. This prepares them for the domestic tasks they will later be assigned; playing with dolls means playing at the care-giving, nurturing (including feeding and diaper-changing) role. Boys, on the other hand, are given "action figures": soldiers and other dynamic characters whom the boys send off into battle or some other challenging activity calling for physical fortitude and courage. Interestingly, the boys' role in this is not to change the figures' clothes or dress their wounds (buying action figures, unlike buying Barbie dolls, does not entail buying endless outfits and accessories for them, too); rather than take care of the figures, boys identify with them. They vicariously participate in the action—they become the soldiers—while girls merely "relate to" their dolls. Even within the same species of toy, so to speak, gender differences abound. The makers of the wildly popular Troll toys, not content with their apparently genderless money-maker, came out with a line of warrior trolls for boys. (They don't say the warriors are for boys, although the children playing with them in the commercials are all boys.) Here there seems to be less cross-over occurring than in the case of clothing. However, we seem to be talking more about the influence of toy manufacturers, advertising, and so on, than of parents. But perhaps this can't be helped: the role of parents, after all, is to—more or less, depending on their income, their parenting "philosophy," etc.—buy their kids what they want, and today what they want is derived more from their interaction with the TV screen than with their parents.

School

Schools teach children by example as well as by explicit instruction. For instance, the disproportionate number of male to female principals communicates to students that the "real world"—of which the school is the first sustained example to which most children are exposed—is run by men. Unless the question why this is so is raised in the classroom (or somewhere else, such as in the home) children are likely to assume what all normal people assume about unquestioned phenomena: they are to be treated as natural, i.e., as the way things are supposed to be. As for explicit content, recent studies of elementary school texts reveal that gender stereotyping is not yet a thing of the past: male leading characters outnumber female leading characters; heroic, adventuresome activities are more often done by males than females; females are still disproportionately cast in a domestic role, etc. (N). Of course it can be said that teachers are very significant authority figures for children, and, since through most of primary school these tend to be women, this must offset the effects of textbook stereotyping or the presence of a male principal. But then throughout early childhood mothers are in most cases more significant authority figures than fathers, yet traditionally their subordinate status in the household (not to mention the outside world) has had a much greater impact on shaping the attitudes of children towards sex roles—convincing girls that they are destined to take care of a husband and children, and boys that they should expect to be waited on by their wives—than their relative power over them has.

But the most pernicious school experiences for girls typically occur later on, in high school. They are: (1) the experience of being discouraged from pursuing subjects that are supposed to be for males only, such as mathematics and science, and even being discouraged from getting too serious about academic pursuits, period; and (2) the overwhelming likelihood of being the victim of sexual harassment at some point or another during their high school years.

Peers

Developing the capacity for normal peer relations is as important an element in effecting a successful transition from childhood to adulthood—a transition in which the child learns to give up its dependency on the comforting, all-consuming love represented by parents and the home—as learning to be a competent student is. They are the precursors of the social skills necessary for adult survival. Of course the home environment itself has a strong influence on the child's ability to develop competency in this area, but here we want to look at the typical influence of peers on the child, i.e., on the gender socialization of the child. The most important thing to note is that peers, notorious for enforcing group conformity, do so in the area of gender, too: they exert tremendous pressure on peer group members to live up to the group's definition of appropriate male or female behavior. This becomes more pronounced as children approach adolescence, and become increasingly self-conscious about their sexuality, but it is present earlier as well. The presence of pressure to follow the rules, as well as the existence of the rules themselves, become evident when violations occur and the violator is punished for it. Violations of group definitions of appropriate behavior typically lead to ridicule, if not ostracism from the group. Girls are routinely disparaged as "ugly"—by girls as well as boys, for both have bought into the wider culture's idea that girls are valuable to the extent that they are pretty (just as "real boys" are tough)—and into its definition of what "pretty" is. Even in the early grades there is sex-stereotyping among peer groups: after all, these are the same children who, at home, were already playing with dolls or G.I. Joes, according to their sex. But interestingly, while girls who deliberately forsake the girl role to imitate boys are not considered serious rule-violators, boys who forsake the boy role most definitely are. Once again, the cross-over only works in one direction. We all know this from our everyday knowledge of playground taunts: girls are tomboys but boys are sissies. Logically, the violators should be treated equally, since the violations are equivalent. Instead, we have a situation that resembles that of the girl in blue vs. the boy in pink. Why the difference? Why is it worse for a boy to want to be a girl than for a girl to want to be a boy? A girl who wants to be a boy is cute; a boy who wants to be a girl is sick. This could only be because the boy role is considered superior or more desirable (by the normal person) than the girl role. This doesn't mean that the girl who wishes to cross over isn't also subject to ridicule if she persists. But refraining, at least in the initial stages, from diagnosing her as sick is a way of acknowledging that her aspirations are understandable: who wouldn't want to be a boy, given their superiority, seems to be the message behind the empathy.

Peers are important in this respect not only because they come increasingly to dominate the child's social scene, as parents increasingly recede into the background, but because their insistence on conformity is actually much greater than that of the typical parents. Parents do not, or do not consistently, convey the message that non-conformity is absolutely unacceptable; they do not go around calling their effeminate son a faggot, or to ridicule him because he has acne. That is left to his "friends." (And when parents do exhort their children to conform, more often than not they justify it on practical grounds—you ought to straighten out in order to survive, not because non-conformity is pathological.)

The Media

Throughout this entire period during which parents, teachers, and peers in one form or another are teaching children what is expected of boys and girls, the TV is on: between the ages of 6 and 18, the average child spends more time in front of the TV than in school (15,000 to 13,000). What impact does this have on gender socialization? First of all, children's toys, and their accompanying gender stereotypes, are advertised principally by means of television. But secondly, the shows themselves are loaded with stereotypes. Let us look only at shows that are usually regarded as good influences, or at least as not being bad ones. All the leading Sesame Street Muppets (Big Bird, Oscar, Grover, Cookie Monster, Telly, Elmo, Bert and Ernie) are boys. The same is true of the Muppet Babies—with the exception of Miss Piggy, who is mainly an object of ridicule. And she is ridiculed in sex-stereotyped ways: as a lovelorn female who must get her clutches on her beloved Kermit (who considers her a pest); as a vain female, obsessed with her beauty (which is illusory) and with material things in general rather than principles (Kermit's domain); as a bossy female, who must always have the last word and have her way. But, as with life in the peer group, sex-stereotyping on children's TV is more obvious and more intense on shows designed for pre-adolescent and adolescent viewers. Here girls are typically treated as being more interested in relationships than boys are, while boys are depicted as typically obsessed with girls' looks ("liberation" for women consists in their ability to be as obsessed with guys' looks as guys are with theirs). The argument that this is merely describing the world as it is, is true but irrelevant: when children learn about our political leaders, for example, they do not at the same time learn about the sex scandals or political corruption enveloping many of them, although adults read about such things. With regard to gendered behavior, the world "is" this or that way largely because boys and girls see certain behaviors as the only realistic option, since it is all they have ever been exposed to. Even characters who allegedly depart from gender stereotypes do so only in very limited ways. Steve Urkel, for example, became famous as a non-macho—"nerdy"—young Black male. Yet his difference with regard to gender roles is consistently treated as a weakness rather than a strength: he has the mind of a womanizer but not the body.

This account of gender socialization does not invalidate the standard sociological theories; instead, it seeks to supplement them by treating the socialized self as a gender-socialized self. In fact the classical socialization concepts can be useful in helping us understand how the gendered self emerges. For example, the process by which the various agents of socialization influence self-development is the same process described by Cooley: children become the male and female selves that they perceive these agents see them as. And that can only be because they agree with them (or don't imagine how they could disagree). A tough boy is a boy who acts tough because he believes he is tough; and he believes he is tough because his parents have always treated him as though he were. The gendered world is no less a world of looking-glass selves than the non-gendered world described in Cooley's own writings. Goffman is relevant, too; he seems to describe actors who have reached a higher level of reflection than Cooley's actors: once we realize that what is real is simply what is perceived as real, then we can attempt to manipulate others' perceptions of us. The gendered world, then, can be seen as one in which individuals strive continuously to create impressions of themselves as, for example, emphatically masculine or feminine—through decisions in the way they speak, dress, and so on; choices, however, which are radically unfree in the sense that they are circumscribed by, and continually refer back to, society's definition of recognizably masculine and feminine looks and behavior, which the impression manager seeks merely to abide by.

Similarly, we imitate, take the roles of, and learn to interact in patterned ways with the gendered selves in our environment—and in this process become competent adult selves, i.e., selves who know how to behave in accordance with the various roles society has assigned to us, not least of which in significance is the role of male or female. But alone among the theories of socialization, Mead allows for the continued existence of a part of the self that has eluded the socialization process. If his scenario is applicable to gender socialization, it would mean that the "I" is, among other things, non-gendered—and that therefore the reader of Mead who finds something refreshing about this concept of the unsocialized "I" would, to be consistent, have to acknowledge the possibility and desirability of a human vantage point that is truly beyond the socially constructed vantage points of male and female.

7

STRATIFICATION

INTRODUCTORY REMARKS

Social stratification refers to the organization of society into different groups such that membership in one brings with it a greater or lesser amount of social rewards than membership in another. In modern societies, these groups are called **social classes.** While the fact that racial and ethnic differences tend to divide us is well-known and highly publicized, the fact that we are divided by class is not—at least not in the United States. Yet sociologists consider these latter differences of equal if not greater significance. It is often said, for example, that there is a white America and a Black America (recently and powerfully by Andrew Hacker; see Hacker, 1992). But it is also true that there is a lower-class America (regardless of race), a working-class America, a middle-class America, and an upper-class America. Imagine two people of the same social class who belong to two different ethnic groups. Then imagine two members of the same ethnic group, one rich and one working-class. Which two do you think would have an easier time becoming comfortable with one another? Looked at this way, it can be argued that our society is more divided (and united) by class than by race.

Depending on the social class you belong to, you receive greater or fewer social rewards than members of other classes. What are these rewards? The most obvious unequally distributed reward in society is wealth. Closely associated with wealth are power, or social and political influence, and prestige, or social standing—"status" in everyday usage. Usually possessing a great amount of one of these implies possessing a great amount of the other two, but not always: an Ivy League university professor enjoys high prestige but may possess merely average wealth, while a plumber may have greater wealth but less prestige than the professor. And a bureaucratic official may possess more power yet less prestige and wealth than either of them. Therefore, in trying to determine an individual's class membership, sociologists take into account these three basic dimensions of class (at least) rather than just wealth.

Among sociologists, the idea that class involves a combination of characteristics and is not reducible to wealth alone was first introduced by Max Weber, and stands as an implicit criticism of Karl Marx's view that all power (including the power to command respect—i.e., prestige) is ultimately based on economic power. Weber's view seems more realistic as a description of modern societies, in which technological and other developments have led to the creation of a new social type—the expert, of which there are, of course, various sub-types—which Marx's analysis of class in terms of property ownership leaves completely out of account. Managers, bureaucrats, scientists, technicians, lawyers—all of these figures are typically employed by others, and may even be at their mercy in the sense of being dependent on them for any possible career advancement. Yet they hardly resemble Marx's "working class." The essential difference is not that they have more wealth than the working class—though that is true, and it is not unimportant—but that **they may possess power and prestige out of all proportion to the amount of wealth they possess.** Thus, the type of work one does translates into a higher or lower level of prestige that doesn't necessarily correlate with income level. And power can result from either wealth or prestige. A recognized academic expert on foreign affairs (low wealth, high prestige) may be able to influence government policy while a successful electrician (high wealth, low prestige)—even one with strong opinions on foreign policy—may not. Yet this too is a matter of degree; if the wealth is great enough, power will surely follow. The owner of a multi-billion dollar business that employs thousands of people and trades on a large scale with various foreign countries will have his views on foreign policy taken seriously by government officials even though he is no more of an expert than the electrician is, and even if the product his company sells is, "objectively" speaking, of less real use to the world than the services provided by the electrician (such that he is "deserving" of lower prestige). Yet the question implicitly raised by the Weberian approach is whether it is the businessman's wealth that gives him power or the perception that he possesses expertise because of his experience in international trade—which would mean that his power reflects prestige more than wealth, since it is based on the type of work he does rather than on the income generated by it. On the other hand, how could one ever completely separate the prestige from the wealth? Would he have as much power if he were a failed businessman with a lot of experience (the way some of the greatest baseball managers were mediocre players)? Is being impressed with the businessman's expertise merely a concealed or euphemistic form of being impressed by his wealth?

Furthermore, wealth can often be "converted" into prestige even in cases where it cannot be converted into power. We might regard an affluent plumber as someone with little power or prestige. But what if the plumber buys a house in an exclusive neighborhood, sends his children to expensive private schools, becomes involved in community affairs, and begins to insinuate himself into the local social network? What would any longer distinguish him from the doctors and lawyers who are his neighbors?

The fact is that sociology cannot quantify, or state in law-like terms, the relation among wealth, power, and prestige; nor can it **disprove the claim that wealth is the ultimate source of class membership.** At the same time most sociologists would maintain that a full description of a particular social class will include a description of the amount of wealth, power, and prestige associated with it.

Weber's composite approach, we noted, is especially useful when applied to the circumstances of modern society. (It is interesting to note that, despite the often bewildering complexity of Weber's work, there is a basic unity to it all. His analysis of the social production of experts in a modern society, in the context of the topic of stratification, is clearly related to his analysis of the development of bureaucracy in modern society as part of the general theory of social organization. And both are related to his analysis of the relation between Protestantism—a peculiarly **modern, rational** form of religiosity—and (modern, rational) capitalism. It has been taken up in recent sociology by a number of theorists—many of whom seek to combine Weber's insights with the earlier model suggested by Marx. The most influential of such attempts is probably that of Ralf Dahrendorf, who argues that modern capitalist societies such as ours invest power in **two separate but connected groups:** large business owners and an elite of experts (including managers, the judiciary, government bureaucrats, and legislators) (Dahrendorf, 1959).

Now aside from wealth, power, and prestige, there are a great many other vitally important goods—for example, **education and health care**—that are, obviously, unequally distributed by class.

But in addition the sociological analysis of stratification includes an examination of the influence of social class on aspects of life which in the common-sense view **might appear completely unrelated to class.** The likelihood of your getting divorced (or, for that matter, getting married in the first place); attending religious services regularly (and the type of services you attend); being the victim of a violent crime; being a smoker or a junk-food "addict"; being politically liberal or conservative; being a jogger; dying of heart disease or lung cancer; living to age 70— all these and more are influenced by social class membership.

Sociologists believe that class inequality is no more "natural" than racial inequality; instead it exists because societies have created it. Therefore it requires justification—or if there is no justification, then at least an analysis of how it originated and how it can possibly be eradicated. Is social stratification necessary? Is it desirable? And if so, how are we to balance its necessity and desirability against the suffering it causes? In other words: what **degree** of stratification is permissible? Does the fact that not everyone can be rich mean that some people have to be poor? If poverty is a problem, is excess wealth too a problem (since the excess could be used to reduce poverty but isn't), even if the excess is "deserved"? These are difficult questions, and it is the business of sociological theory to address them. But first we need to look at some facts—that is, statistics. Why? Of course, statistics are available, especially on people's economic status, but that doesn't explain why it is necessary to look at them. Think of it this way. Someone says, "The existence of poverty in a country as rich as ours is a national disgrace." That may be true; but we are not in a position to decide whether it is true until we know the extent of poverty (and of wealth) in America. Is one out of every 1,000 people poor—or one out of two? Obviously we need to know the answer to this question in order to qualify as competent participants in any debate about poverty; and the answer involves numbers. Statistics are **a way of describing or picturing reality;** at least that is how they will be used in what follows. We don't believe that statistics can prove a point; the actual answer to our statistical question about poverty—not 1 out of 1,000 or 1 out of 2 but about 1 in 7 is poor in America—doesn't prove the proposition that there is "too much poverty" in America.

Yet, for those who do think there is too much poverty in America, the statistic not only can but must be used—**as an indication of what (for them) "too much" means.** And further: to get anybody who is as yet undecided to accept the idea that there is too much poverty, we need to provide these statistical illustrations of what we are talking about. At the very least, then, **the use of statistics is part of the process of communicating meaning.**

This is not to deny that statistics have always to be interpreted, and that they can be interpreted in various ways. Part of the interpretive process is to **assign a context** to statistics—reflecting the recognition that statistics have no meaning in and of themselves. "Context" includes **semantic** as well as **historical** context. For example, when we say that "x% are poor," the interpretation we give to this statistic—whether we see it as indicative of a "national disgrace" or something quite different—depends on the meaning of the word "poor" (=the semantic context). Some observers view the government's definition of poverty, on which the statistic is based, as too generous; that would give them a reason not to consider poverty a serious problem. As for historical context, we would need to ask whether the current poverty rate is higher or lower than, say, the rate ten years ago; if it is lower, then even agreeing that x% poor is too many poor would not necessarily lead us to regard the figure as scandalous; instead, we could interpret it as a sign of progress.

All this is part of the normal give-and-take in the evaluation of statistical evidence in the social sciences and elsewhere. But one thing has to be ruled out of bounds; that is, there is one essential limitation to interpretive freedom: we are not permitted to "interpret" statistics out of existence (unless we have some evidence that they are spurious; preumably U.S. government figures, which we will use for the most part in our discussion of wealth and poverty in America, are not). **There is a difference between interpreting reality and denying reality.** The facts cannot force us to see reality a certain way; but they can—and should—force us to interpret reality **in such a way as to account for these facts**. A common way of violating this rule of reasoned or scholarly debate is to argue ad hominem: instead of refuting a suggested interpretation of the facts, or offering an alternative one, we attack the interpreters—questioning their motives, for example, in digging up these facts, etc.

There are various argumentative strategies—making bold statements without any statistical or other factual backing; presenting statistics as though no interpretation of them, no provision of semantic or historical context, were necessary; "refuting" statistical evidence by personally attacking their source (attacking the messenger rather than the message)—which, to repeat an earlier point, may be the norm for TV and radio talk shows (and, often, political campaigns), but have no place in the social sciences.

THE AMERICAN SOCIAL CLASS SYSTEM

Whether the emphasis is on wealth (what one owns) or income (what one earns), the United States is stratified according to class. 1% of the population owns more than the bottom 90%;

the top 20% of wage-earners earn almost 50% of all income; the rich are getting richer and the poor are getting poorer. Here, then, is a brief description of the social classes in the U.S. today.

Upper Class (about 1% of the population)

If class is defined in terms of wealth, power, and prestige, then belonging to the upper class means possessing all these things in abundance. But in fact we have to be more precise and speak of the privileged few who enjoy such rewards as the **upper upper class**. The upper upper class is the "nobility": a small group of old families who have possessed significant wealth for generations. Every country, no matter how democratic, has its nobility, and ours is no exception. Some of the better-known members of the upper upper class in our society are the DuPonts, Mellons, Rockefellers, Astors, and Vanderbilts. All these families are "old money." While, as we shall see, belonging to the lower upper class and the upper middle class means making a lot of money at work, belonging to the upper upper class means making a lot of money **without having to work**. Present-day members of the upper upper class have inherited their wealth; they live off the profits from assets first acquired by previous generations of family members, and investments made with such profits. Often members of the upper upper class go into politics—the Rockefellers, who have produced a Vice-President (Nelson) and a Senator (John D. IV), are a prime example—thus enhancing the political influence they would have enjoyed anyway just by belonging to the upper upper class. It is one thing to be a bank executive (and to belong, thereby, to the upper middle class); it's another thing entirely to own a bank, as the Rockefellers do (the Chase Manhattan Bank). The upper upper class owns major units of the economy.

One does not become a member of the upper upper class; one can only be born into it. **Even marrying into it is highly unlikely**: more than any other class, the upper upper class is characterized by a kind of self-segregation from the rest of society: members socialize among themselves at exclusive clubs, vacation together at exclusive resorts, and send their children to be educated among their own at exclusive schools. Little is left to chance in the selection of eligible marriage partners.

Finally, a characteristic of most members of the upper upper class is that they are "WASPs"—that is, white, Anglo-Saxon (of British extraction or closely related) Protestants. And, by virtue of their tendency to marry only within their own group, they stay that way. Significant wealth and power in the U.S. has always been disproportionately held by WASPs. For example, most U.S. Presidents have been WASPs. The most obvious exception was John F. Kennedy, who was Roman Catholic; but also included as exceptions would be others such as Jimmy Carter and Bill Clinton, who, as Baptists, are Protestants but, technically speaking, not WASPs, since the "Protestant" in WASP is usually intended to refer to a handful of elite denominations long favored by the wealthy—especially the Episcopal and Presbyterian churches (the American versions of the Church of England

and the Church of Scotland, respectively), while the median income for Baptists is the lowest of any major Protestant denomination.

Not all fantastically wealthy Americans are WASPs; nor have all such people inherited rather than earned their wealth. In other words, there is "new money" as well as "old money." In some cases the new money may even be more substantial than the old. But these "nouveau riche" are not part of the exclusive circle of old families; while they have the wealth, they may not have the prestige or the power (the political connections) that aristocrats have by definition. On the other hand their wealth is so great that it would be absurd to include them in the middle class, even the upper middle class. Thus sociologists have created the category lower upper class to describe them. The lower upper class includes wildly successful entrepreneurs such as Donald Trump, Sam Walton (the late founder of the Wal-Mart chain), and Ross Perot, as well as highly-paid celebrities—athletes, musicians, movie stars, and so on. An All-Star major league ballplayer may be paid quite well, but that doesn't mean that a Rockefeller would consider marrying his daughter, or that a President would consider his advice on how to control the Federal deficit. Of course those members of the lower upper class who are business persons will have more political influence than entertainers will, depending on how many people they employ and how much wealth they control.

Middle Class (about 40–45% of the population)

While not everyone who isn't absolutely poor or fabulously rich is—as the mass media seem to suggest—"middle class," the middle class is nevertheless a quite sizable group, and the one to which most college-educated people (as well as many others) belong. As with the upper class, it is necessary to divide the middle class into two groups—an **upper middle** and a **lower middle**.

Upper Middle Class (about 10% of the population)

An average-income working couple driving past an exclusive suburban neighborhood of attractive Tudor or ranch-style houses with spacious, well-kept lawns is likely to think they are seeing where "rich people" live; but in fact they are seeing where the upper middle class lives. The houses of the rich can't be seen: the roads they're on are private (one of the reasons why the upper class is sometimes called the "invisible class"). Similarly, in daily life the richest people most of us ever encounter are upper middle class. So it is understandable that we think of them as rich; to most of us they are about as rich as actual people ever get. They are high-income professionals (e.g., doctors, lawyers, architects, engineers) and business people; they are highly educated, often with degrees from high-prestige institutions (e.g., Ivy League universities); and they are disproportionately represented in the suburbs (although in the beginning years of their careers, before they marry and form families, they nowadays often prefer to live in or near affluent downtown areas of major cities).

The most obvious advantage of an upper-middle-class job is that it pays exceedingly well. But such jobs are pleasanter than the average in other respects, too: working conditions are comfortable, sometimes even luxurious; an abundant supply of subordinates are on hand to do any menial work that may be required; and the stated salary is supplemented by a variety of perks that may include company cars, country club memberships, free lunches and dinners, and free travel. Physical amenities can be psychologically uplifting as well; for example, freedom from menial labor takes the psychologically gratifying form of exercising power over others.

On the other hand, such jobs involve long hours and often make great demands on the individual's leisure time. As a result, only those who are willing and able to sacrifice their private lives somewhat are able to be high achievers in the professional world. This is one of the reasons women do not often climb as high on the corporate ladder as men. Married fathers can have their wives take responsibility for the children; married mothers rarely have that option.

Lower Middle Class (about 30–35% of the population)

In defining this group we will need to distinguish it both from the upper middle class above it and the working class below it. Unlike the working class, the lower middle class tends to be college-educated; but unlike the upper middle class, their degrees do not usually come from the prestige schools but from state-supported schools or mediocre private colleges. Unlike working-class jobs, lower-middle class jobs usually do not involve manual labor but are, instead, "white collar" jobs that take place in relatively comfortable office settings; but unlike upper-middle-class jobs, they only yield an average income—sometimes lower than a working class income—and carry with them none of the perks associated with high-status professional work. Examples of lower-middle-class occupations include: nurse, teacher, sales rep, technician, lower-level manager, etc. If we look at lower-middle-class working conditions, without for the moment being distracted by the question of income, we can see clearly why the lower middle class is considered to be a notch above the working class but a notch below the upper middle class. The lower-middle-class work setting is clean and comfortable—for example, it is heated in the winter and air-conditioned in the summer—and safe. For many working-class jobs this isn't the case. On the other hand, compared to the upper middle class, lower-middle-class workers are given a minimal amount of private space—a small office or none at all—and little or no support staff (they may **be** the support staff). The terms of employment are also significant: lower-middle-class employees, like the upper middle class and unlike the working class, often have job security; if they work for large bureaucratic organizations (which they are more likely to than the working class), the chances are good that, as long as they behave themselves, some job in the company will always be available to them; and, even if they do misbehave, they usually cannot be dismissed summarily but have certain "due process" rights, just as someone accused of a crime does. Also, like all upper-middle-class jobs and unlike many working-class jobs, lower-middle-class jobs include a range of fringe benefits in addition to salary: paid vacations, health insurance, pensions, stock-option plans, etc. The typical lower-middle-class worker can not only anticipate permanent employment but a continuous, if gradual, expansion in salary and benefits—again like all members of the upper middle class but unlike many in the working class. But while lower-middle-class jobs may involve regular raises, **upward mobility within the organization**, or one's field in general, **is severely limited**—like working-class jobs and unlike upper-middle-class ones. An upper-middle-class lawyer **could** become a judge, and potentially even a Supreme Court justice; a doctor could become a hospital Chief of Staff, and potentially even the U.S. Surgeon General. Mobility for the upper middle class is virtually limitless, and that is one of its most appealing traits. On the other hand a nurse can become—a head nurse; or, to take a working class example, a factory worker can become a foreman. These are certainly examples of mobility, but they do not exemplify the kind of qualitative leap involved, say, in going from attorney to Attorney General. And for most lower-middle-class workers, mobility means nothing more than accumulating seniority and reaching the highest level for the job category or "line" one has worked within from day one.

Just as income is not the only source of job satisfaction or dissatisfaction, the significance of mobility is not limited to its translatability into a potential for significantly higher income. In other words, where "unlimited mobility" means, aside from expanding income potential, the possibility of continuously doing new and interesting things, facing new challenges, and so on, limited mobility means the reverse: doing more or less the same thing day in and day out until the blessed day of retirement comes. In this sense too upper-middle-class jobs are preferable to lower-middle-class ones. To make matters worse, a lower-middle-class job to begin with—even before it begins to seem routine and one yearns for something better—is likely to be less interesting and challenging than an upper-middle-class one. For these reasons—and because they have made as much of an investment in their education as the upper middle class has (often at greater financial sacrifice) but have less to show for it—the lower middle class is sometimes considered to be the least satisfied, most complaining group in the population. An additional reason for dissatisfaction at the present time is that some of the principal advantages of lower-middle-class employment over working-class employment—security and benefits—can no longer be taken for granted. Members of the lower middle class are understandably anxious—they are worried that their jobs, none too thrilling to begin with, may not always be there for them, and will never be there for their children; and that, if they are there, such jobs will not always be as comfortable as they have been.

Working Class (about 30–35% of the population)

This is the **blue-collar** class of skilled tradespeople—plumbers, carpenters, electricians, construction workers, factory workers, and others employed at manual labor. The question is often asked why this group is placed below the lower middle class when, as everyone knows, plumbers make more than corporate executives. Allowing for the exaggeration, there are two answers to this question. First of all, for every plumber (electrician, etc.) who runs his own small company and owns a big house in a fashionable suburb, **there are many more who merely work for such people**. Their incomes are not as impressive as their bosses'. And secondly, even to the extent that their incomes do compare favorably with those of the lower middle class, what is their situation like once we look beyond income? It is just what we described in our discussion of the differences between lower middle class and working class jobs: little or no job security (argue with the boss and be fired); few or no benefits (take a day off and lose a day's pay); an uncomfortable or unsafe work environment. (The last item explains why police officers and firefighters, whose income and benefits are impressive, are still considered working-class by most sociologists. Most lower-middle-class jobs can't really kill you.) Job security means more than protection against arbitrary dismissal. The affluent plumber eventually retires to Florida—rendering all his workers unemployed. Furthermore, working class jobs are more subject to economic fluctuations than lower middle class office work: in times of recession, for example, homeowners may put off doing even necessary repairs, thus leading our affluent plumber to lay off some staff. Or, the work may be seasonal, e.g., construction work.

Our examples of working-class jobs—plumbers, police—should not be taken to imply that the working class comprises only, or mainly, men. Aside from the fact that many working-class jobs that in the past went exclusively to men are increasingly open to women—who, however, face special problems in them due to discrimination—there are many working class jobs that traditionally have been done mainly by women—waitressing, for example. Of course men often wait tables, too; but, in this as in other occupations, the more low-status the job, the more likely it is done primarily by women. Career waiters earning high incomes in expensive Manhattan restaurants are mostly men; their counterparts in greasy spoons across America tend to be women. The same is true of factory work. Women are more likely to be found in low-paying, non-union textile jobs; highly-paid auto workers are mainly men.

Finally, we should note that in our high-tech economy the term "working class" has been expanded by sociologists to include work which, while taking place in white-collar office settings, nevertheless has distinctively working-class characteristics. In fact, as the de-industrialization of society progresses, and the economy produces more service and fewer manufacturing jobs, an increasing number of jobs which, by most of the criteria so far discussed, have to be considered working-class, are taking place in non-working-class settings. Sociologists speak of the "electronic sweatshop." An example is telephone sales work, which is essentially the **post-modern version of early assembly line jobs**, reproducing the latter's stressful pace, low rewards, and norms of capricious discipline. And, as with the assembly line, the stress of these jobs is physical as well as psychological—causing outbreaks of whole new classes of disorders such as "repetitive stress syndrome."

Thus, the shift from a blue-collar to a white-collar world has not necessarily meant a net increase in "comfortable" employment, since it includes the creation en masse of new forms of discomfort.

Lower Class

"The lower class" is not equivalent to "the unemployed" for the simple reason that many jobs, even many full-time jobs, do not place their occupants above poverty. For example, if you work 40 hours/week year-round at the minimum wage—as approximately million people do—your income would be about 25% **below** the Federal poverty line. Non-unionized factory jobs, and low-level service jobs such as fast-food counterperson, often pay the minimum wage or close to it. Furthermore, such jobs typically don't provide health coverage. It is reasonable to assume that the main reason why people are not motivated to get off welfare is not that welfare is so rewarding but that the jobs that are available as alternatives are so unrewarding (assuming a job is available at all). The choice between welfare and work is often a choice between a miserable income with basic health coverage (Medicaid), and a miserable income with no health coverage. When you add to this the fact that non-working mothers can care for their children while working mothers may have to pay for child care, the proposition that remaining on welfare represents a moral failure becomes questionable. It should be noted that the unavailability of desirable work is not something to which only low-skilled, uneducated, single parents are subject. In the 1980s a new breed of welfare recipient emerged: laid-off industrial workers whose skills have become obsolete in a technological age. Yet it remains true that the female householder is more likely to be poor than any other type of adult in America.

But what exactly does poverty mean?

Sociologists distinguish between **absolute** and **relative** poverty. **Absolute poverty** is what is usually meant when we use the word poor: namely, not having enough—for example, being without decent housing or sufficient food. **Relative poverty** means having less than the average person does. In this section, we are discussing absolute poverty. The question arises, can absolute poverty be defined objectively? Isn't "not enough food" relative to the amount you think is enough for you? Indeed, the official definition of absolute poverty is somewhat relative. It is based on the Department of Agriculture's estimate of the annual cost of an adequate diet (multiped by a certain figure). The main criticism of the poverty line, by those who think it is drawn too high, is that the cost of an adequate diet is lower if you are an efficient, knowledgeable shopper with access to large, reasonably priced supermarkets; but, while the government's estimated food budget presupposes such a consumer, the poor are least likely to fit that profile. The main criticism of the poverty line, by those who think it is drawn too low, is that by "income" the government doesn't take into account non-cash transfers such as food stamps, which invisibly inflate the incomes of recipients. (Although it is hard to imagine why the government, which foots the bill, would want to exaggerate the extent of poverty. Could it really be—as politicians running for office often assert—that the government "likes" to spend "our" money?) Since the liberals in this debate contend that the poverty rate should be raised, and the conservatives argue that taking non-cash transfers into account effectively does raise the household income of those designated as poor, we conclude that we will not be far misled if we take government poverty figures as more or less accurate.

SOCIAL CLASS AND EVERYDAY LIFE

Social classes are distinguishable not just by the amounts of wealth, power, and prestige their members enjoy but by a wide range of other characteristics as well. Virtually no aspect of people's thought or behavior remains uninfluenced by the class to which they belong. In this section we look in some detail at the impact class has on various aspects of everyday life.

Health

How is the quality of a person's health affected by class membership? To put it simply: there is overwhelming evidence that wealth is good for your health. There are several reasons for this. To begin with the most obvious one: the higher your social class, the greater your access to high quality health care. Those in the upper class can purchase the best care, and most members of the middle class are usually guaranteed at least decent care through health insurance plans tied to their employment. But there is more to it than that. Those in the middle classes and above can afford health care in the additional sense that they can "afford" to get sick and be taken care of—for example, they do not sacrifice any income by taking time off to visit the doctor. In many working-class jobs—waitressing, for example—the employee who doesn't show up, for whatever reason, loses a day's pay. A major reason why the health of the lower classes is inferior to that of the upper classes is that members of the lower classes are more likely to put off seeking professional help for a problem until it becomes urgent. As a result, death rates from heart and lung disease, ulcers, diabetes, and many other ailments are significantly higher in the lower classes. In fact, life expectancy itself declines as social class declines. (There are various factors at work here, including: a higher infant mortality rate for the lower classes due to inadequate and/or intermittent pre-natal care; the greater likelihood of working under hazardous or dangerous conditions if you are poor; and the greater likelihood of your being a homicide victim.)

There is growing evidence that stress and stress-related disorders are more common among the lower classes. This is true, for example, of high blood pressure. Probably this can be attributed either directly to the stress of being poor (or at least, as in the case of the working class, being economically vulnerable and therefore in a state of fairly constant anxiety), or indirectly to certain "life-style" decisions that are themselves reflections of stress. So, for example, the lower your class the more likely you are to smoke.

If any of this seems surprising, it is probably because of the existence of cultural stereotypes, to which we have all been exposed, associating stress with high-income occupations—e.g., we think of businessmen, not factory workers, getting ulcers. Perhaps this popular association of high achievement with poor health is designed to keep people from feeling too resentful at not belonging to the class of high achievers (at the same time that it is an expression of such resentment). At any rate it is largely based on fantasy. While it is true that many of the highest-paying jobs are also the most stressful—involving, as they do, high degrees of responsibility—they also include more buffers against stress than working class jobs do. For one thing, middle-class, as against working-class, jobs, typically entail a higher degree of job security, which may well translate into lower levels of stress. In addition, the stress of high-pressure upper-middle-class business life is to some extent offset by the various "perks" associated with that life: long vacations in luxurious settings; regular visits to the office health club for a restorative workout; and, not least of all, **complete freedom from menial tasks**—the things secretaries and other "support staff" are paid to do. (Working-class means not being allowed to make a phone call; upper-middle-class means never having to make a phone call.) The young blue-collar worker may indeed seem hardier than the young accountant; but compare them again at age 70. Years of uncomfortable if not hazardous working conditions, of daily physical if not psychological stress, of insufficient medical care, and poor dietary habits—which are much likelier to characterize the life of the blue-collar worker than that of the white-collar worker—eventually take their toll.

Unhealthful life-style patterns among the lower classes may also be attributable to an under-standably weaker commitment to preserving one's health. Bright prospects for the future provide a motive for staying in shape. This may seem like sheer speculation, but consider the following: Over the last twenty years, a health and fitness craze has swept American society. People jog, work out, pay great attention to the nutritional content of foods, and so on. Ask yourself: who jogs? who reads the fine print on food labels? who has given up hard liquor in favor of a little white wine or Perrier? The health and fitness craze is clearly a phenomenon of the middle and upper classes. (Quitting smoking is part of it.) Why? Part of it may have to do simply with money: health club memberships are expensive, as are the prices of many "health foods." Part of it may also have to do with knowledge or lack thereof: the lower your class the less educated you are likely to be, and so the less likely you are to be aware of the dangers of cholesterol, and so on. But it is also possible to be vaguely aware of such things but not especially care about them (ignorance is a result as well as a cause of indifference). Sociologists used to believe that a distinguishing feature of the middle class was its ability to **defer gratification**—to sacrifice an immediate pleasure for the sake of a long-term benefit. It was assumed that this ability—itself unaccounted for—was the **cause** of middle-class success: A middle-class family, for example, now owns a house because it was able to save up for it—which meant denying itself certain pleasures along the way: unnecessary spending on clothes, dining out, etc. The health and fitness craze is like that: a cigarette would be pleasurable but you give it up for the sake of a long-term goal (maintaining your health). Sociologists still see things this way, but with one important difference: **the ability to defer gratification is now seen as an effect of being middle-class— or of the realistic expectation that one will become middle-class—rather than its cause.** In other words, one can defer gratification—organize one's life around pursuit of a future goal— to the extent that one perceives that the goal is realizable. A 25-year-old lawyer fresh out of law school, who takes an entry-level position in a law firm, realistically foresees a steady and substantial increase in her income over the next forty years, culminating in a partnership. Such an individual has every reason to quit smoking, avoid junk food, and the rest. But a person who is unemployed and without skills, who doesn't like to think much about the future because it is likely to be as bleak as the present—such an individual is more likely to feel a need to seek whatever gratification is available now.

Education

In Chapter One we described the ways in which wealth enhances educational opportunity in the form of private schooling, superior public education, and so on. These enhanced opportunities pay off: SAT scores, for example, vary directly with family income. (This is at least partly due to the fact that such tests are culturally biased. But it is also directly due to the influence of money: children of the affluent can pay for courses to help them in taking the SATs.) But there is a further way in which money influences educational opportunity—one that is important not only because it may exert a decisive influence on educational outcomes but because it is difficult to imagine any social policy that could remediate against it.

Affluent parents tend to be highly educated. Their jobs as professionals tend to be "comfortable" in a physical and psychological as well as monetary sense. While they may return home from work tired, they are energized as well—the result of doing interesting, stimulating, challenging work, in physically pleasant surroundings, for which they are being amply rewarded in dollars and prestige. Thus, as parents they are in a position to supplement their children's formal education with extra-curricular instruction. A second-grader has a lesson at school in division. Perhaps it is a good school; perhaps the child is bright. It may still happen that the principle of division didn't quite sink in. Upper middle class parents are able to help out. If they are not exactly walking reference libraries, they know how to help their children find their way in an actual one.

What social class a family belongs to has great predictive value when it comes to answering the following questions: Do parents monitor what their children watch on TV? Do they limit the number of hours their children are allowed to watch? Do they encourage their children to read (which is done in part by being avid readers themselves, thus providing the children with role models in their immediate environment)? Do they regularly engage their children in conversation, drawing out their children's thoughts and encouraging them to express themselves? Is there a personal computer in the home that the children can use? Is the children's after-school program merely a baby-sitting service, or does it consist of extra-curricular "enrichment," e.g., art, music, dance, or language instruction (providing the children not only with meaningful fun but an opportunity to discover artistic or other talents they may have)? Do the children go to summer camp, and if so, what educational experiences does it offer? The list could go on. Nowadays, there is much talk about extending the school year in the U.S. because of a concern that we are losing our competitive edge against the Europeans and the Japanese.

The fact is, however, that education is already year-round in America for many children of the upper middle class and above. Whether or not these children can successfully compete in a global marketplace against similarly highly-trained Europeans and Japanese remains to be seen; but their competitive advantage against American children whose education comes solely from the school system is assured.

Marriage and Family Life

First of all, the very structure of the household is influenced by class: the lower the class, the higher the divorce rate. This fact contradicts the widespread impression that the skyrocketing divorce rate of recent decades is due to the entrance of women to the ranks of professionals—i.e., the impression that the current divorce rate mostly reflects an increase in middle-class, and especially upper-middle-class, divorce. But, while it is certainly true that the middle class divorce rate is higher than ever, and that this increase is largely attributable to expanded career opportunities for women—enabling them to leave bad marriages without necessarily putting their economic survival at risk—the fact remains: lack of economic resources rather than an abundance of them is the principal cause of marital tension in the first place. Further, once the marital relationship is strained for whatever reason, material resources can provide avenues of escape from the harsh reality of an unfulfilling relationship. If frequent vacations and shopping sprees do not cause married people to be happy with each another, the frightening thought of having to give such things up may convince them that they are not too greatly unhappy after all. The higher the social class, the more one stands to lose materially in case of divorce. (The "one" who loses is usually the wife.) By contrast, marriage in the lower class means having little or nothing to lose by divorce—and little or nothing to gain by marrying: just as the divorce rate is higher, the marrying rate is lower for the lower classes. Of course the economically marginal, like the economically secure classes, have the option of marrying strictly for love, without consideration of the long-term economic consequences of their prospective union entering into the equation. But such behavior is rare. The emphasis our culture places on romance keeps us from acknowledging the normal role economic calculation plays in the "dating and mating" process. Very few people would allow themselves to become strongly attracted to someone with little or no income-earning potential. In this sense the poor shouldn't be criticized if it is found that they use the same criteria in marital decision-making that the rest of us do. What makes the poor an easy target is that, given the kinds of potential mates they are likely to meet, their reasoned assessment of the situation is more likely to lead to the decision to divorce (or not to marry at all) than ours is.

Class also influences the ways in which marital partners relate to each other. Here some broad distinctions can be made between behavior characteristic of the middle classes and above, on the one hand, and the working class and below, on the other. For example, below this dividing line married couples tend to engage in sex-segregated leisure activities. Thus, a working class couple invites a few other couples over to their house; before long the husbands go off by themselves, perhaps to watch a ball game, while the wives repair to the kitchen to do "girl's talk." (In an earlier generation, the husbands left the house altogether for a "boy's night out," while the wives stayed home and attended to their domestic duties—further evidence that what the men did from nine to five, but not the women, was considered real work, entitling one to some time off.) In general, members of the working class and lower class are more traditional in their attitudes towards sex roles than those in the middle classes. Why? Possibly because the lower the class, the less likely it is that individuals derive a sense of meaningfulness and self-worth from their work, or any other aspect of their lives in society; thus their self-images depend more on the possession of such "natural" traits as "masculine" strength and "feminine" charm and ability to nurture (men and children). And indeed it is more than just a matter of self-image: these qualities—as against advanced degrees signifying high income-earning potential—are the principal assets such individuals are able to bring into a marriage, i.e., they represent the means by which they are able to lure a partner into a marital commitment. Of course, the man gets more out of this reliance on nature than the woman does: He gets to be the boss (which he doesn't get to be at work).

Finally, the very meaning and significance of family differs according to social class. For example, the working class and lower class are more likely to have close ties to the "extended family" of cousins, grandparents, aunts and uncles, etc., than the middle classes are. There are several reasons for this. First of all, economic necessity plays a role. For the upper-middle-class couple who go out to dinner and a movie, adding an extra $20 for a baby-sitter may mean nothing; but for a working class couple having grandma around to babysit makes it possible for them to afford to go out at all. Similarly, affluent couples can hire contractors to do home repairs, make improvements, and so on, while the less affluent recruit family members to help tackle such jobs. Secondly, there may be a psychological factor at work: working-class and lower-class people often feel, not without justification, that family members are the only ones who understand, appreciate, and respect them. Professionals are typically respected by their clients and colleagues, and so have less of a need for the psychological sustenance that the extended family may provide. For the working class and below, the extended family serves as a buffer protecting the individual from a cold, unsupportive world (Rubin, 1976). In contrast, the lives of professionals revolve around their professional status. Professionals are eager to forge social and personal ties with fellow professionals—for the sake of career advancement, where that is a possibility, and, more generally, because being around colleagues reinforces their sense of the meaningfulness of their lives by reminding them of their occupational status. It is just this that the working class and lower class do not wish to be reminded of.

Child-rearing

The social class of parents exerts a decisive influence on the life chances of their children. The most obvious reason for this connection is that opportunities—the opportunity to receive a high-quality education, to meet influential people who can help you establish yourself in your chosen career, etc.—are unequally distributed by social class. But there is another reason why people tend to remain in the social class in which they were born: **styles of child-rearing differ by social class, and these distinct styles tend to produce distinct types of individuals who are better or less equipped to succeed in the job market.** Sociologists claim that, in general, middle-class parents raise their children with an emphasis on **autonomy** while working-class and lower-class parents emphasize **obedience.** Middle-class children are encouraged to think for themselves and to develop their creative potential; working-class and lower-class children are more likely to be taught merely to stay out of trouble. The sociological explanation for this difference is that the world-views of adults—in this case, parents—are formed by their social, and especially their occupational, roles. Working-class jobs typically emphasize rule-following, with a minimum of independent thinking encouraged or even allowed; just the reverse is true of professional work. The point is that parents inevitably relate to their children in terms of the experiences they have had in the "real world." This makes perfect sense, since child-rearing is oriented to the goal of preparing children to become competent adults. For the working-class and lower-class parent "competent" means "able to survive;" for the middle-class parent it means "able to excel." In other words, parents communicate the skills they have had to use in their real-world adult lives, and these skills differ by class. Child-rearing practices are thus a self-fulfilling prophecy. The professional parents expect their children to become professionals, and therefore act towards them in such a way that the children turn out to be equipped to be professionals; working class parents expect less of their children, and therefore get it (Kohn, 1977).

Leisure Activities

What people do in their free time differs according to social class. This is a significant topic because it deals with what people freely choose to do; to show that such apparently free choices in fact bear the imprint of class is to show just how radically the sociological insight that the individual is a social product is to be understood. It is one thing to note that the individual's "unique personality" does not express itself on the job; but it is quite another thing to make the same observation about the individual's private life. In most cases it is not true that "there is no accounting for taste"; taste is a class phenomenon. Different social classes have a "taste" for different newspapers, magazines, books, TV shows, and movies. In this country, as in others, there are tabloids—heavily illustrated newspapers with sensational headlines, easy to read stories (in terms of length, print size, and vocabulary level), and lots of "features" (horoscopes, comics, gossip columns)—for the lower middle class, working class, and poor; and standard-sized newspapers for the professional class. Advertisers are well-aware of the typical audiences for typical media products, and place their ads accordingly.

Why does it matter who reads what? The fact that the lower classes consume only tabloid journalism means that the upper classes get more complete and accurate information about the world around them (i.e., information less distorted by the need to attract an audience via exaggeration, scandal-mongering, and so on). For instance, many of the examples we have used in this book to illustrate contemporary social phenomena come from articles in **The New York Times**, a prominent "serious" newspaper. Depending on the particular article, a greater or lesser degree of elaboration on our part was deemed necessary to show the sociological relevance of the issues raised in it. But our comments aside, the fact is that a regular **Times** (or **Washington Post** or **Los Angeles Times**) reader is consistently exposed to more or less in-depth coverage of vital issues the tabloids hardly even mention. This discrepancy is greatest when it comes to foreign affairs. The ambiguity of the motives, and the complexity of the events, that led to the Iraq War, was something tabloid newspapers—and network TV news shows—did not feel a need to expose their audiences to.   We all depend on the mass media for most of our knowledge of the world beyond our immediate neighborhoods. The attitudes and beliefs of individuals in society—e.g., political opinions and therefore voting behaviors—are formed in and through the interaction between people and the information made available to them via the mass media. Of course one can question just how one-sided this interaction is. Are we mere passive recipients of media messages? Are we incapable of recognizing sensationalism, distortion, and so on, for what they are? To the extent that audience responses are autonomous and unpredictable, the fact that the lower classes consume journalistic junk food could seem irrelevant. But that would be like saying one is in good shape and exercises regularly, therefore it doesn't matter what one's diet consists of. Can it really make no difference what one consumes mentally?

THEORIES OF STRATIFICATION

Sociology maintains that stratification is a social arrangement; it exists because human societies have brought it into existence. The question then arises: why? What are the reasons for the existence of social stratification? What purposes does it serve? These questions are especially important to raise since stratification produces, among other things, untold suffering: in our society especially, the material deprivation suffered by the poor is compounded by the fact that they face the daily indignity of being blamed for their situation; they tend to be seen as inferior beings in a society where what you are is measured by what you have.

   People often note that, below a certain age, children are not cognizant of racial differences, although we all inevitably become aware of them as we grow up. That is, our awareness of race is a result of socialization. But we ordinarily do not recognize that the same is true of social class: society makes us aware of differences that, in the "natural" state of childhood "innocence," go unnoticed. But, just as surely as a Black child sooner or later begins to wonder why she is treated differently from whites, a poor child will begin to wonder why her friend has a bigger house and nicer clothes than she. "Theories of stratification," then, try to deal with a basic question posed, not by sociology, but by life. Both functionalism and conflict theory have offered explanations for the phenomenon of stratification. We will look at each of them in turn.

Functionalism

The standard functionalist view of stratification, developed by Kingsley Davis and Wilbert Moore, emphasizes the socially useful, beneficial aspects of stratification. Its underlying idea is elegantly simple: Stratification is necessary to society because it motivates individual effort. Only in a society where effort pays off will people be inspired to make an effort. Concretely this means that rewards must be correlated with amount of effort. So, for example, if a certain occupation involves extensive training, long hours, great responsibilities, high levels of stress, etc., a society that wanted people to enter this field would have to ensure that those who do so will be rewarded more than those who do easier jobs. Who would become a medical doctor if it paid no more than being a dishwasher? And, if we look at systems that take an opposite approach—for example, communist states that try to more or less equalize income—we see that they have encountered precisely the problem that this theory would lead us to expect: a near breakdown of the "work ethic." Communist systems were so plagued by absenteeism and other forms of work-avoidance that transforming workers' attitudes is considered a major challenge facing those attempting to manage the "privatization" process. By contrast, the dynamic, innovative, achievement-oriented spirit of our economy, it can be argued, is based on belief in the American promise of reward for effort. We can only go for the gold if there is gold to go for. Actually, the analogy from the world of sports is fitting: teams play harder when a World Series ring is at stake.

But, while the logic of the functionalist theory seems unassailable, a closer look reveals a number of fundamental flaws:

(a) as a sociological theory, and a functionalist one at that, Davis and Moore's theory must show not only how individual effort but **socially useful individual effort** is created. Without that, the rewards for individual effort could still explain the effort but not why society would want, let alone need, to arouse it. Thus, while the production of well-trained, hard-working MDs can be used to justify the high incomes we allow them, what justifies the even higher incomes of business executives, corporate lawyers, movie stars, professional athletes, and others? What vital social roles are they performing?

(b) as a sociological theory, the Davis and Moore theory needs to take into account that any definition of "vital social role" is somewhat arbitrary. While most people would concede that MD is a vital social role deserving of higher-than-average status, a similar case could be made for other occupations that at present don't pay that well. Why shouldn't teachers make more than doctors? (And why shouldn't kindergarten teachers make more than college professors?) The general question here—who decides which social roles are the most important?—is one that Davis and Moore do not raise.

(c) Davis and Moore's theory leaves the upper upper class totally unaccounted for. The theory of effort and reward does not cover those whose present economic condition is based on inheritance rather than work. So the question arises: what theory justifies the unlimited inheritance of wealth (subject to rather modest taxation) in a society in which 36 million people are poor? This is not to say that it can't be justified, only that Davis and Moore do not do so.

(d) Davis and Moore's theory is abstract in the sense that it suggests that **to justify inequality of rewards is to justify any degree of inequality**. Let us assume a functionalist justification for the high salaries of film stars—something to the effect that they have rare talents, and work hard to perfect them; they entertain us, and we need to be entertained (which we prove by our willingness to pay to see their films), etc. For a variety of reasons, then, we agree that actors deservedly make more than theatre ushers. But ten thousand times more? The principle that inequality is justified does not mean that any application of the principle is valid. If we were to say, "Actors deserve to make a lot of money," is it then illogical or hypocritical to continue by saying that $10 million a film is too much and that they ought to be content with a mere $1 million? And if it isn't, then couldn't it also be argued that doctors and lawyers should be content with making only two or three times what nurses and teachers make rather than five or ten or a hundred times?

(e) a related criticism is that the functionalist theory reduces all incentives to the least common denominator: money. Couldn't people be motivated—and aren't they, in fact—by a variety of potential rewards? Of course prestige is a reward in addition to income, but it is so closely tied to income, in our society especially, that it is difficult to imagine it functioning as a separate incentive for entering any particular occupation. On the other hand the (perceived) intrinsic meaningfulness and usefulness of a particular job can and does motivate people—teachers, for example, who know they aren't going to get rich but are often committed to their profession anyway. Why couldn't doctors learn to view medicine, and lawyers the law, in the way dedicated teachers view education? Probably some of them do. But as long as society appeals to the baser motives in people—becoming a doctor=becoming wealthy—base motivation is what is likely to be activated.

(f) finally, the formula that the promise of reward motivates achievement overlooks an equally powerful element in the production of motivation: the threat of punishment. Most students beyond a certain age who study hard, just like their parents who work hard, do so not because they hope to become wealthy but because they fear that otherwise they will not even survive. It could be argued that most of us are impelled more by our fears, which are often quite realistic, than by our dreams: fear of losing a car or a home because of a missed loan payment; fear of unemployment; fear of complete loss of social standing, of the respectability one has so painfully won, and so on. The fact that one can become and remain homeless in America is a major source of motivation for the average person yet it finds no place in functionalist theory, perhaps because to acknowledge it would be tantamount to a functionalist justification of widespread poverty—i.e., it exists as a motivator: if poverty weren't a real possibility, we wouldn't work as hard. Herbert Gans actually formulated a somewhat satirical "functionalist theory of poverty" along these lines (Gans, 1962). Here is where the analogy from sports proves to be inexact. Competition loses its romantic associations when we recognize that those in "last place" in American society, unlike those in last place in the American League, are actually hungry.

Conflict Theory

The Background: Marx's Theory

The conflict theory of stratification is not simply equivalent to Marxist theory; in the century since Marx's death, his analysis of stratification has been expanded, revised, and reformulated by a variety of sociologists. Yet the basic Marxian model remains a major source of sociological insight. This is important to emphasize today because of the widespread belief that the fall of communism testifies to the irrelevance of Marxism. A lot depends on what is meant by "Marxism."

We will begin by describing Marx's view of industrial society. Marx lived most of his adult life in England, at a time when the factory system was first emerging into prominence. This was the world that Charles Dickens also wrote about: a world of sweatshops, starvation wages, and wrenching poverty. Marx argued that the nature of the relation between factory owners (the "owners of the means of production" or the "bourgeoisie") and their workers (the "proletariat") was inherently unfair and therefore inherently unstable. Its inherent unfairness can be seen in the following example: Textile factory workers produce clothes, which the owner then sells on the open market; the difference between the price the clothes command and the amount of money the owner has to plow back into the factory—in the form of overhead and wages—is the owner's profit, or, in Marx's terminology, **surplus value**. The unfairness resides in the fact that, while the workers literally produce the surplus value by producing the clothes, they keep none of it. They do, of course, receive a wage, so any unfairness, one could argue, is only a relative one. But that doesn't mean they are not underpaid. Marx asks the concrete question: what determines the wage the owner pays his workers? His gratitude for their assistance in his efforts to become wealthy? His sense of their dignity as human beings? His awareness of their needs and those of their families? Actually, no; the owner is influenced by only two things: First, he cannot pay his workers less than the competition is paying (in reality this is rarely a problem—big businessmen tend to act in mutually advantageous ways). Secondly, the owner has to pay his workers enough so that they will be physically able to continue working for him. Thus, a starvation wage in the literal sense is out of the question. The crucial point is that the owner has no incentive to increase wages above that minimum necessary to ensure the workers' bare survival. He only would **if they had a choice not to work for him**; but, as we suggested, one employer is likely to be just as stingy as another. Marx's blunt way of putting it was that, in the modern factory system, the average worker has but one concrete freedom as a worker: the freedom to starve. That is the only alternative to working for this (or an equivalent) employer at this wage. The fact that this barely subsisting worker is indispensable to the production and maintenance of the owner's comfortable life-style struck Marx as inherently unfair.

As for the inherent instability of this system, it follows, for Marx, from its unfairness. Once workers become aware that their poverty is not an unalterable accident of fate but is the necessary consequence of their membership in the working class—an awareness which Marx calls **class consciousness**—they will rise up and seize the means of production. Private ownership will give way to collective ownership; and society and economy will be organized, not around the pursuit of individual profit, but by the principle "from each according to his abilities; to each according to his needs."

Now Marx's prediction proved to be almost completely inaccurate. He envisioned socialist revolutions in the advanced European industrial nations and the United States; not one occurred (although in 1848 Germany and France came close to revolution). Instead, revolutions occurred after Marx's death in several countries that were not yet industrialized: Russia in 1917, China in 1949, Cuba in 1958—to give three of the most prominent examples. What occurred in the industrial world to upset Marxian expectations? Two things primarily, both of which were not foreseen by Marx: first, a tremendous expansion of the middle classes due to the development of modern technology (creating a "new class" of technicians, managers, and other salaried experts who, while not rich, are quite comfortably above poverty); and secondly, the rise of the trade-union movement, which meant a rise in the standard of living for millions of members of the working class to a point beyond which revolution in any real sense seemed any longer necessary or desirable. In short, Marx did not foresee how comfortable average living standards would become; a Marxist would say he understimated the extent to which workers would be bought off with token improvements in income, distracted by the mass availability of consumer goods, and tranquilized by the productions of the various mass media. In any case, no one any longer seriously anticipates the outbreak of revolution in the industrialized world—and especially not in the U.S., where the token improvements have been more substantial, the toys more widely available, and the media entertainments more titillating, than anywhere else. But this outbreak of peace among social classes does not invalidate Marx's basic insights about structural unfairness; it only calls into question whether such unfairness is liable to lead to revolt. The irony is that, while Marx is most famous (or notorious) for his theory of revolution, he is actually more valuable as a guide to the dynamics of stability.

Marx accounts for stability by means of his **theory of ideology**. He reasoned as follows: If stratification systems are as unjust as they seem to be—and the bourgeoisie-proletariat relationship under capitalism is merely the latest (although to Marx the most oppressive) in a long series of arrangements throughout history whereby average working people are shabbily treated—the question arises why resistance, let alone revolution, is such a rare occurrence? His answer is that for revolution to occur, the working class would first have to become conscious of its situation. Marx mistakenly believed that, despite all the obstacles that lay in its path, such "class consciousness" would eventually develop. Yet he was also the one who **first identified and focused on these obstacles**, and in that sense he was as much a realist as a visionary. He argued that revolution failed to occur because people remained unaware of the true nature of their situation. To the question which then follows—why aren't they aware?—he answered: **the same system that has the power to oppress people has the power to keep them unaware of their oppression**. Not only the bodies but the minds of workers are held captive by the system. Just as Marxists are critics of the system, those in positions of power—those who benefit directly from the status quo—are supporters of it. Marxists speak and write against the system; those in power speak and write on behalf of it. 'Those in power' include politicians, government officials, and captains of industry, of course; but it also includes a wide range of cultural "authority figures"—religious leaders, educators, and in our day all sorts of media "personalities." The mainstream culture continuously promotes the view that the present system deserves our support. In fact, to Marx the **purpose** of culture is to protect the interests of the powerful by spreading propaganda favorable to the system. The reason people are unaware of their oppression, then, is that they are taught by those in authority that the present system is a legitimate one—that it is more or less fair, just, rational, and in any case the best one can reasonably expect.

Marxism and Stratification Today

Let us now ask how these two basic components of Marxian thinking—the theory of economic exploitation and the theory of ideology—can contribute to an understanding of contemporary society. First of all, it can be argued that the dramatically improved situation of working people in the 20th century has not changed the fact that in our system employers are motivated exclusively by a desire for personal profit, and that any concessions to labor have been based not on employers' compassion but has been dictated by self-interest. By this same logic, as soon as owners perceive that it is not to their advantage to act humanely, they will cease doing so. What does the historical record show? Originally, owners accepted unionization only in the wake of strikes and violent confrontations between police and workers—a situation which, had it continued, could have resulted in economic calamity for the owners. The minimum wage, workers' compensation, unemployment insurance—all these and other measures to promote a tolerable life for working people were instigated by government and accepted by employers in a spirit of resigned realism. There is no evidence to suggest that, in the absence of government and union pressures, any material improvement in the living standard of factory workers from Dickens' time to ours would have occurred. On the other hand, there is abundant evidence that, during periods of economic recession, big business will do everything in its power to ensure that as much of the necessary economic sacrifices as possible are borne by workers rather than high officials. As corporate profits declined in the late 1980s, corporate executive salaries increased—and record numbers of middle and low level personnel were laid off, phased out, switched to part-time, forced to accept decreased benefit packages, and so on. "Economic recovery," furthermore, has not necessarily meant the re-hiring of former employees; instead, the trend has been to try to protect against potentially dwindling profits by making do with fewer workers and squeezing more out of the ones that remain (Uchitelle, 1994).

Thus, the Marxian principle that **the profit motive implies exploitation of labor** seems at least as applicable to the present day as to the 19th century. And the theory of ideology seems even more applicable. Marx, it must be remembered, wrote long before the rise of the mass media—perhaps the most influential institution in contemporary society. He dealt more with the **content** of ideology than with its **form**. He could not describe the Presidential use of TV to "sell" policies; the constant media attempts to capture audiences through the use of catch-phrases and buzz-words that oversimplify complex socio-economic issues; the role of advertising in keeping our minds on the pursuit of things rather than on the possibility of creating a social system in which we would not be obsessed with things.

The content of the democratic ideology in our society involves a variation on the theme of meritocracy: we are taught that we live in a free society with equal opportunities for all; therefore what we make of our lives is what we choose to make of them; therefore success reflects individual excellence while failure reflects individual shortcomings. Of course such notions are especially favored by those in power. The more power and wealth you possess the more it is in your interest to believe that you deserve to possess them.

Yet despite its persuasiveness, the Marxian paradigm betrays a number of weaknesses. First of all, it can convey the impression of a conspiracy on the part of a diabolical elite to dupe innocent citizens into co-operating in their own destruction. Such an impression would be false on two counts: it overlooks the possibility that the evil conspirators **actually believe** the ideas that they are promoting (and so, from a Marxian viewpoint, are themselves dupes); and it assumes that the unsuspecting public bears absolutely no responsibility for being so apparently willing to be taken in by the propaganda assaulting them. The exploiters may be more "innocent," and the exploited less so, than the Marxian theory allows. Secondly, the Marxian theory leaves the phenomenon of progressive mainstream politicians unaccounted for. For example, Marxian theory would lead us to expect government to simply reflect the interests of big business; yet a succession of liberal Democratic administrations in this century, beginning with Roosevelt's in the 1930s, pushed through legislation designed to protect workers—despite the opposition of big business. The Marxian answer to this is that such measures are mere palliatives: they appease workers (which, if workers are in a position to cause trouble by striking, etc., is in the interests of big business) without qualitatively improving their situation. There is no way of settling this argument objectively, since it all depends on how we define real improvement. Marxists would deny that the higher salaries and benefits, and greater availability of consumer goods, for workers has "really" made them better off; workers are, for the most part, still hopelessly dependent on the whims of management for their very survival. But for those who disagree with that assessment, the realization that improvements in the living standards of workers have consistently been fought for by a host of liberal politicians—many of whom are themselves millionaire businessmen—serves to discredit the Marxian view of a monolithic political structure dedicated to preserving the status quo at all costs.

This leads to a third criticism. When we look at those who have advocated social reform in 20th century America, we find that in most cases they have done so by appealing to the same ideology that their opponents have. The American ideology of individual freedom is the source of left-wing as well as right-wing politics. The trade-union movement and the civil rights movement both appealed to the ideal of individual freedom and dignity embedded in the Constitution and the Declaration of Independence—the same ideal to which opponents of government intervention to help workers or minorities appeal. From the liberal point of view, the phrase "All men are created equal" is hollow unless society commits itself to ensuring that Black as well as white men are covered by it (and, since "men" in this context must be understood generically, women must be included as well as men); the right to "life, liberty, and the pursuit of happiness" is meaningless in the absence of decent pay and working conditions, etc. The Marxist theory of ideology does not notice that beliefs are used to criticize as well as justify social arrangements. But, again, that is because the Marxist would refuse to acknowledge that reform equals real change: of course, they would say, critics appeal to the same ideology as conservatives but that is because both ultimately aim to uphold the system (the liberal just wants to tinker with it a bit, perhaps out of a sense of guilt—or naivete: he may be deluded into thinking he really does want change; the conservative, who doesn't want change, at least knows that he doesn't.)

But even if it were agreed that the unionization of workers or civil rights for minorities represented real change, the theory of ideology would not thereby be proven invalid. After all, we began this section with the assertion that the theory of ideology is an attempt to explain the phenomenon of societal stability. Civil rights laws were passed in this country—a hundred years after the abolition of slavery. Trade unions were legalized—a century after the conditions described by Marx and Dickens had become the norm in the industrialized world. This history of unchanged conditions requires an explanation—and pointing to eventual improvements doesn't eliminate the question, let alone the suffering of those whose whole lives were lived in an environment utterly hostile to change.

8

DEVIANCE

THE PROBLEM OF DEFINITION

Deviant behavior is any behavior that violates significant social norms. Since society determines what the norms are, and which ones are to be regarded as significant, society determines what will count as a significant norm violation. In this sense deviance is a purely social phenomenon; what "is" deviant is what is called deviant. And so, what deviance actually means depends on how the concept is applied.

What is called deviant varies considerably from one historical period to another. Deviance is an especially interesting phenomenon to study at the present time because we are living in a period in which society's understanding of what counts as deviant is undergoing constant revision. In the last generation or so a whole series of behaviors that used to be considered normal have come to be considered deviant—and vice versa. Many of these re-assessed behaviors have to do with gender roles and relations. For example, twenty years ago the term "date rape" did not exist. The behavior that the term described existed, but we didn't have a term for the behavior because society did not recognize it as anything noteworthy, let alone as a problem (i.e., as deviant). The same is true of "marital rape"—a term which not everyone accepts even today. The point of controversy is not whether a particular behavior exists but whether it should be designated as deviant or normal—in which case, instead of speaking of "marital rape," we should speak of "conjugal rights," "a husband's prerogative," etc. On the other hand, the term "spouse abuse," like "child abuse," is widespread today—though there is still considerable disagreement over its application. Should it be restricted to cases of actual beating or to subtler forms of degradation as well?

In all these cases, at any rate, the invention of new, pejorative terminology illustrates the societal decision to reconsider the status of a number of previously ignored, denied, or accepted behaviors. In each case a negative label, a mark of disgrace—what sociologists call a **stigma**—has been attached (not without disagreements, inconsistencies, and occasional retreats) to these behaviors for the first time.

On the other hand, in recent years many behaviors that were once stigmatized have become socially acceptable. Births that were once branded as "illegitimate" are now described by the more neutral term "out of wedlock." Sociology argues that the concept of legitimacy functioned traditionally as a kind of moralistic weapon to keep families intact—that is, keep the fathers around—in societies where the father had to be around for the family to survive economically (because only men were socialized to be breadwinners). Thus, as women's educational and career opportunities improved, the concept of legitimacy lost its reason for existing, and so it began to die out. And people who today express concern over the rising proportion of out-of-wedlock births tend to have poor single mothers in mind (rather than either middle-class single mothers or single fathers). In other words, people usually attack single parenthood not for being immoral but for being impractical—in the sense that it may entail disastrous economic consequences for mother and child (and for society, if mother and child need to be subsidized by the government).

Behavior includes speech, and here too major changes have taken place in society's conception of deviance. Language once considered obscene is now permissible—to some extent on TV (imagine one of the children on "Father Knows Best" complaining that homework "sucks") and to a much greater extent in films. The same is true regarding sexual themes and depictions—"suggestive" on TV, "graphic" in films.

Life and death issues—literally—are undergoing a process of re-definition, too. To begin with death: is suicide a gravely immoral act (as it was perceived to be under the influence of the Western religious tradition for centuries) or, instead, the most rational, authentically human, and even life-affirming decision to make under certain circumstances? Is physician-assisted suicide, then, a violation of the medical oath or an especially poignant embodiment of it? And, at the other end of the life-cycle, there is the continuing controversy over abortion. The abortion debate, like the less heated debate surrounding the "right to die," illustrates a further sociological dimension of deviance: **the importance of consensus.** Definitions of deviance are never shared by everyone or understood by everyone in exactly the same way; and they are never free from the possibility of revision. Yet a certain degree of stability in our conceptions is vital to social order at any given point in time. In the abortion controversy a fundamental disagreement exists over the question of the personhood—and therefore the "rights"—of the fetus. Could society function if this kind of fundamental disagreement existed on a wide range of issues? Despite the intensity of feelings on the part of supporters and opponents of abortion rights, it is probably the fact that abortion is not a central aspect of everyday life for most people that has kept this issue from seriously threatening to tear the social fabric apart.

The sociological study of deviance deals not only with the question why people commit deviant acts—a question also treated by abnormal psychology—but, in light of the fact of historical variations in the definition of deviance and differences in public opinion, why particular acts are considered deviant in the first place.

In our discussion of culture, we noted that the concept of **norm** is broader than that of **law;** some of society's most cherished mores are not encoded in law. Conversely, deviant behavior is not always illegal behavior. Mental illness—perhaps the most widespread and perplexing form of deviance in our society—is an example. Incidentally, if you think that mental illness is not deviant, ask yourself how much easier it would be for you to become friends with a non-violent, non-criminal but psychotic ("crazy") person than with a mentally healthy violent criminal. Like criminals, crazy people are ostracized: they belong to "them" rather than "us." If deviants are those who are stigmatized for their behavior, then the mentally disturbed are clearly deviant.

The reason why it may seem to common sense that insanity doesn't really fit the concept of deviance is that the insane are not seen as **responsible** for their insanity: they are not "bad" but merely "sick." But sociology can't accept this common-sense view because it obscures the fact that in reality it makes no difference whether we feel sorry for "them" (crazy people) or want to punish them (criminals). The essential thing is that we have established a boundary between "us" and "them," "normal" and "deviant." Pity may be as denigrating as hatred. The "sick" person can only be helped by us because we are the healthy ones; thus the "sick" person we want to help, just as much as the "evil" person we want to punish, or rehabilitate, is not seen as our equal.

But doesn't it matter that we treat the insane as ill, i.e., that we view their behavior neutrally and objectively—unlike criminal behavior, which we condemn as morally wrong, socially disruptive, and the like? To this the sociologist would point out that the word "illness," as used in the phrase "mental illness," is an **evaluative** term. Think of how often "sick" is used as an insult word. Or how parents often feel whose child has been diagnosed—unfairly, in their view—as having a "learning disorder." (Imagine getting insulted when a medical doctor diagnoses you as having the flu!) Obviously the parents get upset because they know perfectly well, as common-sense members of society, that psychological impairments, however slight, are guaranteed sources of stigma.

WHY A SOCIOLOGY OF DEVIANCE?

The fundamental question in the sociology of deviance is: what are the causes of deviant behavior? This is the question which, in one way or another, all sociologists of deviance address, and which anyone who reads their work naturally wants an answer to. Deviant behavior can destroy individual lives, shatter family relations, and even disrupt social order itself. For practical reasons alone, then—i.e., for the purpose of trying to reduce the amount of deviant behavior—the study of the causes of deviance is obviously important.

But sociology is not the only field that deals with this question; psychology, and even biology, do so as well. So before we describe the various sociological approaches to deviance, we will discuss these alternative approaches in order to try to show why a sociology of deviance is necessary.

Biology

Over the past century various attempts have been made to explain at least some deviant behavior patterns in terms of genetically transmitted, inborn dispositions. Most of these theories have been refuted; some are still being debated. But biological explanations, even if proven valid, would be of only marginal interest to the social sciences. Biological answers are irrelevant because they are answers to a different question than that posed by the social sciences.

For example, one of the more recent and well-regarded attempts at a genetic explanation of crime is the extra-Y chromosome theory. It has been shown that a disproportionate number of males born with this extra chromosome are represented among the prison inmate population; and there is some evidence of a correlation between this genetic trait and violent behavior. The standard sociological criticism of this theory is as follows: the extra-Y chromosome male is endowed with certain characteristics—subnormal intelligence, an oversized and "ugly" appearance—that are likely to make social acceptance difficult for him to obtain; criminal violence, therefore, may be a response to society's rejection rather than the expression of a genetic imperative, as the chromosome theory supposes. A genetic explanation that fails to show that the behavior in question was inevitable does not succeed as a genetic explanation at all.

But this sociological critique points to something more important than the truth or falsity of the biological theory: namely, the irrelevance (to sociology) of the biological question. Biological questions, of whatever kind, try to locate factors which could show deviant behavior in particular cases to be inevitable. But deviance is only interesting—and puzzling—to sociologists to the extent that it is not inevitable. Whoever you are, your child might become a doctor or might become a junkie. Or: you have a good job, live in a nice, middle-class neighborhood, and have a loving spouse and children, as does your neighbor—who, however, has just committed suicide. You work hard and are loyal to the company despite being underpaid and under-appreciated; your co-worker and good friend has just been fired for stealing. Deviance is a profound and difficult topic **because of how alike, not how unlike,** the normal and the deviant are. Only the similarities make the question, "How did it happen?", so troubling and so important—because then it is a question about life as such (we would say: **social life** as such) rather than a question about these or those "freaks," "animals," etc. Sociology can't accept biological accidents as the cause of deviance because it is aware of the fact that deviants are usually just like us—until they behave differently, at which point they become, for us, a "them" to whom we affix all sorts of labels in order to exaggerate our difference from them. Even the "freak" cult leader, if that's what he is, only gets his name in the paper because he has attracted hundreds if not thousands of ordinary people as his followers.

Imagine reading a murder mystery in which there is a whole array of suspects, each with what appears to be a possible motive for the crime; you are absorbed in the book for two hundred pages until, on the last page, it is revealed that the perpetrator was a complete stranger who killed the victim accidentally in the midst of some kind of biochemically induced frenzy. Wouldn't you feel disappointed at such a "resolution" to the mystery? It would be as though the novel gave an answer—to who committed the crime—that wasn't an answer to our question: which of the characters committed the crime for which reason? When we ask "why" deviance occurs, we mean: give us the **reasons,** the **motives;** make it **humanly understandable that this person committed this act.** Thus, like the rest of sociology, the sociology of deviance deals with reasons rather than causes. Animal behavior is caused; human behavior is done for reasons. (Winch, 1958).

There is a second reason for sociology's opposition to biological explanations of deviance: they do not explain why certain forms of deviance become widespread—even to the point of becoming trends. When people say there is a "drug epidemic" in the U.S., they are obviously using the word "epidemic" figuratively. Yet it is a revealingly appropriate figure of speech. A flu epidemic, for example, refers to a situation in which an individual with a perfectly healthy respiratory system has an excellent chance of coming down with the flu. Now this seems to be the situation today regarding many types of deviant behavior: they are so common that they point to an environmental cause rather than an internal individual one. At the same time the environmental cause should not be seen as mechanically inducing individuals to behave a certain way. That would be to treat deviant behavior the way biology does, i.e., as inevitable. Sociology sees the individual's "response" to an environmental "stimulus" as a very complicated process whose results are always unpredictable (because people are not animals).

Psychology

Psychology provides some useful insights for the sociology of deviance but at the same time shares some of the basic weaknesses of the biological approach (as well as containing unique weaknesses of its own). That is understandable given that modern psychology grew out of modern medicine, and thus has always displayed a tendency to emphasize physiological as well as purely psychological factors in behavior.

Both the unique strengths and weaknesses of the psychological approach can be seen, for example, in Freudian theory. We saw above that Freud conceived of the human personality as consisting of three elements: the id, the superego, and the ego. The ego—the rational or realistic part of the self—strives to effect a compromise between the natural demands of the id and the societal restraints represented by the superego. In no human being does the ego completely succeed in governing the id and the superego; in this respect Freud was a firm believer in the merely relative difference between the healthy and the unhealthy individual. Nonetheless, he believed that a person whose ego was helpless before the tyrannous demands of either the id or the superego is in serious difficulty. While the problems that the unrestrained id can cause are obvious, Freud's unique contribution lies more in his emphasis on the disastrous consequences of an overactive superego. In most of us the id has been successfully harnessed in early childhood; under normal circumstances we hardly resemble the impatient, screaming, selfish, demanding infants we once were. The superego has subdued the id; "I want" and "I don't want" has been replaced by "I should" and "I shouldn't." But at what cost? Has the id been **tamed**—adapted to the needs of social survival under the guidance of the ego—or just **suppressed**—driven underground by the sense of shame and distrust of our own desires that an unrestrained superego induces? Have we learned to **moderate** our appetites—or to feel **ashamed** of them? Have we found socially acceptable ways of expressing ourselves—what Freud called "sublimation"—or have we repressed our deep need for self-expression? Freud believed that the id cannot be denied forever; the chronic frustration of unfulfilled longing is liable to explode into aggression (or 'implode' in the form of self-destructiveness). People who do not allow themselves, i.e., whose superegos do not allow them, to be happy, may resent the happiness of others—hence aggression; or else the pain of suppressed desire, together with the shame that makes suppression necessary, becomes so intense that the only solution appears to lie in extinguishing the self altogether—hence self-destruction, e.g., in the form of intoxication and other attempted escapes from reality.

For sociology the psychological insight that frustration leads to aggression has proved quite useful; Merton's **anomie theory,** for example, is based on it. At the same time it typifies certain weaknesses of the psychological approach. First of all, because it does not attempt, as Merton's theory does, to explain frustration in terms of societal factors, it is as unable to explain the "epidemic" character of deviance as biology is. Most psychologists assume that frustration results from pathologically impaired parenting or parent-child communication; but could such pathology be so widespread as to account for the deviant behavior that is all around us? As with biological theories, psychology tends to ignore the fact that most deviants are by all measures perfectly normal. And then there is the opposite problem: not all cases of pathology lead to deviant behavior. All of us know people whose personalities—or the personalities of whose parents—seem so strange as to make the fact that they function as normal individuals in society something to marvel at. Why a particular person seems so happy, so well-adjusted, often seems as puzzling as why another person is depressed. In other words, psychology is able to provide motives for deviance but not an explanation of why, and under what circumstances, the existence of these motives will actually lead to particular behaviors. Psychology can't tell us what **will** happen although it ends up giving a lot of reasons for what **has** happened.

But even its retrospective explanations are severely limited. In explaining a suicide, psychology does not explain why this particular individual committed suicide but rather how, under these circumstances—this kind of parenting, this level of pressure to excel in school, etc.—suicide is one intelligible outcome. But so were others. In other words, instead of explaining suicide as the act of this or that particular individual, psychology describes general background conditions that make the behavior in question understandable as one out of many possible responses.

(The problem is that people expect psychology to be able to do more than this. Whether psychology claims as much for itself or whether the public expectation represents a misperception of the nature of psychology, is an open question.) Psychology does not have very impressive predictive powers in that it is unable to really explain the reasons why this particular individual committed this particular act; rather, it merely describes certain acts as more or less likely under certain circumstances. In this respect psychology is quite unlike biology—i.e., it does not deal with the inevitable—and more like sociology. But now that we know that psychology tends to be non-predictive and generalizing in the ways we have just described, we should not consider the sociology of deviance to be inferior for having these same characteristics. For sociology too merely deals with the general background conditions that make certain behaviors possible, understandable, likely, intelligible, etc.—never inevitable.

Finally, psychology tends to overlook the evaluative nature of its conceptions of "normal" and "abnormal." It acts as though its application of these terms is as objective as, say, a medical doctor's distinction between a healthy and a broken arm. But standards of psychological health are not as self-evident, as universally valid, as standards of physical health. Without recognizing it, psychologists, as members of the middle class, tend to invoke middle class standards of "normal" appearance, behavior, and thought patterns in assessing the mental health of their patients and others. This can have serious consequences, as when psychiatrists testify in custody cases about a particular individual's fitness or unfitness to be a parent. The "Baby M" surrogacy case of a few years ago is often used as an example: many observers were outraged at what they perceived to be the middle-class biases of psychiatric experts who testified that the would-be surrogate parents—an upper-middle-class professional couple—would make better parents than the girl's natural mother (a working class single woman). Everything from the mother's indiscreet shows of emotion at the prospect of losing her baby, to her unsophisticated taste in baby toys, was used against her. And in the initial round of the case, the judge went along with this diagnosis, and even contributed a number of disparaging remarks of his own. (N)

Whether they are successful or not in overcoming their middle-class biases, sociologists at least try to avoid them by keeping in mind that "normal" and "deviant" simply refer to societal definitions and that it is not the business of sociology to either endorse or refute them.

With these preliminary comments out of the way, we can now turn to an examination of some of the major sociological theories of deviance.

SOCIOLOGICAL THEORIES OF DEVIANCE

Anomie Theory (Robert Merton)

Why is there so much deviant behavior in American society? Because, according to Merton, American society promises people more than it delivers; it incites desire but doesn't satisfy it.

Thus it produces more frustration than other societies do. And frustration leads—not necessarily to aggression, but to one of four typical forms of deviant behavior, which we will describe shortly.

It is interesting to note that Merton's theory was formulated before the age of television yet TV more than any other social phenomenon seems to validate it. Even households below the poverty line usually contain a TV set. And what do children see on TV? They see sitcom characters who appear to be middle-class but who don't seem to be working especially hard or, in many cases, to be very bright. (In fact, story lines often revolve around the dim-wittedness of the purported breadwinner.) Combined with the fact that unpleasant or controversial topics—such as racial or gender discrimination, unemployment, the scarcity of affordable housing, etc.—are almost never brought up, the message conveyed is clear: the U.S. is a wealthy nation in which equal opportunity prevails and in which anybody can achieve a middle-class lifestyle with little effort (or at least without having to make an extraordinary effort). Merton puts it this way: our society is more adept at inculcating desirable goals (e.g., a middle-class lifestyle) than at helping people master the necessary means (academic success, job skills) to achieve those goals. Partly this is a question of society's lack of commitment. For example, it is generally acknowledged today that whether a child gets a quality education, or gets the message early enough in life to take school seriously, or develops good study habits, or receives extra-curricular help when necessary—that all of this depends on luck, i.e., it depends on who the child's parents are. This is an indirect way of acknowledging that society does not make it its business to bring about real equality of educational opportunity. Yet is it a matter of chance that these same children grow up addicted, so to speak, to a continually expanding vision of material comfort, according to which the car you were content to drive two years ago isn't good enough now, that DVDs and CD players are not luxuries but necessities, and that you must dress a certain way to look cool no matter what the cost? No, it is not a matter of chance: advertisers try to make sure we get the message. And we do. And the TV shows themselves rarely if ever contradict the advertiser's message (most of them, after all, are dependent upon advertising revenue).

Hypothetically, of course, the same TV shows that depict the good life could also depict the struggle and sacrifice often required to achieve and maintain it, and thus serve as wholesome role models for children. But they don't. Thus, many children grow up in a state of **anomie,** or normlessness: they do not see the sense in behaving normally. Specifically, they do not see the connection between the mastery of particular methods (e.g., disciplined study habits) and the achievement of particular goals (e.g., affluence). Or, they do see the connection in the abstract but feel it is inapplicable to their particular situation (of substandard schooling, for example). The problem is that, while people can give up on "the system"—drop out of school, despair of finding a decent job, etc.—they cannot as easily give up the desires that that same system has been implanting in their minds since early childhood.

Merton formulates four main types of deviant behavior, each of which is to be understood as a particular response to societally induced frustration (i.e., the discrepancy between goals and means). They are attempts, in other words, to cope with desires that can neither be extinguished nor fulfilled. The following chart summarizes them:

	Goals	Means
Innovation	yes	no
Retreatism	no	no
Ritualism	no	yes
Rebellion	no	no

Innovation

This is the most common form of deviant behavior, according to Merton. The innovator is committed to a socially prescribed goal—for example, the goal of becoming middle-class—but, for reasons such as those stated above, has abandoned the socially prescribed means (hard work in school followed by hard work at a well-paying job), and instead achieves the goal through illegitimate means (e.g., theft). Clearly this is one way of dealing with frustration.

One does not have to be poor, or without decent job opportunities, to become an innovator. Affluent individuals can feel frustration too, especially in a society that emphasizes wealth as much as ours does. The affluent may commit crimes because they are not affluent enough. Sociologists speak of **relative deprivation:** the experience of frustration is relative to the level of desire; what we define as failure is relative to what we count as success. And these definitions—of success, happiness, wealth, etc.—are strongly influenced by our peers: it may not be enough to be objectively "middle-class" if we still have less than our neighbors.

Retreatism

Frustration can also be handled by giving up. Instead of satisfying desire illegitimately—which may not extinguish the perception of oneself as a failure in societal terms—we abandon the desire altogether. But this, as we noted above, is difficult to do. The desire for a normal, respectable middle-class lifestyle is so deeply ingrained, extreme measures are needed to erase it from consciousness. For the innovator the end justifies the means; victory is so pleasant—e.g., in the form of material goods—that it covers over the unpleasant memory of how one got there. But for the retreatist this is not an option, either because achieving an illegitimate victory seems to be too difficult or too unpleasant a prospect (unpleasant to the extent that one focuses on the illegitimacy, so to speak, rather than the victory). The thought that the innovator hasn't really succeeded in society's terms, that, while material goods have been secured, the goal of respectability has not, deters some individuals from pursuing that course. Yet what other course is there? The retreatist is someone who sees inevitable failure ahead, and for that reason must escape from reality. Examples of retreatism, then, include drug addiction and insanity.

Ritualism

The ritualist has a decent job, works hard, pays taxes, obeys the law, perhaps raises a family, and in general appears perfectly normal. Yet Merton says that true normality—which he calls **conformity**—includes **a commitment to goals,** and this is what the ritualist lacks. The key to recognizing ritualism as a form of deviance is to recognize that it too is fundamentally **a response to frustration**—only it is a milder, less socially disruptive response. Typically the ritualist's job, while "decent," is not a really fulfilling one. Over the years youthful dreams of career achievement have given way to the resigned acceptance of the fact that one is merely going to survive. No significant promotions or other signs of recognition, no tangible accomplishments, no challenging work projects, are in store. In this situation innovation is of course a possible temptation (you could embezzle company funds), as is a slow descent into retreatism (you could keep a bottle in your desk). But since you are surviving through socially acceptable means—you have a job, are paying your bills, and so on—it is more likely that you will cope, i.e., distract yourself from the reality of your frustration, by throwing yourself into your work and pretending to yourself that you are doing a job which, if not of ultimate significance, at least deserves being taken seriously. Taking the job **quite** seriously is for some a more viable way of coping with frustration than goofing off would be (since to goof off is to admit the insignificance of your job). Examples of ritualists would include petty bureaucratic managers who rigidly enforce the most insignificant organizational rules as though the world depended on it, when the fact is that only **their** world does. Viewed objectively, rules are justified by the fact that they further particular ends. But the ritualist, who has given up on real worthwhile ends, embraces the rules in an attempt to make them a self-justifying end in themselves. As a rule of psychic self-preservation—a defense against the threatening thought that life as a whole has no meaning—the ritualist becomes immersed in life's details.

Rebellion

The difference between rebellion and the other categories of deviance is that rebels recognize their frustration (unlike ritualists) yet (unlike innovators or retreatists) believe that the problem lies in society not them. Innovators do not oppose the law, they merely want to evade it. If you cheat on a test, that does not mean that you think cheating is justified. Retreatists, too, are not opponents of societal norms; they do not think that one should be drunk rather than sober. In most cases retreatists are perfectly willing to agree with society's diagnosis of their behavior as a symptom of moral or some other form of personal weakness. Rebellion is different. Instead of cheating the system or withdrawing from it, the rebel actively criticizes it (for, among other things, leading people into cheating and withdrawing). The innovator steals to escape poverty. The retreatist drinks to escape thinking about poverty. The rebel asks: why am I poor? The trade union movement of the 1930s was a rebellion against the socially accepted, normal yet unfair exploitation of labor by management. The civil rights movement of the 1950s and 1960s was a rebellion against the socially accepted, normal yet unjust treatment of blacks by the white majority.

The rebel does not necessarily speak out on behalf of, or only on behalf of, the outcast. The countercultural rebellion of the 1960s is a case in point. The "hippie" movement was composed largely of white middle- and upper-middle class youth enraged not at poverty but at the spiritual and moral emptiness, as they saw it, of a life devoted to the pursuit of wealth. They were not angry at being excluded from the American Dream; rather, they felt that the dream was more like a nightmare.

As we said, a major difference between rebellion and the other forms of deviance is that in rebellion the actor does not define the behavior in question as deviant; instead, the rebel defines **society** as deviant. Therefore, when Merton lists rebellion as a type of deviant behavior, it is obvious that he merely means to describe society's point of view. The problem, though, is that society's point of view changes. Thus, the labor and civil rights movements were once considered deviant but have since become more or less part of the status quo; and the same is true of many aspects of the '60s counterculture (rock music, environmentalism, long hair for men, etc.). But this means that we must be sensitive to the fact that these rebellious movements "were" deviant only in the sense that they were considered as such by the public. But then why isn't that true of the other categories of deviance, too? And if so, shouldn't the sociology of deviance be about societal definitions of deviance—their origins and consequences—rather than about those whose actions come to our attention simply on account of those definitions? The major charge made against Merton's theory, indeed, is that it pays insufficient attention to **the question of definition,** i.e., it does not take seriously the basic relativity of the concept of deviance.

Obviously, rebellion is called deviant because it calls the established order into question. The deviant label is an attempt by society to direct attention to the rebel's behavior and away from the rebel's question. But, it could be argued, the innovator too raises questions, however unintentionally and indirectly—such as: isn't there something wrong with a society in which poverty and unemployment (which could drive people to crime) are increasing at the same time that the incomes of the wealthy are reaching all-time record rates? (And of course the same could be said regarding retreatism.) Merton's approach, like society's, is to treat the deviant as having a problem. Unlike society, he locates the cause of the problem in society. But then isn't society rather than the deviant individual "the problem," and if so shouldn't it rather than the deviant individual become the focus of the sociology of deviance? **Labeling theory** and **conflict theory** have both, in different ways, built upon this basic critique of Merton. We turn to them next.

Labeling Theory (Howard Becker, Edwin Lemert)

The sentence "Deviant behavior is caused by society" is ambiguous. It could be taken to mean that norm-violations are the result of environmental factors. Or it could mean that society decides which behaviors to designate as deviant. Labeling theory understands the sentence in the second sense. What does this mean? The psychiatrist R. D. Laing wrote:

> Marx said: under all circumstances a Negro has a black skin but only under certain social-economic conditions is he a slave. Under all circumstances a man may get stuck, lose himself, and have to turn round and go back a long way to find himself again. Only under certain social-economic conditions will he suffer from schizophrenia. (Laing, 1972, p. 58)

To say your behavior is "mentally disturbed" is to apply a societal definition to your behavior. In that sense society creates or "causes" mentally disturbed behavior. One focus of labeling theory, then, is the societal definition process. Which behaviors does society view as deviant? Are certain individuals more susceptible to being negatively labelled than others? And what does this tell us about American norms, values, and prejudices? But the principal concern of labeling theory is to show that **labeling behavior as deviant actually tends to reinforce that behavior.** In other words, labeling theory claims society "causes" deviant behavior both in the sense that society causes us to regard certain behavior as deviant and in the sense that society causes those behaviors to occur.

This insight of labeling theory is really just an application of Cooley's theory of the **looking-glass self** to the study of deviance. According to Cooley, we tend to see ourselves the way we think others see us. Negative labeling, therefore, can undermine the individual's self-concept and weaken the motivation to conform. This was dramatically demonstrated in a series of "teacher expectation" studies conducted over 20 years ago in the San Francisco public schools. Researchers provided elementary school teachers with a standardized test to be administered to their students. As a result of the test some of the students were labeled as advanced. The test was a fake, although the teachers didn't know this. Yet the students identified by their scores as "spurters" outperformed their fellow students over the following two-year period. Why? Because the teachers expected them to. In other words, the teachers inadvertently communicated to the students their assumption that some were smarter than others—for example, by listening more attentively when a "spurter" spoke than when a non-spurter spoke, thus encouraging the spurters to get involved in class discussion. People feel more like speaking when they feel they are being listened to. You'll work harder on a report if you think the teacher will be impressed with it, and so on. Of course this is especially true for children, who depend so much on the approval of parents and parent-like figures in the environment. But studies suggest that this need for interactional support does not only exist among children (King, 1992).

Research on gender bias in the classroom has shown the effects of labeling through high school and beyond. For example, recent studies have found that science and math teachers typically pay more attention to boys than to girls—that they call on boys more often than girls, offer them more extensive and helpful criticism, and allow them—but not girls—to shout out answers (thus contributing to their self-confidence as well as reinforcing the idea that the race goes to the swiftest, i.e., the most assertive). And what effect does all this have? "Researchers . . . found that girls had less confidence in their math abilities than boys did, and that as their confidence diminished so did their performance." And: ". . . even those girls who did well in science and math tended not to pursue careers in those fields. Studies of girls who continued to study science after high school showed that encouragement of teachers was crucial in their decisions." (Sadker & Sadker, 1992) In other words, a label is a self-fulfilling prophecy: by thinking of people in a certain way (girls are less competent in science than boys) and thus treating them in a certain way (spending less time encouraging girls than boys) we make them into what we thought they were (girls don't do as well as boys on standardized science tests).

So there is certainly evidence that the self-confidence of adolescents as well as children is effected by labeling. As for adults, **the question itself is less relevant,** since the effects of prior labeling remain with us even if our self-concept improves in adulthood. If negative labeling led you to do poorly in school, that school record is likely to be a burden you carry with you throughout your life. You may decide in adulthood that you have what it takes to be a scientist after all, and begin the serious pursuit of scientific education for the first time; but it is not likely. This illustrates a second theme of labeling theory: regardless of its ultimate effects on the individual's self-concept, negative labeling **objectively reduces the individual's chances of succeeding in life.** No matter how smart you think you are, having been labelled as non-college material and being placed in a vocational "track" will limit your access to the professions. No matter how innocent you know you are, being convicted of a crime can affect your employability. And no matter how sane you know you are, being labeled manic-depressive will affect your chances of winning a custody battle for your children.

Thus, according to labeling theory, the best way to create a career offender is to respond harshly to a first offense—because by doing so the individual becomes stigmatized, and this, as we saw, limits one's opportunity to succeed in normal society, thus maximizing the chances of the person being driven to "innovate" or "retreat." And this will be the result regardless of whether the person accedes to society's judgment, in looking-glass-self fashion, or not.

Of course the labeling theorist does not claim that society necessarily drove the individual to commit the deviant act for which he or she is then punished; the response of authorities is usually a response **to** something. But was what they responded to "really" deviant—or was it just a "mistake," a "temporary lapse," a "momentary outburst," i.e., something that any normal person, in a weak moment, might do? It depends on how it is responded to. You're taking an exam and happen to be sitting next to someone whose answers are written in such large print that they catch your eye as you look up to stare out the window in order to think better. And seeing those answers, and noticing that some of them are different from your own, makes you re-think some of your answers, and to change them accordingly. But the question is: how does the teacher, who happened to notice this, view it? In Edwin Lemert's terms, you have committed an act of **primary deviance**—an isolated, relatively minor deviant act performed in the context of an otherwise normal life. Anyone who has ever cheated on their income tax (which could simply mean not being absolutely honest with regard to income reported or deductions claimed); used an illicit drug (which could simply mean temporarily yielding to the temptation to appear cool); shoplifted (which could simply mean not calling the cashier's attention to an item that she forgot to ring up); had a homosexual experience (which could simply mean momentarily expressing in action the experience of the ambiguity of gender identity)—anyone who has done any of these things is guilty of primary deviance. The fact is that the vast majority of people have committed such acts. **Secondary deviance,** on the other hand, refers to habitual, patterned deviance: deviance not as a mistake or an experiment but as a lifestyle. The point labeling theory makes is that we are all primary deviants simply because we are human. But only some of us become secondary deviants. And the difference between the primary deviant and the secondary deviant is that the secondary deviant has been exposed to a history of negative labeling. Where the teachers may think my child is "having a bad day," they may think another student "has a problem." Where the police send home the middle-class white delinquents to be disciplined by their parents, they arrest the lower-class minority delinquents. (There is an abundant supply of evidence for the differential treatment of offenders by race and class. See Chambliss 1988). These opinions by people in positions of authority have real consequences. They are embodied in official documents—school records and arrest records—that define the individual for society as a whole. The individual is likely to agree with these official opinions—after all, in most cases we go along with what the experts say, so why not in this one? But, as we noted above, whether we agree or not—whether our self-concept changes in order to agree with the concept others have of us—is ultimately beside the point. If we don't withdraw from normal society because we have given up on ourselves, we may withdraw because we recognize that normal society has given up on us.

Conflict Theory

As we have seen, conflict theory focuses on power relations in society. One of the consequences of the unequal distribution of power is that more powerful groups are capable of shaping the public perception of less powerful groups. As we saw in the Stratification chapter, it is in the interest of dominant groups to promote the idea that those with less power are less **deserving** of power. In some cases it is in the interest of dominant groups to go as far as to promote a conception of certain minority behaviors and attitudes as deviant. This is what the conflict theory of deviance examines.

This approach is similar to labeling theory. Where the labeling theorist studies the consequences of negative labeling for the labeled individual, conflict theory studies **the sources of**

negative labeling in the dominant group—raising questions, for example, about the political and economic motives behind the actions of the powerful.

The conflict theory of deviance takes one of two forms:

Cultural-conflict Theory

In this approach ascriptions of deviance are seen as weapons used against groups whose norms differ from, and appear threatening to, the majority. The affected group may be an ethnic, political, or other minority. A classic case in American history was the Prohibition movement of the early 20th century. The crusade against alcohol—which led in 1919 to passage of the 18th Amendment banning its manufacture and sale—was orchestrated by elements of the white Protestant majority as an attempt to stigmatize some of the recently arrived immigrant groups (e.g., the Irish and Italians), in whose cultures alcohol played a more prominent role. The real source of conflict was not alcohol but religion—the targeted immigrants were overwhelmingly Catholic—but alcohol provided the majority with an issue.

How intense cultural conflicts can be—and how serious the consequences for the minority culture—can be seen today in the debate over abortion rights. At the present time the 1973 Supreme Court decision affirming abortion rights remains in place, although no one can predict what will happen in the future. The point is that if the "pro-life" position were to become law the effect would be to render a particular point of view—the pro-choice view—officially deviant (which the pro-life position at present is not: the law states that a person can have an abortion if she chooses, not that it is wrong to choose not to have one).

Marxist Conflict Theory

For Marxists the ultimate source of power in society is economic; "protecting the interests of the powerful" means protecting their economic interests. What society calls deviant behaviors are in reality behaviors which threaten the power structure or call it into question—and in either case are the direct or indirect result of inequities in the system. The powerful respond to these threats by influencing the public (more and more through the mass media) to regard the perpetrators as sick or evil, and by segregating them from the rest of us in prisons and similar institutions (an assignment carried out by the criminal justice system and professional psychiatry) where they are rendered powerless and invisible to the general population.

How does deviance result from inequities in the system? Marxists explain as follows: Capitalist economies, such as ours, tend to generate high levels of unemployment as businesses struggle to secure profits. The tendency for business to try to maximize profits by minimizing costs has accelerated in the present era of global competition. To cut labor costs American businesses have turned to automation, overseas production, and other measures that have eliminated millions of jobs, especially for semi-skilled workers, over the past decade. And, where jobs are not eliminated outright, wages stagnate, workers are hired increasingly on a part-time basis, health benefits are slashed, and so on. This means that unemployment figures drastically understate the dimensions of the problem; they fail to reflect the underemployment or deprived conditions of employment that many workers are forced to accept because of the threat of unemployment that pervades the workplace today. In addition the individualistic ethic of American society has meant that industry feels little social pressure to take responsibility for re-training workers whose skills have become obsolete in a post-industrial, high-tech economy. Those with low skills or antiquated skills become more and more useless as time goes on and the skills required to do decent-paying jobs are progressively upgraded. Our system, in short, tends to produce a **marginal surplus population**—a large collection of individuals that the mainstream economy has no use or place for (Spitzer, 1975). As their misery intensifies, many of these marginal people become desperate or enraged. As a result, they may commit property crimes to obtain material necessities, or violent crimes to express their anger, or they may use drugs or become mentally disturbed in order to stifle their awareness of their hopeless situation.

Now both anomie theory and labeling theory could accept this analysis of the connection between hopelessness and deviant behavior. So what is different about Marxist theory (aside from its emphasis on the sources of hopelessness in the dynamics of a capitalist economy)? The answer is that the Marxist is claiming that by becoming deviant—by committing crimes or by going crazy—members of the surplus population **solve capitalism's problem of what to do with them.** After all, before they become deviant their existence potentially poses a major moral as well as technical problem. People might ask: if this is what our economy does to people (i.e., makes them useless), isn't there something fundamentally wrong with it? And that would lead to the awesome technical question of how to integrate millions of marginalized people into the economic mainstream. But once these individuals commit deviant acts, we no longer ask what's wrong with **society** but what's wrong with **them.** They have a problem. And the solutions are now much less elusive: police and prisons for the criminal, hospitals and drugs for the insane. Deviant individuals, in other words, can be processed fairly routinely without causing much disruption to the system. The public is encouraged to blame crime on the criminal and insanity on genetics, thus absolving the system of moral or technical responsibility. (The criminals can further be blamed for costing us—corporate executive as well as average citizen—a lot of money, in the form of taxes spent on courts, prisons, etc.)

Cultural Transmission Theory (Edwin Sutherland)

Unlike the previous theories, the question for cultural transmission theorists is not **why** but **how** individuals become deviant. And their answer is: individuals become deviant in the same way that normal individuals become normal—by **imitating the behavior of others.** Deviance, like normality, is **learned behavior.** Rarely do people invent behavior patterns; creative genius, like exemplary courage, does not characterize the typical individual. The choices we make—in clothes, cars, or careers—are the same as those made by our peers, or by those invisible yet omnipresent people "like us." Most of our behavior springs not from a sense of what is ultimately right but of what is normal, which means our sense of what those around us do and expect us to do. The only difference between the normal and deviant individual, then, is that the deviant has been exposed to a greater number of deviant role models than the normal person has. While this view may seem rather extreme in the degree to which it eliminates the difference between "us" and "them," it is actually in line with common-sense assumptions about deviance. People assume that individuals become deviant by being exposed to "bad influences"—otherwise it would be hard to understand why parents care so much about who their children's friends are. However, cultural transmission theory does go further than common sense is willing to by insisting that it is not only young people who are impressionable; throughout the life cycle, it claims, individual behavior tends to be modeled on the behavior of others.

To fully understand cultural transmission theory we must first understand what it means by "learning." Groups transmit not only **behaviors** but **attitudes;** we can only behave a certain way if we think there is sufficient reason to. In other words, learning to behave a certain way includes **learning motives as well as techniques; we learn why to act as well as how.** For unlike robots or animals, human beings need to make sense of their behavior; in this respect people never just mechanically obey commands. Cultural transmission studies try to show this dual aspect of human learning. A classic example of such a study is Howard Becker's "Becoming a Marijuana User" (Becker, 1963). That the individual is dependent on the group for technical learning in this case is fairly obvious. For it is from the group that the individual learns how to use the drug competently—by learning how to obtain it, how much of it to use, how to administer it, and so on. All this would apply, of course, to a wide range of substances, from tobacco and alcohol to heroin and crack. In the latter cases, learning the proper techniques is especially important given the potentially disastrous consequences of misuse. Yet whatever the substance the uniformity in our manner of using it is remarkable. Everyone who smokes cigarettes, for example, smokes in more or less the same way.

As for motivational learning, it is from the group that one learns to (1) recognize the state of being high and (2) define that state as pleasurable and therefore desirable (by being around people who seem to be enjoying it). Without this kind of learning the individual would have no reason to use marijuana. The point here is that the group provides the substance with the positive associations necessary to motivate the individual to become a user.

The effects of group definitions on individual behavior can be seen today in the case of tobacco use. As public awareness of the dangers of smoking increases, popular culture provides fewer positive images of tobacco use. Forty years ago, leading characters in films were often portrayed as smokers; smoking was identified with romance, adventure, and sophistication. TV anchormen and talk-show hosts often smoked, thus establishing an association between smoking and intellectual authority, social fluency, and so on. Today we have severed these connections. To the extent that one of the reasons people smoke is because people they admire do, the decline in the percentage of smokers in the general population can be at least partly attributed to this disappearance of role models who smoke. This too is common sense; for example, people often ask: How can we expect kids to stay in school when the only examples of affluent people in their neighborhoods are the drug dealers?

A second type of behavior that has been studied by cultural transmission theory is male homosexuality. This is a more controversial topic than drug use because we are more likely to resist the idea that homosexuality—as against drug use—is learned at all. Even if it is not inborn, isn't a homosexual orientation developed in early childhood? According to the logic of cultural transmission theory, the question is beside the point. It may be interesting to study how a homosexual orientation comes about, but such an investigation could never explain why only some potential homosexuals become actual homosexuals. Some persons with a "homosexual orientation" may remain "in the closet" their whole lives—may marry, have children, and never realize (in thought or action) their homosexuality. (Many people live a typically "straight" life for years, then divorce and begin having homosexual relationships; did they "become" homosexual in midlife?) By the same token, you may be a very aggressive, resentful, even hateful person without ever thinking of yourself that way and without ever assaulting anyone. In this respect, cultural transmission theory represents a strong sociological critique of psychology; it suggests that no personality test could ever predict who, of all the "deviant" personalities in the world, will actually behave deviantly. Yet it is deviant **behavior,** not the abstract potential for deviance that can be found to exist in all of us (depending on which psychologist is doing the looking), that we seek to study and understand. And what cultural transmission theory points out is that, of two men, for example, who are equally possessed of a "homosexual orientation," the one who meets other gays who encourage him, explicitly or just by their example, to "come out," is more likely to do so—and that this encouragement takes the form of a technical and motivational learning process. The technical aspect in this case may include learning where to meet people; how to recognize gays; a specialized "in-group" vocabulary to describe different types of gays, sex acts, etc.; and, especially in the age of AIDS, the latest scientific findings on safe and unsafe practices (something gay publications cover more frequently and in greater detail than the mainstream press).

But, again, the motivational aspect is logically prior; wanting to act leads to learning how to act. An "orientation," an "urge," is not a motive; a motive is something that gives you a reason to act. This the group provides by encouraging the individual to accept his homosexuality. He can accept it when he sees he is not alone, that being gay does not mean being marginal under all circumstances. The fear of being gay can then recede into the background, and the "orientation" is freed to express itself.

Thus cultural transmission theory provides a cogent account of how we learn to become deviant. But where did our teachers learn it from? In other words, cultural transmission theory presupposes the existence of the particular form of deviance it is studying, and then proceeds to show how this form of deviance is spread (transmitted). Thus, no matter how useful it is in other respects, it does not really deal with the question of the origins of deviance in the way the other theories we have discussed try to.

Functionalism

Functionalism holds that if societal patterns—even deplorable ones—persist over time, it must be because they serve certain social purposes. This is true of ethnocentrism; and it is true of deviance. Not that deviance isn't also dysfunctional. In fact, before we describe the ways deviance contributes to the smooth functioning of society, let us briefly describe the more obvious part of the equation—the ways in which deviance is socially disruptive. Among the many harmful effects deviance has on society, functionalists emphasize these:

Deviance Undermines Trust
Orderly everyday life depends to a great extent on our willingness and ability to trust people—including complete strangers. We trust that our bus driver will take the same route as yesterday, even if we have never seen this particular driver before; we trust that the department store clerk will not refuse to hand back our charge card after we've made a purchase; and so on. But as deviant behavior becomes more widespread in society, this basic trust begins to break down. We (probably) still trust the bus driver and the store clerk; yet, if we compare life in a contemporary urban setting with life in a traditional small town, the difference in degree of distrust is remarkable. The costs of this distrust are largely intangible (although we could calculate how much money is spent annually, for example, on home and car alarm systems). But, from the mild anxiety over whether we remembered to lock the front door on our way out of the house to the palpable fear of walking down a city street alone at night, distrust is both a drain on energy (providing yet another set of things to worry about in an already highly stressful environment) and a source of interactional suspicion and hostility (adding a further degree of fragmentation to an already disintegrated social world).

Deviance Undermines the Authority of the Norms
It is difficult for society to effectively condemn behavior that happens "all the time." If respectable—and even admired—people evade their taxes, lie under oath, commit adultery, do drugs, accept bribes, and so on—as the investigative journalism of recent years has shown in the case of numerous politicians, athletes, and entertainers—how can the norms be taken seriously? Parents often wonder how children can be raised to respect norms that adults seem to

routinely disregard. And there is a further problem. Once norm-violations become common, a kind of self-fulfilling prophecy sets in: we excuse our doing it because "everyone does it"—which leads, eventually, to everyone doing it.

The functions of deviance are not as obvious as the dysfunctions—yet they naturally occupy a more central place in functional theory. How can deviance be useful to society?

Deviance Reinforces the Norms

As long as deviant behavior is associated with social ostracism, instances of deviance will remind us of their consequences, and so deter us from breaking the rules. Placing a dunce cap on one child's head inspires all the other children to be on their best behavior. Thus, a little deviance goes a long way. Similarly—as we noted in the Stratification chapter—the existence of poverty is functional in that it provides an incentive for people to study and work hard—in order to avoid becoming poor.

Such reasoning seems to provide a basis for the "deterrence" theory of crime, which states in essence that rules are obeyed in direct proportion to the degree of punishment for violating them. But according to Travis Hirschi's **social control theory** of deviance, a variant of functionalism, the deterrence model is too abstract: it doesn't take into account how much a particular individual stands to lose by being punished. If I have a good job, a loving family, and enjoyable hobbies— example of what Hirschi calls **commitments, attachments,** and **involvements**—the prospect of going to jail for acting on an impulse to break a law may indeed act as a deterrent; but if I am homeless and hungry, why not break the law and take a chance on not getting caught—since, even if I do get caught, life behind bars couldn't be any worse than life in the streets or in a shelter for the homeless? In other words, behavior is effectively controlled by the existence of the actual or potential rewards of rule-following (good job, high social status) as well as by punishments for violations. Our behavior is a response to promises as well as threats. Hirschi's theory, then, can be seen as a critique of the idea that severe punishment alone can reduce the crime rate.

Deviance Promotes Solidarity

Nothing unites people more effectively than a common enemy; a function of deviance is that it helps social groups achieve a sense of community by defining themselves in opposition to those designated as deviant. Solidarity was a major theme in Durkheim's work. He felt that, while it was essential to social order, solidarity was becoming more elusive under conditions of modern industrial society. Today we can ask: In an ethnically, religiously, and linguistically heterogeneous society with increasing competition for decent jobs, what holds us together? If we are so different from one another—and if we are encouraged to **accentuate and celebrate precisely the differences**—what makes us an "us" at all? This sense of disunity, of the U.S. as a collection of warring clans (or "interest groups") can be temporarily broken through by a crisis. As a direct result of "9-11" for example, a majority of people, at least, seemed to have regained a sense of "us"—because there was now a clearly definable "them." But that was a brief interlude, and the problem of achieving solidarity remains an on-going one in American society. A more common occurrence that can be placed under this heading is that of the recent immigrant, well-educated and with a decent job, who, in order to fit in with his conservative suburban neighbors, adopts their attitudes of hostility towards those "animals"—criminals and other deviants—who mar the social landscape in direct contrast to law-abiding people like himself. In general, the less self-confidence a group or individual feels, the more likely will the need arise to derive a sense of strength by attacking others. Thus, adolescents convince themselves they are cool by stigmatizing and harrassing the nerds in their midst. And religions, especially in the period when they are first being founded, tend to define themselves in contrast to what they are not—by defining others as unbelievers, heretics, infidels, and the rest (Gager, 1975).

Durkheim, it should be pointed out, believed that the main function of punishment was to strengthen collective sentiment, i.e., to re-achieve solidarity. In this sense his thinking went beyond that of the "classical school" of criminology, which took for granted that punishment only made sense to the extent that it acted as a deterrent against crime. For Durkheim, punishment not only deters us from breaking the rules but intensifies our commitment to them. In other words, Durkheim argued that the interests of social order not only require that society regulate our behavior but our thinking as well.

Deviance Provides a "Safety Valve"

This means that, as obnoxious as deviant behavior can be, it is often less obnoxious than the available alternatives. Imagine that a group of store owners, alarmed at the increased shoplifting rate in their stores, hire experts to investigate the problem. The investigators report that the increased shoplifting appears to be the result of increased poverty in the surrounding neighborhoods, and they recommend that to eliminate shoplifting the owners should donate a substantial portion of their profits to local anti-poverty programs. The owners' likely response would be "Thanks, but no thanks." The reason is that shoplifting is less costly than eliminating the causes of shoplifting—especially if, as conflict theorists point out, a high crime rate has the advantage of inciting public outrage at crime rather than at the discrepancy between rich and poor.

Deviance Can Alert Society to the Need for Reform

As deviance becomes more widespread, more and more people begin to suspect that the problem lies in society rather than the individual deviant. As we noted above, epidemics point to environmental rather than individual causes. When tens of thousands of people are strung out on drugs, the logic of the sociological approach to deviance becomes more convincing. For, if so many people in our society behave as if their lives are worthless and that reality is something to be escaped from at all costs, even to the point of death, the question naturally arises: what experiences in society have led them to think this way?

LABELING WOMEN DEVIANT

Labeling theorist Edwin Schur has argued that "in our society being treated as deviant has been a standard feature of life as a female." By "treated as deviant" Schur means **labeled** as deviant: women are subject to a wide range of negative stereotypes which, while "they do not put the presumed offender in jail . . . they do typically damage her reputation, induce shame, and lower her 'life chances.'" For example, Schur mentions that "with great regularity women (are) labeled 'aggressive,' 'bitchy,' 'hysterical,' 'fat,' 'homely,' 'masculine,' and 'promiscuous.'" Notice that Schur implies a connection between "micro"-phenomena and "macro"-phenomena: defining women as deviant not only hurts their feelings but their chances of success. Negative labeling not only affects male-female interaction, it affects the position of women vis-a-vis men in the social structure. Schur claims that the negative perceptions of women that infect routine interaction between the sexes "reflects, and in turn reinforces" gender inequality in society at large. In other words, he is pointing to the same process we saw at work in the interactionist analysis of everyday gender rituals such as the door ceremony. Schur suggests that a damaged reputation and deep feelings of shame among women, such as result from negative labeling, are not conducive to high achievement even in the absence of overt obstruction on the part of men.

The negative view of women is so pervasive in society that even when a woman is a victim of a crime she if often treated as the offender: ". . . the female victims in such instances as sexual harassment, rape, and wife-battering have themselves often been treated as though they were the 'deviants.'" It is interesting that in these examples the perpetrator is typically a man. Is it reasonable to conclude that the woman's "offense" has been to make them look bad? Perhaps society lashes out at them because public acknowledgement of their victimization threatens to bring to light many disturbing facts about the behavior of men in society—facts which reflect the disproportionate social power wielded by men. Schur argues that negative labeling of women serves the purpose of re-inforcing male domination. Sympathy for the plight of women tends to undermine that domination, since the latter is the source of women's plight. Thus it becomes important to divert attention from that plight when it threatens to become noticeable—as in instances of harassment, rape, and abuse. (Interestingly, Schur wrote his book before the Anita Hill affair— perhaps the most publicly observable attempt to negatively label a female in our history.) But for the most part Schur deals with normal everyday situations in which male domination of women is legitimated and perpetuated by means of negative definitions, rather than specific crisis situations in which male domination is threatened. In the background, however, there always lies a perceived threat, hence the need for putting women down in the first place. "Recent studies show that efforts at deviance-defining typically are grounded in the definers' perception that the 'deviants' pose some kind of threat to their specific interests or overall social position. . . . There can be little doubt of the relevance of this notion to the situation of women. It is, indeed, axiomatic that male dominance depends upon female subordination."

Schur begins his account of everyday male-dominance-via-negative-labeling by pointing out, in line with a number of other symbolic interactionists, that deviant statuses tend to become master statuses: people who are identified as having deviant characteristics—criminal, homosexual, mentally disturbed, physically disabled, drug addicted, and so on—are seen by others principally if not exclusively in terms of that characteristic. An area of everyday language use in which we see this process at work is the "hyphenization phenomenon." To describe someone as a "woman doctor" or "woman executive" or "woman novelist" is to infer occupational deviance. (Compare "female nurse" or "female prostitute.") These designations do not merely neutrally indicate, as some would claim, that women are a substantial minority in these professions; rather, they imply that the exceptional belong to a different category (woman doctors) than the norm (doctors, i.e., male doctors) and so are not to be assumed to be comparable to—that is, on a par with—the norm.

BOX I: MODERNITY AND PUNISHMENT

Serious inquiry into the causes of crime existed long before sociology did, mainly as a philosophical pursuit. By the mid-19th century the "classical school of criminology" dominated the field. Its leading proponents included the eminent British philosophers Jeremy Bentham and John Stuart Mill. Its impact on both academic and common-sense thinking about crime—even down to the present day—has been enormous. And it has played a major role in shaping those public attitudes that led to the development of the modern criminal justice system.

The classical approach, while it has influenced many sociologists is, in essence, decidedly unsociological, for it locates the cause of crime in human nature rather than culture or social structure. Its basic theme is that crime is an attempt to get something for nothing; crime exists because human beings—at least before social influences are brought to bear on them—desire to obtain their goals with the least possible effort. Crime, in other words, is an expression of natural hedonism. So, for example, the thief acquires in a minute or two what it takes others forty hours of hard work to earn. If you wish to win an argument, striking your opponent may be easier than engaging in debate.

For such a view, it follows that the way to combat crime would be for society to guarantee that it ends up being less rewarding than costly for the criminal: i.e., society has to ensure that crime doesn't pay.

Underlying this way of thinking is the idea that criminals, no less than law-abiding citizens, are **rational actors who freely choose their courses of action.** More specifically, their criminal behavior is the result of a **rational assessment of the costs and benefits** of various possible behaviors. The purpose of punishment is to prove to them that their assessments of the advantages of criminal activity are incorrect.

But the modern prison system, which was designed to implement the classical theory, actually embodies a **distinctively modern notion** of the nature of crime and the purposes of punishment.

That, at least, is the theory of the influential French historian and philosopher Michel Foucault. According to Foucault, the prison is a total institution that has the power to coerce the mind as well as the body. Sociologist Stephen Pfohl writes that "Foucault suggests that prisons were initially filled up with persons sentenced for rational punishment, but that the raw power of prison technology soon produced a new theory of social control, one based upon strategies of manipulative change, one suggesting that deviance results not from free rational choice but from observable and changeable defects or pathologies" (Pfohl, 1985, pp. 63–4). In other words, the prison represents a transition from the classical model of crime as rational action to a modern model in which it is seen as "disturbed" behavior. The goal of "corrections," consequently, becomes more ambitious: instead of merely trying to get prisoners to renounce the life of crime on practical grounds (i.e., it doesn't pay), the system tries to influence them to **embrace conformity on moral grounds.** The ideal rehabilitated criminal is a "well-adjusted" person, one who can be counted on not only not to break the rules but to stand up for the rules as well. To be well-adjusted means not only obeying the police but agreeing to help police oneself and others. (We "police others" mainly by disapproving of their deviations from the norm, i.e., by means of ostracism, ridicule, and so on.) Two important points emerge from this analysis:

a. The prison system can only be fully understood when it is seen as part of modern capitalist society. That is, the prison is a social institution, and like other social institutions (education, science, family, etc.), it exists in order to serve the needs of the system. What our self-policing and our policing of others is designed to ensure is that **we become and remain functioning, productive units of society.** Pfohl writes:

Productive efficiency is a cornerstone of the capitalist economy. The more efficient that capitalists are in exercising rational control over both material and human resources, the greater will be their profit. This demand for efficiency precludes the possibility that capitalists will maintain direct physical control over the work of each wage laborer. This would be too costly. Under capitalism the centralized management of labor cannot be secured efficiently by the threatening hand of the boss. This is replaced by the "invisible hand" of a more subtle and omnipresent form of control—the technology of inner discipline. According to Michel Foucault this new internal technology of human subjugation produces the rationally self-controlled worker needed by capitalism. It permits the capitalist system to accumulate a self-disciplined workforce in much the same way that individual capitalists accumulate a mass of raw materials or natural resources. (Pfohl, p. 106)

(2) The prison system reflects the modern **medicalization of deviance**. Everything from alcoholism to overeating to sexual promiscuity is treated as a disease rather than as what they would be for the classical school—moral failings. Thus, the prison system reflects the view that deviants are disturbed individuals who are to be cured rather than punished. (It thus reflects

not only a perspective on the nature of deviance but on the nature of normal society: that society's goal is to cure rather than punish demonstrates that society is essentially humane, having progressed beyond more 'primitive' epochs in which justice took the form of seeking vengeance.) The problem with this model lies, again, in its totalitarian implications: society now determines not only what behaviors are requisite for social order but the proper **attitudes** that are to accompany those behaviors. Medicalization is based on the idea that deviance does not represent a (conscious or unconscious) **critique** of the normative order, but merely an **incapacity** to conform to it. So, medicalization is totalitarian in the sense that it disallows any difference from the system; it writes off all differences by labeling them as pathologies. To connect this point with the preceding one, we could say: the ultimate victory of capitalism would be to produce a population of robotically co-operative and cheerful workers, indistinguishable from one another in terms of personality traits. And this victory has been at least partly achieved already: we see it today among chain store employees, fast food workers, and telephone salespeople—all of whom have been trained in the art of being impersonally personable, i.e., the art of appearing to be expressive when in fact they are expressing not their own unique particularity but, rather, the company's conception of a "pleasant" personality. And the feeling of being told how to feel may extend even into our private lives, where societal definitions of emotional well-being, internalized by all of us to one extent or another, may lead many of us to see ourselves as deficiently assertive, happy, independent, or whatever else we are supposed to be.

BIBLIOGRAPHY

Adorno, Theodor W. *Negative Dialectics,* trans. E.B. Ashton, NY: Seabury, 1975.

Adorno, T.W., et al. *The Authoritarian Personality.* NY: Harper and Row, 1950.

Bauman, Zygmant. *Modernity and the Holocaust.* NY: Cornell University Press, 1991.

Becker, Howard S. *Outsiders.* NY: Free Press, 1963.

Casey, Maurice. *From Jewish Prophet to Gentile God.* Louisville, KY: Westminster John Knox Press, 1991.

Chambliss, William. *Exploring Criminology.* NY: Macmillan, 1988.

Cooley, Charles H. *Human Nature and Social Order.* NY: Scribner's, 1902.

Coser, Lewis. *Masters of Sociological Thought.* NY: Harcourt, Brace, 1975.

Dahrendorf, Ralf. *Class and Class Conflict in Industrial Society.* Stanford: Stanford University Press, 1959.

Davis, Kingsley. "Extreme Social Isolation of a Child," *American Journal of Sociology,* 45:4, January 1940, pp. 554–565.

Davis, Kingsley, and Wilbert Moore. "Some Principles of Stratification," *American Sociological Review,* 10, 1945, pp. 242–249.

Denzin, Norman. *Symbolic Interactionism and Cultural Studies.* London: Blackwell, 1990.

Durkheim, Emile. *The Rules of Sociological Method,* trans. by S. Solovay and J. Mueller. NY: Free Press, 1966 (1938).

Durkheim, Emile. *Suicide.* Glencoe, Ill: Free Press, 1951 (1897).

Freud, Sigmund. *Beyond the Pleasure Principle.* trans. by J. Strachey. NY: Norton Books 1961 (1920).

Freud, Sigmund. *The Ego and the Id.* trans. by J. Riviere. NY: Norton Books, 1960 (1923).

Gager, John. *Kingdom and Community.* Englewood Cliffs, NJ, Prentice-Hall, 1975.

Gans, Herbert. *The Urban Villagers.* NY: Free Press, 1962.

Garfinkel, Harold. *Studies in Ethnomethodology.* Englewood Cliffs, NJ: Prentice-Hall, 1967.

Gilligan, Carol. *In a Different Voice.* Cambridge, MA: Harvard University Press, 1982.

Goffman, Erving. *The Presentation of Self in Everyday Life.* NY: Anchor Books, 1959.

Heidegger, Martin. *What is a Thing?* trans. by R. Barton and V. Deutsch. Chicago: Henry Regnery and Co., 1967.

Johnson, Elizabeth. *She Who Is.* NY: Herder and Herder, 1992.

Kellner, Douglas. *Critical Theory, Marxism, and Modernity.* Baltimore: Johns Hopkins Press, 1989.

King, Mary C., "Occupational Segregation by Race and Sex, 1940–1988," *Monthly Labor Review,* 11: 30–36, 1992.

Kohlberg, Laurence. *The Philosophy of Moral Development: Moral Stages and the Idea of Justice.* NY: Harper & Row, 1971.

Kohlberg, L. and Carol Gilligan, "The Adolescent as Philosopher: The Discovery of the Self in a Postconventional World," *Daedalus,* 100, p. 1051–1086.

Kozol, Jonathan. *Savage Inequalities.* NY: Harper Perennial, 1992.

Kuhn, Thomas. *The Structure of Scientific Revolutions*. Chicago: University of Chicago Press, 1962.

Laing, R. D. *The Politics of the Family and Other Essays*. NY: Vintage Books, 1972.

Lasch, Christopher. *Haven in a Heartless World*. NY: Norton, 1977.

Lemert, Edwin. *Human Deviance, Social Problems, and Social Control*. Englewood Cliffs, NJ: Prentice-Hall, 1966.

Marx, Karl. *Capital*. ed. F. Engels, trans. by S. Moore and E. Aveling. NY: Random House, 1906.

Mead, G. H. *Mind, Self, and Society*. Chicago: University of Chicago Press, 1934.

Merton, R. K. *Social Theory and Social Structure*. NY: Free Press, 1968.

Merton, R. K. *The Sociology of Science*. Chicago: University of Chicago Press, 1973.

Milgram, Stanley. *Obedience to Authority: An Experimental View*. NY: Harper and Row, 1974.

Mills, C. W. *The Sociological Imagination*. NY: Oxford University Press, 1959.

Mortmann, Jurgen. *The Crucified God,* trans. by R. A. Wilson & J. Bowden. NY: Harper and Row, 1973.

Niebuhr, H. R. *The Social Sources of Denominationalism*. NY: World Publishing Company, 1929.

Niebuhr, R. *Justice and Mercy*. NY: Harper and Row, 1974.

Nietzsche, F. *The Will to Power,* trans. by W. Kaufmann. NY: Vintage, 1967.

Phan, Peter. *Christianity and the Wider Ecumenism*. NY: Paragon House, 1991.

Piaget, Jean. *The Origins of Intelligence in Children*. trans. by M. Cook. NY: International Universities Press, 1952.

Ruether, R.R. *Faith and Fratricide*. NY: Seabury, 1983.

Sanders, E. P. *Jesus and Judaism*. Phila: Fortress Press, 1955.

Schaberg, Jane. *The Illegitimacy of Jesus*. San Francisco: Harper and Row, 1990.

Skinner, B. F. *Science and Human Bahavior*. NY: Macmillan, 1953.

Skinner, B. F. *Walden Two*. NY: Bantam Books, 1967 (1947).

Spitzer, S., "Toward a Marxian Theory of Deviance," *Social Problems* 22, June 1975.

Sutherland, Edwin and Donald Cressey. *Principles of Criminology*. Phila: J. B. Lippincott, 1960.

Troeltsch, Ernst. *The Social Teaching of the Christian Churches*. NY: Macmillan, 1931.

Veblen, Thorstein. *The Theory of the Leisure Class*. NY: New American Library, 1953 (1899).

Weber, Max. *The Theory of Social and Economic Organization,* trans. and ed. by A. M. Henderson and T. Parsons. Glencoe, Ill: Free Press, 1947 (1925).

Weber, Max. *The Protestant Ethic and the Spirit of Capitalism,* trans. T. Parsons. NY: Scribner's, 1958.

Index of Terms

Index of Names